FLORIDA STATE
UNIVERSITY LIBRARIES

NOV 0 7 2000

TALLAHASSEE, FLORIDA

Remembering the Boys

Remembering the Boys

A COLLECTION OF LETTERS,

A GATHERING OF MEMORIES

EDITED BY *Lynna Piekutowski*

The Kent State University Press 🝒 Kent, Ohio, & London

© 2000 by The Kent State University Press, Kent, Ohio 44242
All rights reserved
Library of Congress Catalog Card Number 00-038459
ISBN 0-87338-664-7
Manufactured in the United States of America

07 06 05 04 03 02 01 00   5 4 3 2 1

Library of Congress Cataloging-in-Publication Data

Remembering the boys: a collection of letters, a gathering of memories /
edited by Lynna Piekutowski.
p. cm.
ISBN 0-87338-664-7 (alk. paper) ∞
1. World War, 1939–1945—Personal narratives, American.   2. Western Reserve Academy—Alumni and alumnae—Correspondence.   3. Western Reserve Academy—Faculty—Correspondence.   I. Piekutowki, Lynna, 1951–

D811.A2R46   2000
940.54'8173—dc21   00-038459

British Library Cataloging in-Publication data are available.

In remembrance of the forty-six Academy boys who lost their lives
while serving their country during the Second World War

The Boys and the College Street Elms, Winter 1929. *Western Reserve Academy Archives*

It is certainly nice to be remembered.

—*John H. Noyes ('40) to Joel B. Hayden, March 13, 1945*

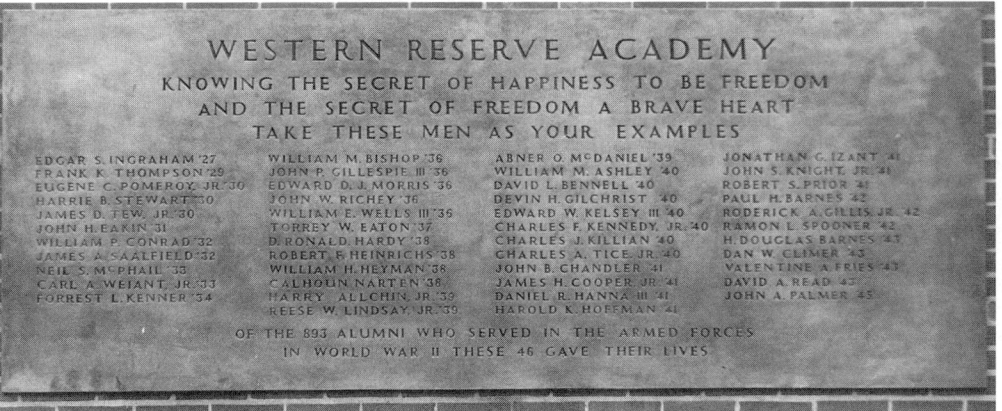

The bronze World War II memorial plaque, dedicated in spring 1951. *Western Reserve Academy Archives*

Contents

Foreword *by Lt. Gen. Daniel W. Christman*   xiii

Preface   xv

Introduction: Western Reserve Academy, the Boys and Administrators   xix

1 The School Year 1940–41: Much as Usual   1

2 The School Year 1941–42: No Longer a Small World   8

3 The School Year 1942–43: This Is a War Year!   36

4 The School Year 1943–44: Busy and Tired   92

5 The School Year 1944–45: The Greatest Loss   153

6 The School Year 1945–46: The War Is Over   251

7 Aftermath: If Your Boy Has Not Come Home   282

Appendixes

A: Gold Stars   287

B: Faculty Masters, 1940–46   288

C: Board of Trustees, 1940–46   291

D: Academy Boys Who Died during Military Service after World War II   292

Index   295

Foreword

Lynna Piekutowski captured a magic moment for many Western Reserve Academy alumni— indeed, many of my generation—when she included in her marvelous collection of letters the closing thoughts of Stephen Lamb, WRA '40, who returned for his fiftieth reunion in 1990. Standing amid "the lawn's wide sweep," Lamb was transfixed by the timeless beauty of Reserve and by the memories of those who had gone before—to fight in World War II, or to remain at Reserve and shape those who would follow in Lamb's footsteps. "Not a thing had changed," concluded Lamb in 1990. He was, of course, both right and at the same time, very wrong. *Remembering the Boys* captures this irony in a powerful, yet tragic way.

What has not changed in schools like WRA, which are committed to holistic development of young people, is the passion of a faculty and staff to educational growth. Joel Hayden, Reserve's headmaster through the Second World War, reflected this commitment. He knew and wrote to each of the "boys"—soon to be soldiers, sailors, airmen, and marines—like a proud father. And how robustly and movingly he and his faculty wrote! From letters of recommendation for flight school to morale-building notes to prisoners of war, Joel Hayden and the Reserve administrators and masters maintained a globe-spanning intimacy with those they had warmly nurtured during their younger years in Hudson, Ohio. I knew many of the teachers personally; they taught me when I was a Reserve student: Parker, Jones, McGill, Mickel, Roundy. Their passion towards those of my generation had not ebbed from the war years, nor has Reserve's to this day. In this critical respect, "not a thing had changed."

But in one critical respect, *everything* had changed. Reserve's losses during World War II totaled forty-six, a remarkably high number for a school of such small size. Disturbingly, memories of these sacrifices are growing dimmer and dimmer. Even in my Reserve days in the late fifties, the names on the plaques by the alumni gymnasium were scarcely mentioned, and certainly no serious effort was ever made to research these "boys" who gave the supreme sacrifice and what that sacrifice represented. In the four decades since my departure from Reserve, this understanding has virtually disappeared. Lynna's manuscript is a wonderful effort to rekindle those memories and reawaken the importance of selfless service to nation. To its credit, our country has tried to keep alive the memories of those who served and sacrificed—parades, plaques, monuments, films, songs. My own college alma mater, the United States Military Academy at West Point, uses the symbolism of the "Long Grey Line" as a means to connect with those who have gone before. One touching phrase from a West Point song comes to mind in this context. The relevant words are, "Grip hands with us now though we see not, Grip hands with us, strengthen our hearts—As the long line stiffens and straightens, With the thrill that your presence imparts."

It is this unseen presence that Lynna Piekutowski is trying to recapture in her collection. She does so marvelously. By way of reminder of those who served so selflessly at a time of enormous national peril, and of those who prepared and nurtured them during that service, *Remembering the Boys* is a moving reminiscence and a worthy complement to Tom Brokaw's, *The Greatest Generation*. That is exactly what these "boys" were—and are.

Lt. Gen. Daniel W. Christman ('61)

Preface

During the winter of 1994, I was recruited by the Western Reserve Academy Alumni and Development Office to process the files of one thousand deceased alumni, ranging from the classes of 1893 through 1993, for the Academy archives. Since 1984 I had been the school horticulturist, and it was generally in December that I scouted around the campus for a winter project while the grounds slipped into a season of dormancy. I discussed the project with Secretary Blanche Burns, who had worked with the files for a number of years and was familiar with their contents.

"There is so much history in these files," Blanche told me, "especially the letters written during World War II. It would be interesting to put them all together in a book." Through this simple exchange, the seed was planted for this collection.

As I organized and arranged the contents of each file, I discovered a number of letters within them and became especially captivated by the correspondence between Dr. Joel B. Hayden (headmaster 1931–46) and other school administrators, and the Academy boys who were serving in the armed forces during World War II.

In May 1996 I resigned as horticulturist and proposed to organize the files of over three thousand surviving alumni from the classes of 1918 through 1969 in the same manner as I had organized the deceased files—with one main difference: Correspondence relating to World War II would be copied and saved for this project. At the end of the six-month undertaking, I had gathered 850 pieces of correspondence.

I compiled the letters in chronological order by school year before I began to transcribe and edit them. I then turned to the school newspaper (the *Reserve Record*) and the alumni magazine (the *Alumni Record*) from the years 1941 to 1946 to gain further insight into the effects the war had on the school, its faculty and administrators, and the current students. As my editorial work was underway, Academy archivist and historian Thomas L. Vince discovered a collection of letters within the files of Lucien Price ('01) written during the war by Dean of Students Harlan Wood; I have included these in the present volume.

To date there have been five histories written about the school. School historian Helen Kitzmiller's *One Hundred Years of Western Reserve* (1926), published to celebrate the school's centennial year, and 1888 alumnus Dr. Frederick C. Waite's *Western Reserve University: The Hudson Era* (1943) detailed the school's early years. J. Fred Waring's *James W. Ellsworth and the Refounding of Western Reserve Academy* (1961) was written about the Academy benefactor and the years of the school's renewal (1916–25). Waring's second volume, *The Growing Years, 1926–1946,* published shortly after his death in 1972, continued the series of published histories of the school by exploring the period spanning the depression through the World War II years. French master (1957–95) Robert F. Pryce's *The Hallowell Years, 1946–1967* (1980), detailed events that occurred during the twenty-one-year tenure of Headmaster John W. Hallowell.

Unlike these preceding histories, the present volume has been written by the boys and administrators. Although I have provided a connecting narrative, the story is, for the most part, told through their correspondences to and from the warfront and in articles written for the student-run school newspaper on the home front.

The entire collection is arranged by the school year (September through August). An "x" following a student's class year indicates he attended the Academy but did not graduate. I have included each boy's age at the time he wrote the letter, and his class year. Errors in usage, spelling, and punctuation have not been corrected. Negative references to the Japanese and the Germans, though considered politically incorrect today, were part of the vocabulary of a nation at war and have not been altered.

During my attempts to contact available correspondents and family members of the deceased to request permission to use the letters, I invited the living correspondents to relate memories of their school days at the Academy. Those who wrote shared one common bond: appreciative recollections of their faculty masters and the school administrators, Headmaster Hayden, Assistant Headmaster "Scotch" McGill, Dean of Students Harlan Wood, and Dean Raymond Mickel.

The most fascinating aspect of the project was meeting some of "the boys" in person. I knew them only through their school files, their senior class pictures, and their letters. However, as we sat and talked, and as they reminisced about their years at the school, I saw these men—now in their seventies and eighties—as the teenaged youths and college students whose future plans

George Manlove ('32), left, at a 1931 track meet. *Archives*

were put on hold so they could serve their country. Their memories proved to be my greatest source of reference.

In the fall of 1998 I drove to Vermont to meet Dr. Hayden's daughter, Jean, and George Manlove ('32) and his wife. Mrs. Manlove reminisced as she sorted through photographs that had been put away years before. Dr. Manlove had suffered a stroke the previous spring, but his memory for his years at the school, the war years, and Dr. Hayden himself were as clear as the tone of the chapel bell. As he shared his memories, I saw the same twinkle in his eyes that I had seen in a photograph of him in the early 1930s as he raced toward the finish line at a school track meet.

My visits with Jean and Joel, Jr., answered and clarified many of my questions. The warmth of our conversations confirmed for me that Dr. Hayden's spirit, which I have come to know through my research, is still very much alive in his children and grandchildren.

My involvement in the creation of this book has truly been a privilege. A special note of gratitude to Blanche Burns for "planting the seed" for this project and her continued support throughout, and to Emily Schiavone ('97). Emily was a great help in gathering and copying the correspondence during her senior year, and her enthusiasm and interest served as an inspiration to me.

Throughout the project I was fortunate to know a variety of people who took the time to read and edit the manuscript as it continued to unfold. Each was a stickler in his or her own way: John Shaw ('40), Marje and Bill Danforth

('34), Velia and Bob Pryce, Hudson resident and Kent State University Press board member Henry Leonard, Helen Gregory, and Christine Bradbury. Everyone contributed his or her knowledge of the English language and its proper usage in the early stages of development. To them, and to family and friends who contributed their editorial advice as the collection evolved, a most heartfelt thank you.

Thanks also to Tom Vince, archivist and historian, for his input and the use of the archives; to the Alumni and Development Office staff for their support; to Cal Frye in the computer lab, as I struggled to understand the jargon of 1990s technology; to John Hubbell, director of The Kent State University Press, for his guidance and editorial comments; and to Business Manager Len Carlson and Headmaster Skip Flanagan for appreciating the importance of this project.

Introduction

 WESTERN RESERVE ACADEMY, THE BOYS AND ADMINISTRATORS

School life on the campus of what is now Western Reserve Academy began in the fall of 1827. Originally established as the college preparatory department of Western Reserve College, it remained in Hudson, Ohio, when the college moved to Cleveland in 1882 to become Case Western Reserve University. The Academy struggled along on its own for twenty-one years. It closed in 1903 due to the lack of funds.

For thirteen years the buildings and the campus fell into decay. However, because of a generous endowment from benefactor James W. Ellsworth, an 1867 alumnus of the preparatory department and a Hudson-born multi-millionaire coal baron, the school reopened in 1916 as a college preparatory academy for both boys and girls. In 1922 the Academy trustees voted to no longer accept applications from the girls; Western Reserve Academy was to become an "all boys" college preparatory school. It continued to be coeducational until the end of the 1925 school year, after which it began a forty-seven-year period when the alumni were known collectively as "the boys." In 1972 girls were once again admitted, and the school continues to be a private coeducational college preparatory school for grades nine through twelve, accommodating both boarding and day students. Faculty members live in homes and dormitories surrounding the thirty-two-acre main campus.

World War II had a significant impact on Western Reserve Academy. Eight hundred and ninety-three alumni and eleven faculty served in the war. There were no casualties among the faculty, but forty-six alumni lost their lives.

On the home front there were changes in curriculum, calls to conserve, to "Buy Bonds," to "do your part for the war effort," and, in the fall of 1942, calls from the government, as the minimum draft age was lowered from twenty-one to eighteen. The machine shop, under the direction of Louis

Tepper, went on a "war-time basis" and filled war contracts from nearby production companies.

The *Reserve Record*, the school newspaper, which still runs today, was published each week for the duration of the war; hundreds of copies were sent to the Academy boys serving in the armed forces. The *Alumni Record* was also mailed around the world to servicemen hungry for news of their classmates and from the campus. In addition, many letters were exchanged between the boys in action and the administrators of the school. The bulk of correspondence from the school to the boys was written by Headmaster Joel B. Hayden and Dean Harlan N. Wood. Assistant Headmaster Ralph W. McGill wrote letters as well. Although Dean Wood retired at the end of the 1944 school year, he continued writing to the boys until his death early in 1945. Appointed new dean of students upon Wood's retirement, Raymond A. Mickel continued the correspondence.

In 1982, alumnus John B. Shaw, who attended the Academy from 1935 through his graduation in 1940, received the Waring Prize, the Academy's annual award recognizing lifetime achievement, given in the name of English and history master J. Fred Waring (1935–67). The following excerpt from his acceptance speech (discovered in his school file) paints a vivid image of the Academy boys on the eve of World War II. Shaw was twenty-two years old when he was wounded in action on Christmas Day 1944 during the Battle of the Bulge.

> There I was on a bright fall day, relaxed, confident, lounging between the goal posts on the soccer field below to the west of us. I am alone; that superb forward line is down at the other end of the field, incessantly punching the ball at the opponent's goal. I stand idly, directly beneath the goal bar, yawning, lifting my arms lazily and putting my fingers into the netting. I breathe in the delicious air, fragrant with the whiff of burning leaves. I hear the far-off shouts and whistle, the boot of the ball. The late October blue sky stretches above me endlessly and forever. I am confident because I have Tien Wei Yang ['41] for a fullback[,] with legs like marble posts. He'll break up any attacks. The goal is safe; I am safe. We'll win again.
>
> Another time, on a warm May evening, we sneak past Shirley Culver's [French master 1935–57] door and out of North Hall, and run northwards to the hockey pond and on into the field of fresh new grass beyond. We giggle and laugh; mirth wells up in us until we can hardly breathe.
>
> "I'll bet old Shirley knows we're out!" we pant in whispers.
>
> "No, he won't, but maybe the Commodore [E. Mark Worthen, history and English master 1938–71] knows."

The Gymnasium. Hardscrabble *1942*

North Hall.
Hardscrabble *1942*

"Oh, shoot, they don't care—let's go!" and we run across the field, silly and joyous. Someone tackles me from behind, and we roll on the dew-wet ground. We wrestle and tickle each other, and then we get up and race off eastward, diving down when the beam of a turning car headlight reaches across the field and moves toward us. We are helpless with naughtiness and nonsense and boyish happiness.

In Chapel we harmonized splendidly to "Fairest Lord Jesus" and "Now the Day is Dying," and we sang "Once to Every Man and Nation" at the top of our voices, grinning at each other when we caught one another's eye, and we were eager, excited, happy. "What we changed was innocence for innocence; we knew not yet the doctrine of ill-doing." [William Shakespeare, *The Winter's Tale*] But was it really like that? Were we really as "happy as the heart was long"? . . .

Do I remember fighting one sombre afternoon in the empty hall of Seymour with my roommate, Joe Weitz, both of us little boys dressed in knickers, furiously swinging our heavy briefcases at each other, tears in our eyes, both miserable?

Or the final soccer game with University School, played the morning of November 11, 1939 [Veteran's Day]. Do I truly remember that Dr. Hayden, our Headmaster, came out onto the field at exactly eleven o'clock, actually stopped the game, which we were not winning, and while we stood angrily panting and sweating in the dim morning haze, said a prayer of homage for those killed years before in far-off Europe in the First World War? Could that have really happened? Later, before the game was over, a ball kicked at close range, in front of the goal, struck me in the face with such a slap that I staggered back into the netting. I can still feel that sting. . . .

I came into this Chapel, I should guess, during my five years at the Academy, more than 700 times. Do you know that, with one exception, I cannot recall a single sermon or talk! How can that be! Did I not listen to those talks? Did I learn nothing? Am I not the same person who first sat there, then there, then there and finally there?

The one Chapel talk I recall out of all those 700 was Rabbi Silver's description, late in the fall of 1939, of London, that most civilized of cities. Though still innocent of bombing, the city had everywhere stacks of sandbags, ready to be placed in church choirs and chapels; stained glass windows had been removed; air raid alerts were constantly sounding; air raid shelters were being built. It would not be long before the deadly assaults would begin. . . . The world began to change at about that time for all of us, and some of our classmates on the playing fields at University School, when the game was stopped, were victims of these changes.

Soccer team captain John Shaw ('40), front, center. *Senior Annual 1940*

For the duration of the war, as the boys left the Academy's playing fields for battlefields around the globe, the following school administrators wrote numerous letters to their former students who were in the service: Headmaster Joel B. Hayden, Dean of Students Harlan N. Wood, Assistant Headmaster Ralph W. McGill, and Dean of Students Raymond A. Mickel.

THE ADMINISTRATORS
Dr. Joel Babcock Hayden, Headmaster, 1931–46

Nineteen forty-one saw both the beginning of World War II and the beginning of the last five years of Dr. Hayden's fifteen-year tenure as headmaster of the Academy.

His feelings for the boys can best be described in a letter written to a parent in the fall of 1944.

> Please be assured that Western Reserve Academy "hangs on" to every boy who has ever lived here and with whom we have associated in any way. All the boys are part of our bloodstream. We older folk are simply a sort of temporary-continuing form of life here—always temporary but continuing for a longer time than the average boy. There is something filial in our feeling and thought and devotion about and for the boys.

Dr. Joel B. Hayden, Headmaster.
Hardscrabble *1942*

Harlan N. Wood, Senior Master,
Dean of Students. Hardscrabble *1942*

When he sent letters and handwritten birthday greetings to the Academy boys serving in the military, many of them responded with stories of their war experiences, reminiscences of the Academy, and expressions of gratitude for his guidance during their days as students. Many visited him at the school while home on leave. When he became ill, not long after the end of the war, the boys would visit him at Pierce house, his home on the school campus.

As the servicemen returned home to begin their lives in a world at peace, and as the class of 1946 prepared to graduate in June, Dr. Hayden was given the title of Headmaster Emeritus. He and his wife, Hazel, left Hudson in July 1946 for "Bridge's End," their Middlebury, Vermont, home, where he died in 1950.

Harlan N. Wood, Dean of Students, 1931–45

An 1888 graduate of the Academy, Harlan Wood became professor of Latin at his alma mater in 1893, and continued teaching until the closing of Reserve's doors in 1903. When James W. Ellsworth refounded the Academy in 1916, Wood returned to teach ancient history, American history, and Latin. He began the glee club in 1916 and was in charge of the library until 1924, when Mary B. Eilbeck arrived as the new librarian. In 1929 he was named acting headmaster, a position he held for two years while a search for a new headmaster continued. When Dr. Hayden came to the school in the fall of 1931, Wood was appointed dean of students, a position he held until his death in 1945.

Word of his death evoked an outpouring of letters from battle stations around the world. A former student remembered "a kindly gentleman, full

Ralph W. "Scotch" McGill, Assistant Headmaster. Hardscrabble *1942*

Raymond A. Mickel, Faculty, Dean of Students. Hardscrabble *1942*

of understanding to all boys. A father to all, that was Dean Wood." He was the last living link between the old Academy and the refounded school. His loss left a void impossible to fill.

Ralph W. McGill, Assistant Headmaster, 1940–59

Ralph W. McGill came to the Academy in 1928 to teach math. Known as "Scotch" to students and alumni, he was responsible for many of their nicknames; he had one for each of them. He was a confirmed bachelor until, in June 1942, he married Bernice Cromwell, a secretary in the administrative offices.

In 1940 he became assistant headmaster, and when Dr. Hayden fell ill in mid-October 1945, McGill served as acting headmaster through the end of the school year.

Scotch McGill was one of four housemasters who presided over the boys residing in Cutler Hall (currently known as Ellsworth Hall). The boys who lived there undoubtedly have at least one tale to tell about their attempts to outwit him.

After thirty-one years of devoted service to the school, McGill retired in 1959, settling with his wife into their new Atwater, Ohio, home. He continued to be involved with the school until his death in 1974.

Raymond A. Mickel, Dean of Students, 1944–60

When Harlan Wood was given Dean Emeritus status in June 1944, Ray Mickel became dean of students. He had been with the Academy for sixteen years. Well known as a track and soccer coach, he taught history and social studies in addition to chairing the social studies department. He held these positions and that of dean of students until his retirement in 1960.

In 1945, with both the death of Dean Wood and the sudden illness of Dr. Hayden, Mickel's duties were further increased by the handling of the correspondence that continued to pour in from the boys in the service. Generations of students remember him as the "Chief Potentate" and later the "Grand Bamboozeleer" of the "Secret Order of Siam," a traditional initiation for the "new boys."

When he retired in 1960, four of his former students were serving as trustees; six were faculty members. He died in Hudson in 1974.

These four men, along with a dedicated and loyal faculty, shared the boys' triumphs and tribulations and saw them through the angst of their adolescence. By their own actions, they taught respect and proper manners. They prepared the students for college. And in those war years, when word came through of their "boys" dying—forty-six at war's end—they wept as parents at the loss of a son.

In the meantime, in the common room at Cutler Hall (known today as Ellsworth Hall), the boys attending the Academy listened to their favorite records on the Victrola and gathered around the piano for after-dinner sing-alongs. It seemed a simple, innocent time, yet it was one complicated by a world at war. It is a time to be remembered.

THE SCHOOL YEAR 1940–41

Much as Usual

On October 29, 1940, in Washington, D.C., Secretary of War Henry L. Stimson drew the first lottery number in the newly instituted Selective Training and Service Act of 1940. All males between the ages of twenty-one and thirty-five were required to register for the first peacetime draft in the history of the United States. Only alumni of the Academy classes from 1923 through 1937 needed to be concerned about the drawing.

For the boys currently enrolled, the draft law would be of little interest. Certainly by the time they reached draft age, the "conflict" would long be over. Other than the announcement in the school newspaper, the *Reserve Record*, that nine of the masters would probably be deferred, no mention was made of what had occurred in Washington that day in October.

Nonetheless, Dean Harlan N. Wood (class of 1888) sat at his desk in Seymour Hall and wrote to Lucien Price ('01), his longtime friend and former student, to express his concern for the boys currently enrolled for the school year. The dean was seventy-three; Price was fifty-seven.

October 29, 1940

My dear Lucien,

... I have come to rather count on a visit from you along in October when the foliage is rich in color and the rides along the country roads interesting. A few of the trees on the old campus still hold the yellow and brown leaves, but the flowers are gone and for the most part we are surrounded by reminders of the approach of Thanksgiving and then of winter.

But it has been a pleasant fall. "The noisy ballfield's throng" has been just as eager and just as noisy as ever and it is a glorious sight to drive out to the new field back of Pierce House and then to the one in front of my house and see them all at play. There are times when I shudder, as you do, at the thought of the world into which they are going. But then I think that, after all, we are living in an ordered universe and nature is bringing on this new generation of fine young men to set things right in a world

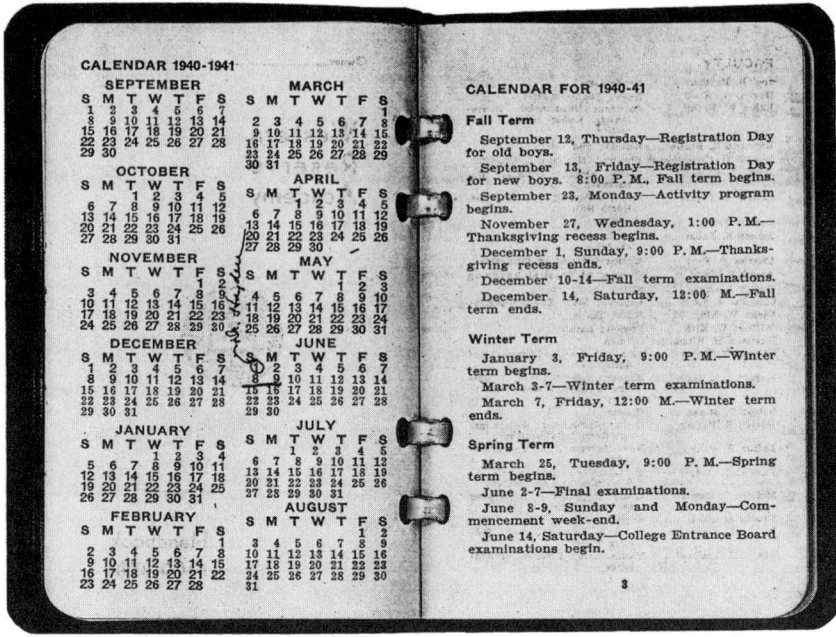

School calendar 1940–41. *Student Handbook*

Hitchcock House (known today as the President's House), campus home of Dean Wood. His front door is on the left. *Archives*

Harlan N. Wood, Class of 1888. *Archives*

Harlan N. Wood, Dean of Students. *Archives*

Lucien Price, Class of 1901. *Archives*

Lucien Price, *Boston Globe* editor. *Archives*

Dr. Hayden at the pulpit with the new Palladian window as backdrop. *Archives*

where the present and former generations have turned things upside down. Changes must come in this ordered universe so far as man and nations are concerned and eventually they will come about in a human and organized way without war and the slaughter of the helpless. Of course, some of us say, "why can't that happen right now?" Well, I suppose we have got to admit that human beings are still ruled in their actions too much by the lust for power, by selfishness and by greed. . . .

School is moving along very well with 202 boys enrolled. It seems strange not to have regularly scheduled classes. I occasionally take over Mr. Parker's classes for him, but most all my time is taken up with work of a Dean and in committee work of various kinds. Today the midterm grades came to the office and I have been busy with my share of them. . . .

I am glad to know that you are getting a needed rest. As a newspaper man[1] you will need all the strength you have to cope with the questions ahead. Poor little Greece! If Hitler drops his bombs on Athens I think I will be ready to shoulder a gun. . . .

                      Very sincerely,
                      Harlan N. Wood

1. Lucien Price was an editor at the Boston Globe from 1914 to 1964.

The top choice in school activities that year was Louis Tepper's machine shop, where the boys were given an opportunity to work with power tools. Although Tepper's inventions and innovations would later prove invaluable in the war effort, this year he was concerned with the creation of several pieces of "conditioning machinery" for use in beautifying the campus.

In December major alterations to the school chapel were nearing completion—enough to celebrate the wedding of headmaster Joel B. Hayden's daughter Jean to Samuel Guarnaccia. The chapel had been extended twenty-two feet to the east in order to accommodate a large Skinner organ, a gift of Mrs. Dudley S. Blossom. The extension also allowed for an enlargement of the library downstairs as well as the addition of choir stalls in the main chapel. The crowning element of the alterations was the Palladian window that served as a backdrop for the pulpit at which Hayden and others gave their morning talks.

On January 7, 1941, the headmaster was ordered by his doctors to take an "indefinite vacation," in hopes that it would reduce his high blood pressure. In his book *The Growing Years*, J. Fred Waring observed, "Dr. Hayden's absence from the campus from January through June 1941 had one curiously valuable result: it threw the running of the school into the laps of the faculty, thus requiring them necessarily to think of the whole school and not of their particular functions; it required them to operate as a team. . . . It was good experience for the efforts the faculty would have to make after Pearl Harbor."

According to the May 29 issue of the *Record,* which presented a detailed account of the trip, Dr. and Mrs. Hayden left the campus on January 10 "with no specific destination in mind and with no guides except two books, *Adventures in Good Eating* and *Lodging for the Night.*" They traveled to Pennsylvania, "where their black Lincoln-Zephyr streaked over the new Pennsylvania turnpike at an average of 65 miles an hour," then on to Atlantic City. Following a trip to Vermont to see their daughter Jean, they traveled westward across the country.

After two weeks of sailing on the Gulf of Mexico, they spent three weeks in Mexico City, then set sail to Hawaii from Acapulco on the steamer *America*. They spent a month in Honolulu, where they met or heard about several Reserve alumni. The article in the *Record* closed with Dr. Hayden's prophetic observations. "Hawaii is no longer simply a romantic island of the sea but has lately become a great outpost of the United States in the West. The size of the population has increased fifty per cent within the last two years with the advent of nearly 125,000 army, navy, and airmen. Planes were in the air day and night even close by the hotel. The inland volcanoes have been converted into tremendous arsenals." When the Haydens retured to the campus late in May, Dr. Hayden was well-rested and healthier.

The June 9 issue of the *Record*—the last of the school year—carried an editorial titled "The Future Calls." The anonymous author called on his fellow

The Haydens in Hawaii. *Courtesy Joel B. Hayden, Jr.*

graduates to accept their destiny: Graduation was not an ending but a beginning. Although the majority would be going on to college, that beginning was destined to end abruptly, for the fall of 1942 would bring a major change in the draft laws, and most of the boys would find themselves in some form of preparation for military training.

May 6, 1941

My dear Lucien,

Early in April the crocuses pushed their way up through the cold ground and gave us a brilliant display of color out here on the lawn between Chapel and Seymour, and Chapel and North. But today the land out here between Chapel and Seymour is a blaze of color with tulips in their prime—red, lavender, pink, etc. The trees are rapidly expanding their foliage and the lawns look beautiful.

How many, many times I have thought of you in recent weeks as, from day to day, I have read of the battle around Mount Olympus, then at Larissa, where I hoped that some modern Achilles might arise who with his myrmidens might smite the advancing foe. Then at Thermopyle and finally at Athens where the German Swastika floats from the sacred walls of the Acropolis.

Down here at Ravenna [Ohio] 21,000 acres of fertile farmland have been purchased by the government and a perfectly enormous munitions plant is being erected. At one time 16,000 men were working there, and it is expected that by July first the plant will be ready for the delivery of shells. Another similar project is being developed out here west of Cleveland near Sandusky. It is sickening to see these farms and homes being appropriated for such purposes. And the end of it all will not be in my day and perhaps not in yours.

Meanwhile life goes on here on the old campus much as usual.

Very sincerely,
Harlan N. Wood

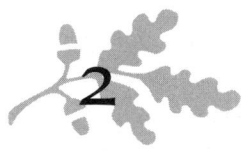

2

THE SCHOOL YEAR 1941–42

No Longer a Small World

❦ FALL TERM: SEPTEMBER–DECEMBER 1941

As the school year opened, the majority of alumni were in college, pursuing careers, or serving in the military. The draft age was still twenty-one, the current world situation still a crisis. An editorial in the October 16 *Reserve Record* paid tribute to William M. Bishop ('36), a member of the American Eagle squadron, who died when, en route to "join up" with the Royal Air Force in England, the fast freighter carrying him was sunk. A related article in the same issue reported that Frank K. Thompson ('29) died in the spring of 1938 while flying in Texas with the Army Air Corps, and that John H. Eakin ('31) was killed in the winter of 1940 in a midair collision while instructing a cub cadet. Two boys were listed as missing: Jim Priestley ('34)[1] and Edward D. J. Morris ('36). Both were exchange students from England who had graduated from the Academy. Although these five alumni were unknown to most of the students, the vespers service honoring them brought the "world crisis" a little closer to home.

In the meantime, the first official yearbook since the school's refounding had begun production. The staff had chosen the name *Hardscrabble* in honor of *Hardscrabble Hellas,* Lucien Price's account of Academy days gone by, first published in the *Atlantic Monthly* in February 1927.

The call to rally at what was called "The Largest Pilgrimage in the History of the University School–Reserve Rivalry" was a success. Reserve's football team tied University School 13-13, and the soccer team tied 2-2, giving Reserve undisputed ownership of its third league title in five years. The annual Fall Sports Dance was announced, complete with date list and rules of proper conduct.

On October 3, the *Record* featured coverage of a visitor from China who had predicted that the war there was nearing its end. "The Japanese army is having more and more trouble obtaining supplies and food, and the Japanese people are tiring of war. . . . Also, the decrease in help from the United States has done a great deal towards stopping their aggression. . . . it is believed that it will end within the next year."

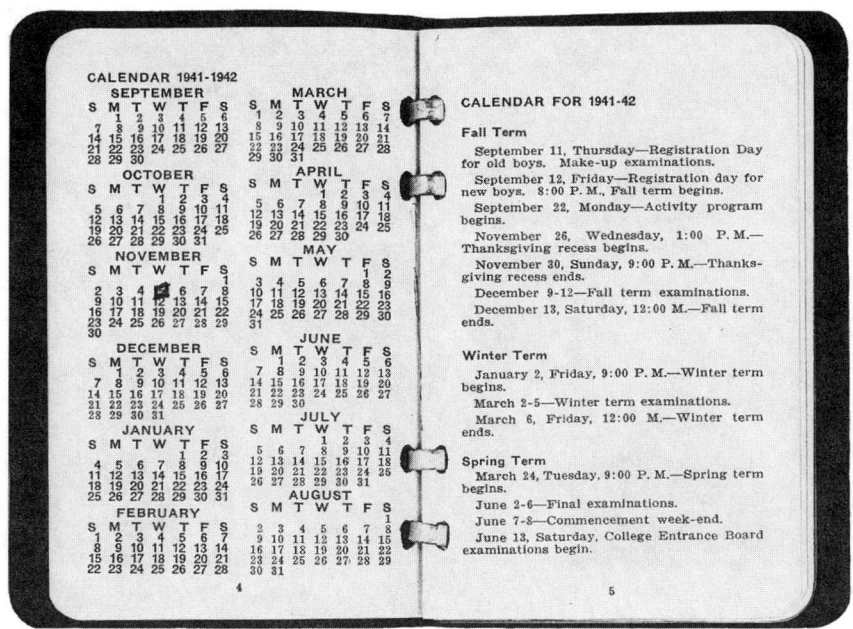

School calendar 1941–42. *Student Handbook*

William M. Bishop '36. *Archives*

John H. Eakin '31. *Archives*

John H. Eakin '31. *Archives*

Frank K. Thompson '29. *Archives*

The soccer team was faced with a shortage of leather cleats. "There were none to be had at the sporting goods stores for miles around," read an article in the October 30 *Record*. "In a weak moment [the coaches] bought a dozen or two from the University School supply." The situation was soon remedied by Louis Tepper. "If we can't buy them, we'll make them," he said, and he taught the team to make their own.

By the end of October the guidance committee, which included Dr. Hayden and six faculty members, met to discuss the school's policy with regard to college planning. Their findings were sent to the parents and included a summary of the draft regulations affecting college boys. The best advice the guidance committee could give was that "students should plan for their college education as they normally would do. . . . a boy can serve his country and himself best by calmly evaluating his abilities, his preferences, his aims, and the institutions that seem most likely to further his development, and then, disregarding mere military exigency, plot his educational course accordingly."

On November 6, 1941, the U.S. cruiser *Omaha* and the destroyer *Somers* captured the *Odenwald*, a German-armed merchantman in the Atlantic. Joseph S. Allen ('38) wrote a letter to his parents with a limited account of the action—as much as he could give in consideration of national security. His sister forwarded a copy of the letter to the school.

1. Priestley was the first English-Speaking Union (ESU) student to attend the Academy. He was also the first English fellowship boy to attend an American prep school west of the Allegheny (*Reserve Record*, June 13, 1933).

USS Omaha, Somewhere in the Atlantic
November 19, 1941

Dear Mother and Daddy:

You must know by now that we captured a German ship with a very valuable cargo. Unluckily I wasn't aboard for the fun, but met the *Omaha* at sea just a few days later. However, I have been aboard since—while we were taking the prize into port.

All the press reports I read did not mention the name of our ship, but some radio reports did, so I presume it's okay to tell you. There's a lot more to the story than the papers gave out, but until they come out with the full report, I can't say anymore.

While the prisoners were aboard we had to wear our guns. Incidentally, we just got rid of the prisoners yesterday. The officers were fairly free to move around, but they were well guarded, of course. I played a few chess games with some of them and picked up a few tricks about the game.

I also listened to their Nazi philosophy. They make it sound pretty logical, but I often wonder if they actually believe in it. The German captain told me he was plenty worried about his wife and family back home. You see, his orders were to scuttle the ship, if capture looked inevitable. He tried to carry out those orders, but failed because our men fixed the damage soon enough to keep her afloat—and because his Japanese dynamite did not all go off. He said he didn't think our men could save the ship and insisted on staying in his cabin to go down with it. Shucks, they not only stopped it from sinking, but had it running after eight hours. Luckily, there's a man aboard who knows German.

There's only one of those officers I didn't like. That was the Gestapo agent. On the surface he was the smoothest and most likable—but too much so—that was the trouble. I didn't trust him and I think the other Germans were afraid of him. Perhaps that's the reason why I think they were afraid to say anything against the Nazis. They were in too much hot water already.

They were a pretty good bunch of fellows, and if all Germans are good, I hate to think that I'm taking part in killing a few. War is war, I guess. . . .

Your loving son,
Joe [Age 21]

In December, the first issue of the *Alumni Record* magazine was published. The twenty-page publication, with Marvin Walker ('35) as its editor, carried news of the campus and the alumni. It is doubtful that it was read by the current students, whose main source of news came from the *Reserve Record*.

The final issue of the *Reserve Record* for the fall term came out three days before Pearl Harbor and was filled with newsworthy information. In addition to announcing the school events that were to occur the week before

Christmas break, it also contained an editorial, which spoke fervently about the world situation and issued a call for the students to count their blessings, and concluded with the author's solution to the crisis:

> The way that you'll see easiest the blessings that are yours is to look at the rest of the world. China has been suffering for five years because of torture, starvation, threats of plagues, homeless millions, no medical care . . . no medical equipment, almost no hope. . . . Germany, or rather Hitler and his gang of crooks, are torturing the conquered peoples. . . . England . . . has lost a huge amount of her beautiful buildings; her homes have been demolished; her countrysides have been bombed. . . . She's suffering, but she's willing to suffer to wipe out the great evil—Hitler and what he represents. Therefore, as you receive your Christmas gifts, remember the stake America has in this world affair and slaughter. . . . The only true and manly thing to do is to declare war, and immediately.

The issue also carried Dr. Hayden's announcement that classes were canceled on January 2 in honor of Roger Clapp ('37). Roger, who had graduated from Harvard the previous spring magna cum laude and Phi Beta Kappa, had also won the Parker Fellowship for the year 1941–42. The boys could thus enjoy an extra day of holiday vacation.

Finally, the issue announced that plans were being made for the February House Party—the biggest social event of the year. The freshmen and sophomores would receive a free double weekend, as only juniors and seniors would be eligible to attend. Athletic competitions and plenty of activities, including a scavenger hunt, games in the common room, and, depending on the weather, skating and sleigh rides, would serve as entertainment. The highlight would be the formal dinner dance on Saturday evening, followed by a Sunday morning chapel service for the boys and their guests.

On December 7, 1941, at 7:50 A.M. in the Hawaiian Islands, Japanese planes attacked Pearl Harbor. On December 8, Congress adopted a declaration of war against Japan, and Prime Minister Winston Churchill informed Parliament that Britain, too, was at war with Japan. Germany and Italy declared war on the United States on December 11, and two days later Hungary and Bulgaria did the same. The "world crisis" suddenly became the "world war."

At the Academy, the boys were preparing for their fall term exams when news of Pearl Harbor came. At five o'clock in the chapel during the Christmas vespers service, Dean Wood delivered his message of peace; the girls from the Laurel School glee club sang with Reserve's glee club; and Dr.

Hayden gave his final address of the term. The school, the boys, and the world would never be the same.

Five days after Pearl Harbor, English master Brooks Shepard sent a letter home to Blaine Rawdon ('42), which serves as an example of the military terms that suddenly became a part of the vocabulary of a nation at war.

Western Reserve Academy
December 12, 1941

Dear "Bucket",

I'm giving you a rotten grade on your examination, and I hate to do it. Your war essay "Ready, Reserve?" is intelligent and courageous, but it's very badly written and organized, and it bristles with freshman errors—spelling, punctuation, organization, and the rest of the technical necessities for limpidly clear communication.

You probably realize that I wouldn't write you this sort of "Merry Christmas" note if I weren't fond of you and if I didn't feel, as you do, that we must all get on the ball and stay on it. Right now the order is: "Every man to his station, at once." Right now your station, like mine, is education. Right now you've muffed your job in rushing to the gun called "English"—you've run in circles, you've stumbled, you've damn near dropped the shell. You didn't quite drop it, but it was a close squeak.

Blaine: pull yourself out of these juvenile hysterics and make a calm analysis of your present job. You have the sort of mind that this country needs to train for future usefulness—not to draft indiscriminately for immediate military service. Have faith. All the information I can get encourages me to believe that the draft isn't going to be run by government clerks on the basis of mere chronological age; exemptions will probably be provided for youngsters like you whose academic record seems to justify postponement or deferment. But don't be childish in your faith, dear boy; those of us who respect our profession, and those of us who have loved the United States longer than we have loved Blaine Rawdon, will scrap you if you can't meet this emergency.

Affectionately,
Brooks Shepard

P.S. Please give my regards to your very charming mother. It's rather comforting to learn what a handful of U.S. Marines were able to do in defending Wake Island before its final capture, which will take place in a week or less. God help the Axis!

Shortly after the school closed for the holidays, Dean Wood wrote to Lucien Price.

Christmas 1941

My dear Lucien,

. . . About all we can do at present is to hope and pray that it may not be as bad as the present outlook indicates. Anyway I wish for you a larger measure of good health and the satisfaction of feeling that you are contributing to the success of a cause which any admirer of the Greeks of old would consider a very worthy one. It may be that we older men will have to step in and take the places of those who are called away. I want to keep feeling fit and I know you do. . . .

In November I enjoyed a visit of several days with Mr. and Mrs. Barnes.[1] They were in New York when the disaster hit Honolulu. They were planning to return in January. A letter from him a few days ago said he was unable to get any chance at a return passage. His whole school has been closed and the buildings turned into hospitals. It's a tough ordeal for him to have to stay here when so much needed there. He said he thought Honolulu as safe from an attack as Omaha, Nebraska would be. Well, we know now that "it can happen here . . ."

Faithfully and sincerely,
Harlan N. Wood

1. Homer F. Barnes, former head of the Academy's English department (1926–30), was the headmaster of the Kamehameha School in Honolulu, Hawaii.

Winter Term: January–March 1942

The Academy closed on December 12 and the boys went home for the holiday. On December 13, Dr. Hayden attended a meeting of the headmasters of the Interstate Association of Independent Schools: Cranbrook, Shady Side Academy, Nichols School, University School, and Western Reserve Academy. Together they devised a "tentative general policy" concerning the responsibilities of these schools in light of the "new national emergency," which was sent to parents on January 1, 1942.

Western Reserve Academy and the New National Emergency
(A Statement to the Parents of Western Reserve Boys)

On December 13, 1941, the headmasters of the Interstate Association of Independent Schools . . . conferred at length on the general problem of the new responsibilities of these schools in light of the emergency now confronting the nation.

Lacking as yet specific information of any kind from the military and naval authorities . . . certain considerations soon emerged from these deliberations as logical and basic in the determination of school policy. They were:

a) Despite the fact that virtually all of our boys are below the age of present and probable future military service requirements, we, as co-directors with the parents of most of their thinking and planning, owe them a serious responsibility with respect to their relationship to the national emergency.

b) ... A pell-mell rush of teenage youth to enlist at once would not only seriously lessen the probability of further educational growth for many of them, but it would certainly deprive their country, in many instances, of their maximum contribution to the nation's welfare both during and after the conflict. ... It seems evident that the boys in our schools should be thought of logically as potential leaders of considerably greater promise than the "run of the mill" of adolescent youth. ... But our responsibility to them now seems obvious: to do the best educational job we can with them from the standpoint of academic thoroughness, physical fitness, and morale, with carefully considered emphasis on such matters as:

  a) The duty of every American to view the present conflagration as public-spiritedly and as patriotically as he can.

  b) His obligation to give concrete expression to this thinking by helping the Red Cross, public health agencies, movements for the conservation of material, air raid protection, and all other essential war efforts.

  c) The advisability of some specific training, where possible, which will be generally helpful to most boys who are called to the colors, such as the construction and operation of the internal combustion engine, map making ... radio ... photography, first aid, etc. ...

  d) Advising and assisting all of our older boys to secure summer employment in war production industries. ...

  e) Stressing at all times the necessity of a calm, sober, and confident outlook with regard to our nation's task, based on the conviction we all have of ultimate victory where might and right go hand in hand.

... We want our institution to be a real part of our country's war effort, but we also want it to maintain the high quality of its educational service in order that its boys may be well prepared later to serve the best interests of peace. We know that you will all work with us whole-heartedly toward these ends.

                Joel B. Hayden
                Headmaster

With the reopening of school on January 3, Hayden received a flood of requests from alumni for letters of recommendation to be used for their entrance into military service. The individuality of these recommendations was indeed testimony to the fact that he really did know his boys. No two letters were alike.

Akron, Ohio
January 4, 1942

Dear Dr. Hayden:

I am preparing to decide within the next ten days what line of war service I want to apply for, and I wondered if you would write a letter of recommendation on my behalf that I could submit to the final selection boards of either the army or navy. . . .

The Akron Draft Board has advised that I will probably be called within the next three months, and I have decided to try for either the Air Corps or the Naval Supply. For application to these services I need sound reference. If you agreed to it, I would appreciate such a reference from you. . . .

    Sincerely,
    Tom Babcox ['37; Age 22]

January 7, 1942

Dear Tom:

Enclosed you will find the recommendation in triplicate to whom it may concern. I hope it hits the bullseye. . . . I am awfully glad you got back for the Christmas holiday. We need a family reunion, just on general principles, in this topsy turvy world. Speaking of the world, I am profoundly relieved that a decision has been reached. I have felt since 1936 that we should do something to meet the basic issues involved in human slavery. Now we are going in for keeps. And we are going to stay in on a planetary scale for decency, intelligence, and the development of freedom regardless of race, creed, and color.

    Ever yours,
    Joel B. Hayden

Albion College
January 20, 1942

Dear Dr. Hayden,

This letter is to ask if you would write me a letter of recommendation for the U.S. Army Air Corps. . . . I have already enlisted as a flying cadet. However, at the present time I am finishing the first semester of my sophomore year at Albion College. I expect to receive my appointment to leave for the basic training shortly after the first of February.

For your information I might say that the letter should contain something about my character, the activities I engaged in while at Reserve, and your own personal opinion as to my qualifications or prospects of becoming a good flying cadet.

    Yours sincerely,
    Harry Allchin, Jr. ['39; Age 21]

January 22, 1942

To Whom it May Concern
In re: Harry Allchin

    Harry Allchin, Jr., at present a sophomore at Albion College, Albion, Michigan, is making application for the U.S. Army Air Corps. Harry spent four years at Western Reserve Academy, graduating in the spring of 1939.

    He did a steadily improving job in his academic program. He played football, baseball and basketball and always showed himself a first class sportsman. He has a fine body, well cared for, and has learned the fine art of self-discipline. He was an excellent all around athlete, game and tireless.

    A rather quiet boy, he was always a good mixer, and became a school leader in terms of morale and School Council leadership.

    He has a fine disposition, and as headmaster, I always found him exercising balanced judgment in matters of discipline touching the individuals in the student body.

    I have no reservations whatever in making the statement that he would be an excellent flying cadet, with latent capacities in him which will underscore and confirm what I have said about him at the secondary school level of experience.

    I shall be very happy to add information if there is any request for it.

    Very sincerely yours,
    Joel B. Hayden
    Headmaster

    Articles in the *Reserve Record* suddenly went beyond the normal coverage of campus events. Along with the news of a new bowling alley opening in downtown Hudson and a mad rush to Freddie's Barbershop to get the new "crew cut" hairstyle, the paper printed announcements of changes to be made in the curriculum (including a new "war-training activities" program), a list of twelve students who had enrolled in the Civil Defense Program, and patriotic editorials. There were calls to conserve and calls for each boy to give forty cents a month toward the purchase of war bonds. Air-raid wardens were assigned to each dorm.

    The January 8, 1942, issue of the *Record* displayed a copy of a postcard from Scottish exchange student Brian Brough ('39), written and mailed from Scotland fourteen hours after the events at Pearl Harbor. "Up and at the Beggars, for all you're worth," the postcard read. "Give them all you've got and more. We're with you every time. Good fighting to all Reserve Alumni."

    One editorial headline exclaimed, "United States Fights All-Out and Long War as We Remember Pearl Harbor." "War, and every horror with it, is upon us at last," the writer declared.

The point concerning us is, "Where do we stand? What are we to do? What can we do?" . . . We may be asked to give up our spring vacations . . . if we are, let it go at that. If we do have to sacrifice vacations and maybe the houseparty and dances, it is because Washington and the military department of our government feel it necessary. The least we can do is to obey their orders and not utter one word of complaint, especially when thousands of Americans are dying to "lick the beggars."

There was also news of the establishment of a "News Room" in the chapel library. In this room, which was lined with maps of all theaters of war, copies of newspapers and periodicals were made available to keep students informed of current events.

The January 22 *Reserve Record* listed results of an all-school meeting held to discuss students' suggestions as to the school's contribution to the national defense. The student council suggested eliminating the popular orchestras hired for the proms and dances, investing the money saved into defense bonds, and to present the girls at the dances with defense stamps in place of corsages. Others suggested substituting square dancing and using recordings in place of live music for the more expensive proms, using cheaper paper for the *Record,* and omitting table flowers in the dining hall.

In the midst of all the excitement, Dean Wood wrote to Lucien Price.

January 24, 1942

Dear Lucien,

. . . How quickly life can change. It seemed to me that last term was one of the best terms I have ever seen in the school. We had a fine group of boys, there was a good spirit, good work was done, there was progress and growth. "Pearl Harbor" happened just about the time we closed. We reopened on January 3rd. We had not been in session a week when it was possible to feel a different atmosphere. Perhaps my having lived in a school atmosphere so long makes me quite susceptible to changing conditions. But there was no mistaking it. There is a restlessness, an uncertainty, to a certain extent an indifference, although the latter is limited to a few. Then there is the faculty to deal with. "Something must be done about it at once." There must be something spectacular so that the world will talk about what is being done at Reserve. All this is with good intentions, but the trouble here is the same as it is in the nation. Some are so eager to let the clutch in, that the engine is likely to get stalled, or the starter flooded with too much gasoline (talk-talk). One master proposes a series of ten lectures over a period of two weeks for the entire school on the general subject of the background and the causes of the war. Notes to be taken and reports required. These lectures to be given each morning during the

Ramon Spooner's prize-winning photo of Blaine Rawdon drinking a Coke. Hardscrabble 1942

third period and the regular daily schedule adjusted to fit. Can't you imagine about how cordially a disrupting of our schedule for such a purpose would be received by two-hundred adolescent boys? Fortunately the plan has been quite considerably modified, but not without some clouded glances at those who are too old to really grasp the necessity of immediate action along such lines. Some projects have been undertaken which will doubtless be of some value and which will not disrupt the regular progress of the work of the school. I enclose a sheet which each boy was asked to fill out and hand in this morning. These activities are all to be scheduled on free time and will not disrupt the orderly daily program. As you will note, they are worthwhile activities—especially such items as "First-Aid" instruction. . . . This is a beautiful day. Bright sunshine and mild temperature. . . .

                Very sincerely,
                Harlan N. Wood

In February the "40-cent Defense Plan" went into effect. Students and faculty alike were asked to donate forty cents a month, the goal being to raise a fund to buy defense bonds. Similarly, the Red Cross and USO inaugurated a national campaign to collect books for use in army camps. The school cooperated with Hudson village and township officials who were trying to "provide army men with literature." A box was placed in Seymour Hall to receive the books.

The February 5 *Record* announced the first-prize winner of the photography contest sponsored by the *Hardscrabble* to get pictures for the new yearbook. Photographer Ramon Spooner ('42) was awarded a free yearbook for the winning photograph, an informal pose of his classmate Blaine "Buckets" Rawdon drinking a Coke.

The February 12 issue detailed the need to conserve. It cited the new ruling by the executive committee with regards to the restricted use of Academy autos: "Not only is school transportation of Reserve rooters to cease, but also students having dental or other medical appointments must attend these while on Saturday leaves or weekends."

In morning chapel it was reported that Mr. McGill urged students to avoid breakage and waste in the dining hall and to use sugar sparingly. Nan Lingle, the school dietician, was busy studying the dining hall budget "in order to get more for the money." Savings from these conservation efforts went to three separate funds: school protection against rising prices, the Scholarship Fund, and the purchasing of Defense Bonds.

The long-awaited House Party weekend in February was a huge success, far exceeding the boys' expectations. Dr. Hayden wrote a special message welcoming the guests, which appeared on the front page of the February 20 *Reserve Record:* "The backdrop to our little stage is grim war," he wrote. "May the remembrance of these days of fellowship and fun be part of the strength we can all take into whatever future awaits us." The collage of photographs that appeared in the following issue left no doubt that a good time was had by all. It was the last House Party until its 1946 postwar revival.

In the meantime, Dr. Hayden received an update from Harry Allchin, Jr. ('39).

Albion College
February 17, 1942

Dear Dr. Hayden,

I want to take this means of thanking you for your very nice letter of recommendation.

I have successfully qualified for the Army Air Corps, and at the present time I am waiting for my notice to report for training. I will probably leave about March 1st or shortly after. I feel very grateful that I was able to qualify. My only hope is now that I will be able to make a good pilot and to serve my country to the best of my ability.

Sincerely yours,
Harry Allchin, Jr. [Age 22]

The winter term sports season came to a close, with school swimming records broken by seniors Lewis Ball and Ralston Hayden. Coach Ed Caldwell's wrestlers took the league championship. It was the last competition for the coach, who soon took a leave of absence to enter the service.

RESERVE RECORD

VOLUME XVIII—No. 18
FEBRUARY 26, 1942

Stunt Night, Sleigh Ride, Bowling Contribute to Houseparty Weekend Fun

23 Hathaway-Brown Girls To Attend Dance Here Saturday

Reserve will play host to 23 Hathaway-Brown dorm girls Saturday afternoon and evening. This will be the first time that Reserve has had a party of this kind.

The girls will arrive shortly before supper, eat with their dates, and then be part of the cheering section for the Reserve-Cranbrook basketball game. After the game there will be informal dancing in Cutler Hall for the girls, their dates, and the Cranbrook boys.

The girls are: Seniors—Molly Kramer, Patricia Williams, Suzanne Caughlan, Mary O'Ferrall, Betty Cowdery, Jean Marshall, Patricia Montenyohl, Jane Anne Anderson, Helen Hildreth, Joan Henry; Juniors—Marilyn Gernhardt, Suzan Van Cleve, Ruth Wiener, Shirley Gibbs, Marilyn Schumacher, Jane Dunbar, Barbara King; Sophomores—Jane Brouse, Peggy Lou Anderson, Peggy

Guests Leave After Full Entertainment Program

Here are shots taken of Reservites and their dates during the House Party: Jim Stevenson and Mary Ellen Wier, Judy Simon and Bill Crisp watch the amateur keglers at the bowling alleys; top center—Ken Goldsmith helps Nancy Rowell, his date, by carrying some of her luggage to her room; top right—John Dickerson, Friday's M. C., and his sister-brother, Dick; lower left—Gene Lindsay and Kitty Cockley on Carrol Cutler's front steps; lower left by center—"Looie" Ball and John Clark watch a figmentary wrestling match on the stage on Friday night; lower center—a sledload of snow fiends tour the campus; right center—Bob Boyer and Jane King, Doug Abbey and Alma Foster; and, lastly, lower right, Walter Haggardy goes into a "Spirit of Sports" routine.

Lucas, Joan Fishgrund, Florence Robinson, and Marilyn Lavin.

By Edward Howard

The Winter Houseparty received, before it occurred, more build-up and publicity than any event remembered recently at Reserve. It has received, since then, plaudits enough to make the advance notices seem inadequate.

Significantly well-managed was the time element; when most of the Reservites and their dates wanted something to do, there was given them the fullest opportunity—and when they wanted 15 minutes or three quarters of an hour which was untouched and unmarred by the minds of those who planned the week-end, it was there for them.

A summary of the high-spots of the high-point would be incomplete as a record and a review of the three days; for an accurate picture involves a great many things more than the few which took the most time and made the most noise. The vaudevillian show

(Continued on Page 3)

Reserve Record front page (February 26, 1942).

❦ Spring Term: March–June 1942

In a normal school year, spring break lasted for three weeks, but this year it was shortened to two. School was to be dismissed one week earlier to enable graduates to take advantage of the plans initiated by many colleges whereby freshman classes would begin in June rather than September. For the rest of the student body it would mean an extra week of summer vacation. In the temporarily slowed pace of activity during the break, Dean Wood again wrote to Mr. Price.

March 18, 1942

My dear Lucien,

Things are moving along in about the usual manner, now that the first shocks of the war have been absorbed. We are all looking forward with some forebodings as to what the economic situation may do to our enrollment. At present it is not quite up to what it was at this time last year. But it is better than I feared it might be and here is hoping that we may be able have an enrollment somewhere near our present one. . . .

I was in Cleveland yesterday and when returning I met Mrs. Hayden and Mrs. Tepper at the Euclid station and sat in a seat back of them on the way out. They had been to hear Professor Nicholas J. Spykman of Yale who spoke at the Foreign Affairs Council luncheon. She, Mrs. Hayden, had heard and was bringing home all the answers. "For you know, Mr. Wood, that Prof. S. is a great scholar and he must understand about the situation." Of course, all wars have been settled in the past by great scholars and economists—this was my thought as I listened attentively. She was riding the train to save tires and the car, but the first day out she raised a blister in her heel and loaded Mrs. Tepper with so many bundles that I could hardly recognize her. Well, this is still a land of freedom and each of us can win the war in his or her own way. As I sit here at my desk I can look across the athletic field to the main highway and it is difficult to note any decrease in the number of cars passing over the number a year ago. It is a genuine March day, raw, chilly, considerable wind and flurries of snow. However, the grass begins to take on something of the color of spring and it won't be long now.

. . . I hope you are well and that the duties of your office are not too heavy. I dare say we shall all be witnessing news such as the world has never known before. I dare not allow myself to think of all the horrible possibilities of the coming summer months. I believe everyone feels a sense of relief in the thought that perhaps an offensive may be approaching and that MacArthur will be the chief. . . .

Very sincerely,
Harlan N. Wood

Toledo, Ohio
March 25, 1942

Dear Mr. Hayden (I think of you always as "Doc" or Joel),

I feel very guilty not having been to Hudson at all this school year—but being in Toledo has made it almost impossible. I haven't driven home since Thanksgiving and I hate to use up the rubber on Mother's car. I have been reading the *Record* regularly, though, so know a little about what has been going on. There is no question about WRA's cooperating with "the nasty job" and it's probably for the best now, despicable as the whole mess is.

I have been in personnel work ever since last February (1941) with Thompson Products and like it a great deal. The time is fast approaching, however, when my deferment will no longer be tenable and I shall be faced with a few alternatives in the Service. Right now—fantastic as it sounds even to me—I am considering the Navy Air Corps, and one of the requirements is the presentation of a "To whom it may concern"—a brief recommendation. You probably know me as well as anyone, Doc, and if you could squeeze in a moment to do this, I should be more than grateful. If I decide against the Air Corps—or it is decided for me—the note will still be good for some other branch. In the meantime, I'd rather nothing is said about it, one way or another.

If I thought eight years ago I could even consider a move like this I'd probably have fallen through the ground, but time and circumstance change many things, it seems. It's been very difficult, to say the least, and it will be more so, to make the necessary adjustments to wartime thinking. I haven't thought any more about the murderous side to the situation than I could help knowing it would only make participation that much harder. . . .

Sincerely,
Bill Danforth ['34; Age 25]

April 1, 1942

To Whom It May Concern
In re: William H. Danforth

It is a real pleasure to write a letter of recommendation for Bill Danforth. I have known him for fifteen years, and that really means something, because I was close to his family before I came to this school; and I was his headmaster here for the three years which he spent in Hudson before going to Yale. He was a top boy in the school. Unquestioned integrity, splendid courage, a disciplined mind, a capacity for hard work characterizes Bill.

And when it comes to personal charm, unselfishness, and the approval of his fellows, he is also tops.

He has got good stuff in him. His mother and father built a home which has stood the stress and strain of great shocks, and never once did they run up a white flag.

I would not hesitate to send Bill on a confidential commission to any spot on the globe. He could be trusted implicitly and some day he would show up with a complete report and the same straight look in his eye and the same straight backbone under his shirt.

       Very sincerely yours,
       Joel B. Hayden

               April 8, 1942

Dear Dr. Hayden:

Am in General Air Corps Administration and will be here in Flight A of Jefferson Barracks, Mo. for another three to four weeks. Then they say to some air field "somewhere." It is really a new life for many like myself here. Uncle Sam is really building an Air Force these days and it should show results soon. Imagine there are many from WRA in the services now. There are a fine bunch down here.

       Regards,
       Reid B. Babcox ['29; Age 30]

In April Louis Tepper's duties changed drastically. The boys in the machine shop, under his guidance, began a monumental effort to fulfill a war contract from the Bardons and Oliver Automatic Screw Machine Company of Cleveland. The April 9 *Record* carried the news of the machine shop gearing up for production: The shop was redesigned to meet wartime demands of fulfilling a 2,300-part order received by the company from the government. The order included a request for eight hundred gear shafts and fifteen hundred steady-rest slides for box-turning tools. Tepper arranged the specifications for the work, which was to be done by the boys who were taking machine shop as one of the new "war activities."

Thirteen boys volunteered for the villagewide scrap drive, initiated by Hudson's mayor Guy F. Garman to raise money "to use in preparation for possible attacks on Akron factories or the . . . ordnance plant at Ravenna." Two and one-half tons of cardboard and newsprint were smashed flat and baled tight by some of the volunteers; others baled and loaded "a couple of tons" of magazines and newspapers, with the purpose of separating pulp paper at $12.50 per ton from glazed rag paper at $16.00 per ton.

Charles Tanner ('44), a sophomore attending the Academy, received a letter from his brother Harvey ('38x), who was "Somewhere in Iceland" serving with the army.

April 9, 1942

Dear Charles:

This letter might seem funny to you, but I want you to take it for just its face value.

You are old enough to know what the Hell is going on, so before you do anything, think and then think again. In the near future you will most likely be able to get a job that will pay you plenty. Remember this though: it will only be temporary. When the war is over, the people who will feel it the most are the ones who are laid off and have nothing to fall back on. They might be making "big" money now, but when it is all over, only the best will be kept on. That is when the kids that are making money now will be sitting on their tails, with no money, no jobs, and nothing to turn to. The boys who have turned down the money, and have taken advantage of their opportunities for education will have a better chance.

If you will only go to summer school from here on in, it will only make your odds better for a good living. (It will not be long now before you will be in the army, too.) In summer school you can "pick up" at least a half year before you graduate from high school. You can pick up some more in college before you are "picked up". . . .

You have been my greatest worry since the U.S. entered the war, and now with the fall of Bataan it bothers me more. By going to summer school you will be cut out on a lot of fun; your summer vacation will be shortened, you will not be able to do the things you have in the past; but now is the time to give up a few pleasures for something more worthwhile, not only for yourself but for your country. The U.S. needs more trained men. We might think things are hard now, but just wait! . . .

If you do the things I have requested and do as Mother and Grandmother wish I will let you have anything you want.

The things I have said might carry some weight and then again they might be just words, but now is the time for you to look ahead and get ahead. For the first time in my life I am looking ahead and when you get right down to it, there could be no worse time. Our time here is limited from day to day. We have our work to do—no change during the week at all. We have no idea what the next day might bring and there is no point in trying to figure it out either.

Harvey [Age 22]

P.S. Remember this—your first duty is to Mother and Grandmother—then think of yourself. H.

April also brought about the second issue of the *Alumni Record,* the first to be published after Pearl Harbor. It was sent to all alumni, most of whom were preparing to enter the service. The issue is a curious one in that there is

James D. Tew, Jr. ('29x); front row, center. *Archives*

(Left and right) Carl Weiant, Jr. ('33). *Archives*

only one copy in the archives. Some years after the war the alumni magazine, in two separate issues, put out a request for additional copies for inclusion in the archives, apparently with no results.

The issue contained a message from former *Reserve Record* advisor and alumni secretary LaRue Piercy, who was working in personnel at the Martin Bomber Plant in Maryland. "There goes another P-40 pursuit ship now, the second since I've been writing this afternoon," he stated. "More and more bombers go roaring away for army delivery every day."

Dean Wood's message reminded the alumni, "This is by no means the first time the shock of war has been known to this campus. During the period

Harrie Stewart ('30) and Frank Thompson ('29) playing handball at the Academy, 1929. *Archives*

of the Civil War this campus was almost deserted. The first World War found the re-established Academy in its opening years and with difficulty did it survive the shock of those days. . . . The same old spirit that has so often shown itself in winning victories on field or track is the spirit with which Reserve will do its part in winning this war."

Separate articles noted the deaths of James Tew ('30) and Carl Weiant, Jr. ('33). James was killed in action over Malta, where he had been serving as a member of the Canadian Air Force. Carl was lost in naval action in the vicinity of Iceland. This brought the number of alumni lost to five.

April 11, 1942

Dear Mr. and Mrs. Weiant:

One of our students from Newark [Ohio] has just given me a newspaper article which tells of the message you have recently received from the U.S. Navy. Needless to state, I am deeply moved.

Though Carl was graduated from Western Reserve Academy a number of years ago, we remember him very well for the sterling lad that he was. Quiet, dependable, conscientious and capable, he was always willing to go "all out" in the performance of his duty. We know that he unhesitatingly and unreservedly turned his talents and his energies to the service of his country.

We want you to know that we feel a deep sense of loss, as you do, but also that we share the profound pride which is rightfully yours for the splendid life this boy lived, a life that he has given up that his country may live.

Dr. Hayden is away from the school for a few days. When he returns he, too, will communicate with you. I know that he remembers Carl well, for he has spoken of him several times in recent months. Boys like Carl make an imprint that lasts.

We want you to know that we are thinking of you and that in a very real sense we are with you.

Yours sincerely,
Ralph W. McGill

Another article in the *Alumni Record* mentioned two alumni who were known to be located in the Philippines: George H. Fairchild ('88), who had been living in Manila for several years, and Lt. Harrie B. Stewart ('30), whose last known address was Bataan, where he was a first lieutenant with the Army Engineers. On April 9 Bataan fell to the Japanese, who inflicted the "Death March" on American and Filipino prisoners. It was later learned that Harrie was among the thousands of prisoners. He survived for two years through the horrendous experience of a Japanese prisoner of war until his death in 1944, when the prisoner ship in which he and others were being transported was sunk.

May 6, 1942

Dear Dr. Hayden:

... Am at Ft. McDowell on Angel Island in San Francisco Bay. This is West Coast port of embarkation for either Australia or Hawaii. I am leaving any minute now with my gang of about four hundred Air Corps men. Yes, I'd say WRA is doing its share in this mess. Have all new equipment now including one of the new type steel helmets. Heavier but more protection. Hope to God this won't last too long. Have many things still to do. A year or two of this would be plenty. It is new to most of us. Good luck to you and best from me to WRA and Hayden family.

Reid Babcox ['29; Age 30]

Early in May it was announced that the government had instituted a sugar-rationing program. The boys who had turned eighteen were required to register for rationing cards, being allowed one sack of sugar per week. The younger boys were exempt.

Later in the month plans for the following year's curriculum were laid out for the returning students in the May 14 *Record*. The editorial the following week took a look back on the year, while the one by senior John Dickerson ('42), published in the final issue for Commencement Day on May 31, looked toward the future and cited the primary task facing the graduating class: winning not the war but peace. As the graduating class marched in

Hardscrabble advertisement. Hardscrabble *1942*

procession towards the chapel on Commencement Day, Congress was already making plans to lower the draft age to eighteen.

> Somewhere in England
> June 23, 1942

Dear Dr. Hayden,

When Sherman said "War is Hell" he made a gross understatement. If only those strikers could spend five months up here with us; we wouldn't have any more labor trouble at home. The more we see the more we marvel at the ability of the human body to take punishment and still keep ticking.

The infantry used to make fun of the medical troops; but now we hear nothing but praise. The first-aid men are doing a wonderful job. They walk out past the doughboys who are hugging their foxholes and pick up the wounded as soon as they fall. It makes us all fight harder to watch men like that.

> All my best,
> Harvey [Tanner, '38x; Age 22]

> June 23, 1942

Dear Dr. Hayden,

. . . I joined the army last May 27th and have been living quite an interesting and different life ever since.

They placed me in the Military Police and I've been learning and practicing their particular art of warfare ever since, which by the way, is very interesting. At the present time I'm stationed about a mile from the Martin Bomber Plant, which is about five miles outside of Baltimore, Maryland. We live in tents right in the heart of a large woods under more or less simulated battle conditions. So far it's been a lot of fun, but they certainly do keep a fellow on his toes around here, and one of the first things I learned was the fact that when we play a game, we play for keeps, by either fair means or foul. I really do love the life and work though. Of course there are a lot of bumps, but I guess you can find those anywhere.

Last week I walked a "beat" in Baltimore just about every night. . . . This week I am acting as a machine gunner on an armored scout car doing patrol duty, and next week, I do patrol duty by myself on a motorcycle. We get a hand at just about every type M.P. duty pulled. I get a big kick out of directing traffic on street corners, but I don't know how good I am. Our scout cars are just like the ones that are continually rolling through good old Hudson.

In a few months I will be eligible for Officer's Training School, which I am certainly looking forward to. My commanding officer said I shouldn't have any trouble either getting in or through it, and I certainly hope he's right.

Torrey Eaton ('37), building a model battleship, during his senior year. *Archives*

Most of the fellows here are from the Middle West, which of course just makes this the best darned fighting outfit ever.

      Sincerely,
      Bill Glover ['42x; Age 19]

JULY–AUGUST 1942

Following commencement and the closing of the school year, the Haydens went to Vermont and Maine for the summer, but not before Dr. Hayden united Assistant Headmaster Ralph W. "Scotch" McGill and Secretary Bernice Cromwell in marriage in the Academy chapel. They set up housekeeping in McGill's recently remodeled apartment on the second floor of Cutler Hall (present day Ellsworth Hall).

The number of faculty members leaving to enter the service was growing, necessitating the hiring of replacements. Dean Wood tended to the search, though replacements were increasingly difficult to find.

In June Japanese planes attacked Midway Island, Rommel and his Afrika Corps captured Tobruk in North Africa, and Dwight D. Eisenhower was appointed commander of U.S. Forces in the European theater of operations.

On July 15 it was reported that two thousand Jews, believing they were being sent to labor camps, were deported to Auschwitz. News from Poland on August 22 estimated that seventy-five thousand Polish Jews had been deported to "labor camps" since August 10. An estimated four hundred thousand Jews were reported slaughtered in occupied Europe by the end of the month.

On August 7 the 1st Marine Division landed on Guadalcanal in the Solomon Islands. Torrey Eaton ('37) wrote to McGill from the vicinity.

Somewhere in the Pacific
July 3, 1942

Dear Scotchman,

Your letter of the second arrived this afternoon, and I was so surprised and pleased that I hasten to answer forthwith.

You probably remember Chayney [Charles Cheyney], '35 I believe. He's a reserve officer on the U.S.S. *Maury*. Day before yesterday I had a long chat with him about old times at Reserve. We quite picked the old place apart, but we seemed to find many pleasant remembrances too. I wonder if the poor Reservites are as henpecked as in years past. I should very much like to see the old place again.

I've been on the *Smith* since graduation [from the U.S. Naval Academy] a year ago last February and am quite convinced that the navy is tops. Also, the first day I get back to the states I'm going to be married to a very lovely and charming army brat.

I've been following in the masters' footsteps lately teaching math to a young quartermaster of mine who wants to get into the [U.S. Naval] Academy.

Censorship regulations prohibit any interesting news. Give my best to Messrs. Hayden, Piercy and Waring. Also my thanks to Mrs. Kitzmiller[1] for her note. Thanks again for your letter, and please do write again when you are able.

    Best of luck,
    Toreador

---

1. Helen Kitzmiller, the school historian, wrote *One Hundred Years of Western Reserve*, a brief history for the school's centennial celebration. She was married to Harrison Kitzmiller, German and French master (1925–54).

Torrey's letter to "Scotch" McGill was forwarded to Dr. Hayden in Vermont by Mrs. McGill. Dr. Hayden wrote her a note on the back and returned it to the school.

July 1942

My dear "Mrs. Mac,"

Thanks for everything—stamps, news, general dependability in keeping things a-going.

Faraway Farm, the Haydens' summer home in East Stoneham, Maine. *Courtesy George Manlove ('32)*

This Eaton letter is good and typical. I'm glad he's found his girl and wife, because now he'll really begin to live and meet the normal responsibilities of life.

Chan has kept me well posted.[1] Just enuf, not too much.

Really resting. I still have some back and shoulder tension pains, but the gardens and Gina and "Million Acres" and "Faraway Farm" are gradually softening me up.[2]

Had a good letter from Teb.[3] Boys want some early practice as last year. O.K. Ask Mac to set it up with Teb, in the last year's pattern. School council and the prefects should be back Monday night, September 14th.

Glad you're going to have your home and may all good things be yours and Mac's. This little Vermont home is a wonderful tonic to us.

                Best,
                Joel Hayden

1. English master Chandler T. Jones (1926–61).

2. The Haydens' daughter Jean, her husband, Sam Guarnaccia, and their eighteen-month-old daughter, Gina, lived in a little red cottage on the outskirts of Middlebury, Vermont, which they lovingly called "Million Acres." But "Faraway Farm," the Haydens' summer home in East Stoneham, Maine, provided what Dr. Hayden called "the vagabondage of isolation."

3. Roscoe J. "Tebbie" Thiebert (Math, Physical Education [1931–59])

Somewhere in England
July 18, 1942

Dear Dr. Hayden,

We are finally becoming accustomed to our new type of life. It was a difficult transformation but very necessary. The two main sources of discomfort now are artillery and bugs. I think the bugs are on the go all the time. The non-biting types are just playful, but as bad as their ferocious cousins. At night, when it gets cold, they just are not happy unless they are in your clothes and next to the skin, and it seems as if everything that crawls is determined to be happy. . . .

Harvey [Tanner, '38x, Age 22]

July 19, 1942

My dear Dr. Hayden:

I thought you would be interested in knowing that [my son] Torrey was married on July 16th to Miss Gerda Elizabeth Miller, the daughter of Major George Miller, U.S. Army, and Mrs. Miller, of San Francisco. Also, that Torrey was recently promoted, and is now a Lieutenant (j.g.) in the navy.

. . . Mrs. Eaton and I often think of the days when Torrey was in Hudson, and of your kindness, particularly your help in getting him an appointment to the Naval Academy. He is very enthusiastic about his naval career. He has not yet been in any of the actions, having been on a convoy and patrol work off this coast, between here and Honolulu. He is on a destroyer. Of course, he may be sent to the Far East, or other scenes of action, at any time, but we are thankful that he has not been so far.

Cordially,
Wm. W. Eaton

As the summer vacation period drew to a close, Dean Wood took a break from his duties of enrollment and faculty concerns and wrote a letter to Lucien Price.

August 26, 1942

My dear Lucien,

. . . Here at the school things are beginning to liven up with the approach of Sept. 1st. The outlook is that our enrollment will be nearly or quite up to capacity. Strange as it may seem we have the largest freshman class enrolled that we have ever had. Of course, we like to see that, for it is much easier to keep the school filled when it builds from the bottom up. Members of the faculty are beginning to filter in one by one. There will be three new men on the faculty.

Mr. King has been in the Service since the first of June.[1] Mr. Waring is somewhere in Africa in the Ambulance Service. Mr. Eaton will not return, due to the death of his mother and serious illness of his father.[2] Morse has been called and will leave before many weeks.[3] Likewise, Walker.[4] Others may go before the year is over. So it casts a shadow of uncertainty over all as we approach the opening of this new year.

. . . I have missed the freedom with which I formerly used my tires. You will remember that I have always enjoyed exploring the country. But that is no sacrifice when one thinks of world conditions and of what the day of reckoning may be like. Will the tide never turn? While in Chautauqua I heard a lecture by Mr. Hill, for many years manager of the American Express Co. in Athens. He was there through the days of German invasion and for some time after. He escaped after Jan. 1st and came to this country a few weeks ago. When the history of this war is written the story of Greece—her courage, her suffering—will be one of the tragic chapters. . . .

                    Faithfully yours,
                    Harlan N. Wood

1. Glenn W. King (Music Department 1933–71).
2. Stacey E. Eaton (French, Spanish 1934–42, 1943–44).
3. Robert T. Morse (History 1937–42).
4. Marvin E. Walker '35 (Alumni secretary, director of publications 1941–42).

THE SCHOOL YEAR 1942–43

This Is a War Year!

🍂 FALL TERM: SEPTEMBER–DECEMBER 1942

"This is a War Year!" proclaimed the headline of the first *Record* editorial of the school year. On September 23, Dr. Hayden wrote in a letter to Trustee Harry L. Findlay, "This is a devastating time for the alumni of the school." Findlay knew this well, as his son Malcolm ('38) and several of his nephews were of draft age. His letter continued: "One hundred-eight names appear on our Service Honor Roll and they are coming in at the rate of several a day.[1] One hundred-eight was the score last Sunday afternoon. Graduates from the class of 1923 down to date are in the thick of it. Those of us who are older and who are devoted to the school must keep the core of affectionate loyalty going in such a way that it is positive and articulate and far-sighted."

In a letter written earlier in the month, to the father of one of the boys, "Scotch" McGill spoke of changes in enrollment for the coming year. "We have had such a strong enrollment pressure during the last month," he stated, "that we have closed enrollment with 170 or 172 boarding students on the bottom line. Without checking to make sure, I believe this is the largest number of boarding boys we have had for several years. We feel in these uncertain times a good many prep schools are not finding themselves so fortunate."

---

1. In the fall of 1942, Arts and Crafts supervisor Charles T. Mears designed a scroll bearing the names of ninety-two alumni and masters who were in the war. It was framed under glass and was hung in the Cutler Hall common room and referred to as the Service Roll of Honor.

Hyde Park, N.Y.
September 15, 1942

Dear Dr. Hayden,

Just a note to let you know that I have changed my address again. After having been lucky enough to attend the Military Police School at Ft. Riley Kansas, I was sent here.

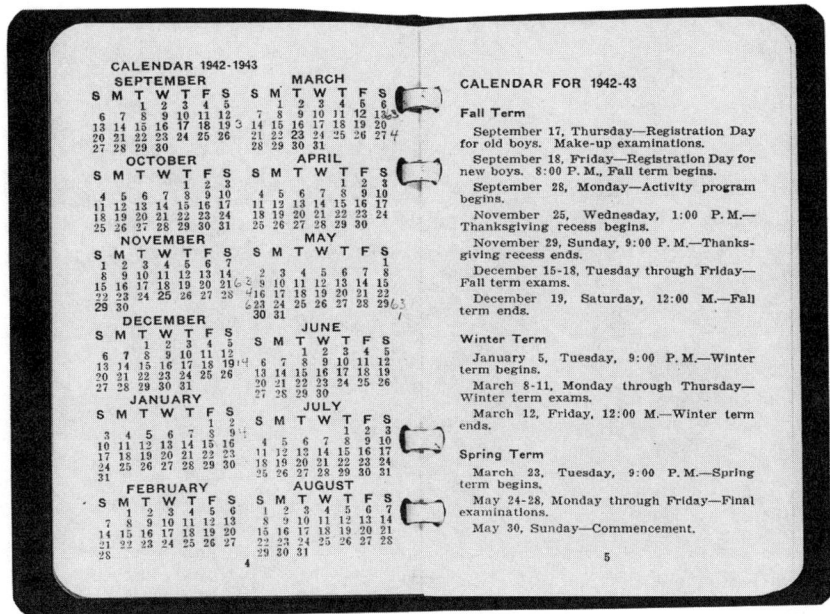

School calendar 1942–43. *Student Handbook*

The work is of such a nature that I am not even allowed to mention it in letters of any sort, including those to the family, which is a big problem at times. I believe the address alone [the home of FDR], though, makes the basic idea of the job quite obvious.

I am actually in love with my work and the army as a whole. I have certainly been getting some marvelous breaks. I was ordered to apply for officer's school at Ft. Riley, but unfortunately I couldn't make up my mind what I wanted to do. While doing so, the next I knew I was on a troop train headed for we knew not where—but here we are. I plan upon placing an application in the future—but I know my chance for acceptance will not be nearly so great as it would have been at Riley.

Best wishes,
Bill Glover ['42x; Age 19]

As the class of 1943 entered its senior year in September, the draft age was still twenty-one. This changed in November, when Congress lowered it to eighteen and raised it to forty-five. Suddenly, not only were recent graduates and alumni (from even the earliest days of the refounded school) affected by this change, so were the majority of the current seniors, for the new amendment stipulated that "any person 18 or 19 years of age who, while pursuing a course of instruction at a high school or similar institution of learning, is ordered to report for induction under this act during the last half of the academic year." However, induction could be postponed by request until

Bill Glover ('42x) at Hyde Park, New York, Fall 1942. *Archives*

the end of the academic year. With the amended draft law came a new round of requests for recommendations from the school.

Princeton University
October 4, 1942

Dear Dr. Hayden,

    I realize that I've been very disloyal in not writing you of recent developments but trust that [my brother] Bradford ['44] has kept you at least a little informed of me. At any rate I am very seriously considering and fully intend to join the American Field Service which is now operating in Libya and Egypt this coming February. However, as you might have already guessed, I need some sort of a letter of recommendation to even be considered for a position and I immediately thought of you. If you think you can jeopardize your reputation I would appreciate it very much if the letter were addressed to me. I'll see that it reaches the proper hands.

    I have given the whole matter of leaving school some very serious thought. I know that I cannot possibly remain in school another two or three months with things as such. The branch that offered noncombatant service and immediate service was what I have chosen. Father thought that if that was what I really wanted I should go ahead and make plans for it—a generous and considerate attitude, I believe. I'll need another year of pre-med work when I get back anyway, so that the other half-year I was originally planning for next spring will not be wasted—nor will the present one.

Cordially,
Howard M. Wells, Jr. ['41; Age 18]

Williams College
October 5, 1942

Dear Doctor and Mrs. Hayden,

Since I saw you last . . . I have become a naval aviation cadet and, as a result, a very pleased young man. Thanks to your swell letter of recommendation, and also my other ones, I went through the enlistment process in four days and was sworn in on Thursday, Sept. 17. The mental and physical exams went without a hitch and my eyes were the best among the group I went through it all with.

As things stand now I will apparently be called to active training duty on or about November 15. There are about twelve other fellows from Williams [College] going on that date also and it appears that we will be allowed to live together as a "Williams Squadron." I can't wait to go and if everything comes off on schedule I should be ready for combat in thirteen or fourteen months.

I am busily engaged in taking my mid-year exams at Williams at this point and this Thursday will be my last day. After that there will be plenty to do in the next five weeks, including saying goodbye to my relatives who are scattered hither and yon. . . .

Remember me to all the masters. Tell Mr. Culver that I'll shoot down a "Jap" for him just to prove that my special "flying permits" were worth it. I hope all the boys at school are applying themselves to their war courses because they are certainly a vital necessity.

Perhaps I won't see you for sometime to come so here is many thanks for all that you and Reserve have done for me during my "incubation" period.

        Yours sincerely,
        Dick Marshall ['41; Age 19]

Once again, the *Reserve Record* continued to report events on the school campus. The October 1 issue brought the news of the death of Frederick W. Ashley. From 1892 to 1897 he had been the principal of the "old" school; perhaps more importantly, he authored the alma mater, which was set to music by Ralph Clewell, head of the music department, in 1932 and is still sung today.

The editorial in the October 8 issue asked students to cooperate with the adoption of required athletics five days a week: "At a time when almost every young man of Western Reserve Academy may look forward to service in the armed forces of the nation, physical fitness is more than essential; it may mean the difference between life and death in hand-to-hand combat." The issue also noted that the Academy boys had collected nearly a truckload of phonograph records and books for the USO the weekend before. On that same weekend, Hudson held a scrap-metal drive, "adding to the huge pile collected in the town which has given Hudson Township the reputation as a

The Alma Mater, words by Fred W. Ashley, music by Ralph E. Clewell. *Archives*

national leader." Every Sunday carloads of scrap metal were loaded by "townsmen and many Reserve masters." The scrap was then taken by train to Cleveland, divided into steel and miscellaneous scrap, and sent on to the steel mills for re-melting.

The front page of the October 15 *Reserve Record* contained excerpts from a letter received by sophomore John Winterling ('43) from English master J. Fred Waring describing his experiences as a driver in the Ambulance Corps in Syria.

> I've learned a lot in the past couple of months, not about the specific job I'm out here for . . . but about people and places: how for instance,

Fred W. Ashley, Dr. Hayden, and Lucien Price in 1932. *Archives*

people, (including myself) behave in an unpleasant situation and how places really look that I've heard about all my life. . . . just out to the right is our headquarters . . . where nearly 2,000 years ago, Roman legions were forted and magnificent temples were built, now all in ruins, but no end impressive.

John Ashton ('38) had just begun his teaching career at Reserve's rival, University School, when he enlisted in the army.

Camp Campbell, Ky.
October 1942

Dear Dr. Hayden,

It was nice to have a note from you—although a lot more has happened to me in the last few months than you suspect. Wish I could have been able to get down to see you before I left, because I still harbor many happy memories of WRA and of association with you.

Managed to get in just about one month of teaching up at University School and thoroughly enjoyed it. Was teaching in the seventh grade—math, English, and general science and also eighth grade English. Found working with boys of that age very inspiring and remunerative on the plane of human relationships. I know now, more than ever, that I wish to do teaching as my life work. There's something in it that gets ahold of you.

Jack Gillespie ('36), U.S. Marine Corps captain. *Archives*

Also was very glad to get a chance to help coach soccer—only wish I could have still been there when we came down to see you in Hudson. The school gave me a very nice send off in Chapel—something I deeply appreciated.

As you can see from the address, I am connected with the headquarters section of the service unit, which takes care of the administrative work of the camp. Camp Campbell is a new camp, only some three months open—and still an archipelago of yellow barracks in a sea of red mud. At the present time I am working as a clerk in the orderly office—not very strenuous work, but an excellent place to find out about how the details of administration of an army work. I hope after three months or so to be able to go to Officers Training School, in which case I shall be very glad I had the experience as an enlisted man. . . . How's Joel doing?[1] . . .

          Sincerely,
          John Ashton ['38; Age 22]

1. Dr. Hayden's son, Joel Jr. ('39), was in his senior year at Oberlin College.

A new feature in the October 22 *Record* was "The Question Box." Answers to the first question posed to the current students, "What do you think of the 18 and 19-year old draft law?" appeared on the front page. Seven respondents agreed it was necessary; some expressed the hope that it would not affect their education. One of them added, "A younger soldier should be better anyhow." In this issue, the school learned that Marine captain Jack Gillespie ('36) was involved in the fighting in Guadalcanal. He was the highest-ranking member of his class upon graduation from Marine Officers Candidate School.

The editorial on October 29 was another call for the boys to give—this time for the War Chest. The writer assured them that once they were approached, they would not be asked to give again but reminded them, "This is War! We must now have war measures!" Later in the editorial, he pleaded, "When the representative sees you, give for the men in the service, the men in prison camps, the relief for the suffering peoples in the war stricken areas and for the Red Cross. Now is the time to give."

An announcement on the following page alerted the boys that "Every Reservite from now on will participate in a series of mass calisthenics to be held every Tuesday afternoon on the lower football field. . . . The purpose of this program is naturally that of physical fitness brought on by the increased demand for healthy young men." Above it was the WRA Honor Roll, which in past years listed the names of students for their academic achievements. This year the 121 names that appeared were those of alumni and faculty in the service. Five had an asterisk next to their names, denoting that they had lost their lives.

November was both a very busy and a highly emotional month for the headmaster. Just as he was absorbing the details of the draft-age changes, he received news that two more of his boys were lost to the war. Throughout the month, his thoughts were focused on composing a proper memorial service for them as well as corresponding with parents and alumni. His was not an easy burden to bear

On November 7, U.S. Army, Navy, and Air Forces began landing operations in North Africa. George Manlove ('32), who was with the First Army, described that area in a letter to the Haydens.

> Somewhere in North Africa
> November 16, 1942
>
> Dear Dr. and Mrs. Hayden:
>
> Just before I got on the boat—on the "boot" rather—leaving England, I got a note announcing your gift of *Fortune*. Thanks so much—it was like a handshake at the last minute. I presume it will follow me about and it will be read from cover to cover many times over. We devour anything to read. Mother sent me a box which arrived just the morning the boat sailed. She stuffed old newspapers around the edges—the *Cleveland Plain Dealer*—and that paper went all over the boat in scraps! Funny, mother slipped in a can of meat, some tea and sugar and a small cheese. She felt sorry for me, I guess, living in rationed England. Well, I had to go for two days on that when we landed here.
>
> You probably are far better informed of this African move, its statistics, etc., than I. It was beautifully planned, a complete surprise, and it gave us a very thrilling boat trip. We were on a little ship that plied the sea

between Belfast and Liverpool in eight hours. So we only got water, cold water, for a half-hour twice a day for over a month—but she rode the waves like a match box, and the crew, English navy, were grand. Some had been on Russian convoys; one had the DSO [Distinguished Service Order] which he won on the Malta convoy; one had taken the landing craft in at Dieppe, another was at Dunkirk, so there wasn't a nervous moment the whole voyage. I slept in my pajamas and soundly every night. I can't say the same after landing though. Now after several days of action, everyone is our friend, even the French soldiers. Yesterday they were fighting us—today in Tunisia they are fighting the Germans. Strange, too, that our armistice here happened to fall on November 11th. We are camped in the hills—it might well be New Mexico or Colorado—small hills, mountains in the distance, sage brush, jackals creeping up close to scare the guards—the days warm, like Maine, and the nights cool. . . .

People here, the Arabs and French, are quite poor. They have been stripped of nearly everything and have been sending 80% of all products—fowl, wine, oranges, olives, spices—to France and thence to Germany. They listen to the news from America via short wave and Boston—so do we every evening at 5 o'clock, how good it seems—and when they heard that President Roosevelt was going to send them food and clothing under the Lend-lease, we all became heroes, or Santa Clauses. Fifty Arabs appeared on donkeys all driving sheep and goats and cows, mixed, and calling out "Comrades, Brudders, amiis—avez-vous du sucre, cigarettes, chocolates?" They all speak French. I feel very much at home among the Arabs—we both speak about the same amount of French. Again—thanks for *Fortune,* and have the happiest of Christmases. I shall be with you often in my thoughts.

My love to all,
George [Age 28]

In light of shortages and gas rationing, the *Reserve Record* announced that the annual father-son banquet was changed into a Parents' Day gathering and that only parents of the students could be accommodated at the 6:30 P.M. dinner. After the presentation of sports awards, the crowd shifted to the chapel to hear a talk by James H. Powers of the *Boston Globe*. A colleague of Lucien Price, he spoke of the war situation and what it meant to the "draft age men of the Academy." Dean Wood referred to the talk in his letter to Price.

November 16, 1942

Dear Lucien,

Just a few lines this afternoon to tell you what a wonderful address Mr. Powers gave us last Saturday evening. The old Chapel was filled nearly to its capacity. It was just what we all need to hear in these days when we are rushing into things as though this war would last forever. His talk was so sane, so convincing, so sound.

It is true, we must drive ahead at a terrific pace in order to cope with a situation we were wholly unprepared to meet. However, we do not need to lose our heads and allow ourselves to be swept away by the tide of military propaganda. A better day is coming and that better day will dawn a little sooner and we will be better prepared to live it if we do not allow the finer things of life to be included in the scrap drives. . . .

Here on the campus the rising sun was greeted with a tremendous shout from the lungs of two hundred youths to whom an announcement was made by the Headmaster in his usual clever and dramatic manner that in view of the wonderful job the boys did on Saturday all along the line he declared this to be a "Free Day." Shouts, woofs and immediately for the hours of one day the humanities were forgotten. However, they will be revived tomorrow with just a little more spirit and interest for the interim. . . . But this is a free day, I must not be found even writing a letter, so my best wishes to you.

   Sincerely,
   Harlan N. Wood

On November 19, a telegram drafted by the commandant of the Marine Corps was sent to the parents of Jack Gillespie ('36).

              NOVEMBER 19, 1942

DEEPLY REGRET TO INFORM YOU THAT YOUR SON CAPTAIN JOHN B. GILLESPIE III U.S. MARINE CORPS WAS KILLED IN ACTION IN THE PERFORMANCE OF HIS DUTY AND IN THE SERVICE OF HIS COUNTRY. TO PREVENT POSSIBLE AID TO OUR ENEMIES PLEASE DO NOT DIVULGE THE NAME OF HIS SHIP OR STATION. PRESENT SITUATION NECESSITATES INTERMENT TEMPORARILY IN THE LOCALITY WHERE DEATH OCCURRED AND YOU WILL BE NOTIFIED ACCORDINGLY. PLEASE ACCEPT MY HEARTFELT SYMPATHY. LETTER FOLLOWS.

   T. HOLCOMB, LIEUT. GENERAL U.S.M.C.

On that same day Dr. Hayden wrote to Tom B. Babcox ('37), who was "somewhere" in the Southwest Pacific.

              November 19, 1942

Dear Tom:

Thanks for the card. We are delighted to know that you are settling into your responsibility for the reason that that is the way your mind works and you do not like to be marking time on the sidelines.

Have just heard that Torrey Eaton's ['37] torpedo boat suffered some severe deck casualties. We are anxiously awaiting further news. It was the Solomon Islands punching party and the *Smith* had more than a ringside seat!

We think of you, your mother and father, and the whole family and, somehow or other, the Haydens are drawn more closely into the lives of all the young men we have seen grow up on this familiar campus. Remember that everything we have belongs to you and the young men like you, and that the resources of your friends here are at your disposal in every way, shape, and form. Blessings on you.

    Ever yours,
    Joel B. Hayden

The following day, Dr. Hayden received a telegram from Torrey Eaton's father. It is unclear how the headmaster learned the news about Torrey on the nineteenth.

    November 20, 1942

Wire to Dr. Hayden received today:

Navy Department has reported Torrey missing in action. There is still possibility of his being safe. Will advise you when we have definite information.

  W. W. Eaton

    November 21, 1942

My dear Mr. Gillespie:

It is a source of profound regret to me and to his brother officers of the Corps that your son, Captain John B. Gillespie III, U.S. Marine Corps, lost his life in action against the enemies of his country and I wish to express my deepest sympathy to you and members of your family in your great loss.

There is little I can say to lessen your grief but it is my earnest hope that the knowledge of your son's splendid record in the service and the thought that he nobly gave his life in the performance of his duty may in some measure comfort you in this sad hour.

    Sincerely yours,
    T. Holcomb
    Commandant, U.S. Marine Corps

    November 22, 1942

My dear Dr. Hayden:

Unhappily, all hope about Torrey must now be given up. This morning we received a telephone call from Mrs. Hunter Wood, wife of the captain

Torrey Eaton ('37) on the WRA football field. *Archives*

Torrey Eaton ('37). *Archives*

Jack Gillespie ('36) on the WRA football field. *Archives*

Edward D. J. Morris ('36). *Archives*

of his ship, saying that she had a letter from her husband, confirming the loss of Torrey and three other officers, in the action of October 25th, when a Japanese torpedo plane crashed on the deck of the *Smith*. Accounts of this action have already appeared in the papers, and it was no doubt because of this that you sent me your telegram.

Our bitter grief in the loss of our only child is tempered by a fierce pride, a pride that I know the school will share, that Torrey died magnificently, and that his death is one of the many that will bring about, eventually, a better world where free men can live.

Sincerely,
W. W. Eaton

November 1942

Dear Dr. Hayden,

Jack's death is an awful thing to his mother and me—but so many others are sharing our grief and that softens the blow.

Jack died doing what he wanted to do, defending a cause he utterly believed in. He was killed on October 14 on Guadalcanal while in command of a unit of heavy artillery.

His was the finest character I have ever known and you and Reserve contributed mightily to that and his other accomplishments. . . . My deepest sympathy to the family of Torrey Eaton.

Affectionately,
John B. Gillespie, Sr.

Then, on November 25, in Cheltenham, England, Mrs. Lesley Morris wrote a letter to Dr. Hayden. After over fifteen months of waiting, word had been received that her son, Edward D. J. Morris ('36), had been officially listed as killed in action on June 15, 1941, while attacking a heavily defended position during the British and "Free French" attack on Syria. One more Gold Star on the Service Honor Roll. "It is true to say," Mrs. Morris wrote, "that everything worth having is at stake and for the sake of the future everything must be sacrificed if needs be. It is not always easy to keep one's eyes on the stars but it's the only way." Dr. Hayden apparently did not receive her letter until later in December. (His response was written on January 14, 1943.)

The front page of the December 3 issue of the *Reserve Record* brought the war home with the news of the deaths of Torrey and Jack. Dr. Hayden sent a letter to the Gillespies, who lived in Columbus, describing the memorial service that was held in the chapel in honor of the boys.

December 3, 1942

Dear Mr. and Mrs. Gillespie:

I want to thank you for your thoughtfulness in sending me all the pertinent material about Jack so that I could give the school and all his friends a fairly complete picture in terms of your own insight and your own information.

It was a bitter evening. A regular blizzard raged when we gathered in the Chapel at six o'clock. . . . We used the grand hymn, "For All the Saints Who From Their Labors Rest." The scripture was a selection from the Old Testament, the New Testament, some lines from Milton, from Shelley, from Traherne, and from Tolstoy. I gave the story of each boy's experience here, in college, and on the field of action. I then gave a brief talk, a copy of which I enclose. There were various forms of emphases in the talk, and one or two minor changes in the delivery, but as it stands it will give you some idea of what we were thinking about when we shared with you the bitterness of your experience and the victorious promise of your own great hope.

Please know that the Academy is a shrine for youth and Jack will be forever remembered on this old campus.

The president of the senior class, John Jahant of Akron, who is getting ready for Annapolis, placed a Gold Star opposite Jack's name at seven o'clock last evening.

     Devotedly yours,
     Joel B. Hayden

The December issue of the *Alumni Record* contained extracts from a letter written on October 7 by J. Fred Waring, who was still in the Middle East: "Dave Dennison ['36]," he wrote, "I haven't seen for a month: he's been out in the middle of nowhere hob-nobbing with the Bedouin's." Another article carried a detailed account of the circumstances of the death of James Tew ('29), lost in action earlier that year.

Assistant Headmaster Ralph McGill included a message to all alumni, assuring them that "Here at Reserve we gladly join the increasing throng of men and women all over the world who are quietly resolving that the quickened conscience of mankind must wring from the bloodsoaked ashes of the present conflagration a just and permanent peace. . . . With all her strength and her best thought, Reserve carries on."

Before the boys went home for Christmas vacation, the "Headmaster's Christmas Message" on the front page of the December 10 *Reserve Record* reminded them: "This is the Christmas for tightening belts. This is the Christmas for restraint in the getting and giving of material things. This is the Christmas for memories and dreams, both rooted in meditation, in appreciation of home and love, in deep resolve that we become disciplined for the understanding and vigorous use of liberty."

Somewhere in the Pacific
December 28, 1942

Dear Dr. Hayden,

It was good to hear from you again. Now a days mail is so welcome there is a race every time mail call blows. One thing about this army life I can say is that we sure do see a lot of the world. First the United States, then an awful lot of water to our tropical paradise (?). As yet we haven't run across anything like home although we wonder when we'll get back to that home. . . .

Bob Bluem ['39x; Age 22]

By the end of the first term, seven masters had gone to serve in the armed forces. Earlier in the fall, faculty master J. Fred Waring had written of his experiences as an ambulance driver in Syria. Later in the term David S. Dennison, Jr. ('36), an ambulance driver in the American Field Service, wrote two lengthy letters to his parents, describing the area where he and Waring, David's former English teacher, were serving in the same unit. Believing the school would be interested in seeing the letters, written during the Christmas and New Year's holidays, David's father passed them on.

You don't know how surprised I was to receive mail today. I am surprised because I received these at a place where a month ago no man would have dared to tread. From this you can gather that I am in the desert and that I am actually a very long way from base. . . .

What I have seen in the last few days is something that words and pictures will never tell. The sight of wrecked equipment of war—tanks, guns, lorries—stretching as far as the eye can see—is so ghastly it's almost unreal. It's true that they are all German and Italian. I have seen airfields simply littered with wrecked Stukas, fighters and bombers and some gliders—all bearing the swastika or black cross. Perhaps, however, the most graphic evidence of this campaign are the graves which one finds everywhere. British graves bear the customary white cross while the Germans are more elaborate, decorating the crosses with swastikas or iron crosses. It's pretty damn dreadful, but if anything can be consoling in war, it's good to know that this theatre of war consists of nothing but waste land.

I arrived here looking like a real desert rat because coming up (which means down) I always managed to sit on the rear of the truck so as to get a good look at things of interest. Inasmuch as it seems to rain most of the time, the back wheels of the car kept me well lathered with mud. Our water supply was low so I had a very good excuse for being dirty. I assure you, however, that the morning after arriving I shaved and bathed, not in a bath tub or shower, but with a wet washcloth moistened via water bottle.

At present our water difficulties are not bad and we have as much as we need within reason—that is for tea, drinking, and moderate bathing. To give you an example of water conservation I'll give you a play by play of my most recent bath. First, I fill my canvas bucket about 4" then I brush my teeth. Next comes shaving, followed by washing face right on down. After putting on clean clothes I wash my feet and dry them with my towel which is then washed in the same water along with underwear, shirt, and socks. It isn't bad at all and appeals to my lazy spirit, as I don't have to go carrying fresh water all the time.

Most of us sleep in our clothes, but I find it more practical to put on my flannel pajamas. It gives the fleas a chance to leave and gives me a chance to scratch. Honestly, I'm quite allergic to insects of all kinds. Bed bugs raised merry hell with me in Syria and now fleas are taking up where the bed bugs left off. One can't actually get rid of them because they live in the sand. My present method of retaliation is to ignore them and hope they gorge themselves to death. Slowly I am beginning to take a dim view of that procedure. It's quite a game here to try to figure out which bites are old ones and which new ones. You can usually tell them by the type of itch—the new ones won't stay scratched as it were.

I am writing in the front seat of an ambulance which I share with a very nice fellow from Concord, New Hampshire. He's a Dartmouth man. The ambulance is our home out here. We sleep in them on stretchers, use the back of them for all sorts of purposes such as washing and drying clothes, shaving, and bathing. At night we play cards or read in them. It isn't a bad life and my experience on the desert in Syria north of the Euphrates River up to the Turkish border served me in good stead. . . .

You might want to know about our meals. They are surprisingly good. We have a couple of "Tommy" cooks who seem to have our interest at heart and, by bargaining with the "wogs," whom one will find at any spot in N. Africa if he stops more than five minutes, they manage to get us eggs in considerable quantity. The cooks are very good at making pastry so that we are well supplied with all kinds of tarts. The meat course is always bully beef (corned beef to you) which is usually fixed in a rather appetizing way. We all consume quantities of bread and jam (usually marmalade manufactured from surplus oranges from Palestine); also tea. Boiled potatoes and carrots and onions are also the normal complement to any meal. This morning for breakfast we had the most marvelous oranges

I've ever tasted—as big as grapefruit and seedless. Though our rations are always the same—bully beef, bread, carrots, onions, and potatoes and flour—an imaginative cook such as we have can make life quite pleasant.

The one big thing we have to watch out for is dysentery which is generally carried by flies. Some say dirty mess kits, bad water ad infinitum. The fly, however, is the main culprit. We are not seriously threatened by this disease now that the flies have pretty well died out and the rainy season has begun.

Curiously enough, ever since I left Syria I've felt that I'm on my way home. Perhaps I'm a silly optimist, but I can't help but feel that equipment is not only going to win this war and the U.S., Britain and Russia have it. The superiority is not only in quantity but in quality and the end of this mess is in sight. Once I get home I'm never going to leave again and furthermore I'm going to do all I can to see that no one else has to leave again. . . .

Private David S. Dennison, Jr.

December 30, 1942

Since I last wrote you I have spent my first Christmas away from home. Who would have guessed that I would ever spend Christmas in the Lybian desert.

By the way, I'm wondering if you are able to keep any kind of a scrap book of such things as news items about the Field Service. I know that *Life* magazine, for instance, printed some pictures of the boys supposedly in action. If you have seen them, you can realize that they were not taken under fire and in fact nowhere near the front. But such things as that, however, would be nice to have and it will be a great deal of fun to see actually how glorious the newspapers are making this war.

So far, I, myself, have neither been heroic nor glorious. I'm hundreds of miles from the front sitting around doing nothing. Any cases we do carry are sick or burned. The "Tommies" often burn themselves making tea over a gasoline fire. I suppose when the statistics of this war are used to define methods of the next, tea drinking will be abolished because of the unnecessary risks involved. On the other hand, the British would probably abandon gasoline in the cars first.

To go on, the closest to danger I have been was the first week out of New York. I saw one ship go down and saw plenty of depth charges and bombs dropped. Out here I've seen plenty of German planes—all on the ground. Once a plane came over and dropped some flares which were rather pretty, but he was shot down. Since then nothing in the nature of action has occurred.

Mind you, I'm not being facetious about war and action. The endless stream of wreckage for hundreds of miles is silent testimony to the fact that war is hell. The little graveyards full of German, Italian, and English dead (many of them unknown) is even further proof of that fact. The point, however, is that if a few moments of action are glorious then 99.8% of a man's time is spent in drab, monotonous existence. I suppose I'll always quarrel with propagandists and they're probably right.

How else except by propaganda are people thousands of miles from the scene of action going to be made to realize that their efforts can win or lose the war. That their efforts can win or lose the war is absolutely true. The war is rather like checkers—when one team has (or thinks he has) more guns, tanks, and planes than the other boy, he moves in and takes over. If the other guy knows that he is short on these things he bluffs and waits for the other guy to attack and then retreats. And that's exactly what has happened out here.

The British had the stuff. Rommel knew it. The British attacked. Rommel retreated and the British are still trying to engage the main German army. The Germans will have to fight when they get cornered. He'll be licked if there are enough American goods at the front. Whether there are enough American goods available or not depends largely on how much the people at home are producing.

This place is full of American equipment. You just wouldn't believe it. I know (as I have always thought) that without American production, England would be out of the war by now. I'm sure I never really appreciated what that word "production" meant. But I've always been a reasonable man and seeing that I, as a reasonable man, did not fully appreciate the importance of our industrial energy, I doubt if many other reasonable men who have not had my experience can appreciate it.

To get back to normal. How in hell do you wash woolen socks? I find it satisfactory either to boil them or to dip them in gasoline. A certain party, namely, my driving partner, Greer Taylor, says I'm wrong and that I should scrub them in luke warm water. What is the answer? I hope my method is okay, because it's much easier than scrubbing. . . .

With this I come to the Christmas story phase of this letter. I'm awfully sorry that your package didn't arrive but most of us were disappointed in the same way. I have received two packages which were Godsends. In spite of the package shortage our Christmas was really swell. The Field Service gave us "backshee" (free) two bottles of beer. Greer doesn't drink beer and Walt doesn't so I had theirs, which I assure you I didn't drink at one sitting. They were quart bottles.

The Field Service also gave us each a package made up of nuts, a bar of chocolate, a can of pears, a piece of mince pie, a piece of fruit cake, and a package of Benson and Hedges cigarettes. The canteen allowed us to buy all the fruit and chocolate we wanted and I indulged to the extent of about $8.

Christmas Eve was very nice. We all sat around in one of our two tents, listened to "Command Performance" via the radio, which was hitched up to the battery of the water truck, and later heard some Christmas music and sang a few carols in between "I've Been Working on the Railroad" and "My Father Makes Two Kinds of Whiskey." The tent, of course, was blacked out. It is usually used by our NCO's as their sleeping quarters since they do not have ambulances.

I got in the Xmas spirit and let the boys have a pack of Aunt Fran's Chesterfields, which they went for in a big way. Curt Rodgers, Greer's former cabin mate, contributed a Christmas tree about a foot high and a can of popcorn to the cause. We popped the corn over a primace stove scrounged in the vicinity of a wrecked German truck. There were a couple of Englishmen in the crowd and they had never tasted popcorn before. They remained rather non-committal about it, though I think they liked it. You see, the British have a sort of polite contempt for American goods. It's probably because everything they use is American and they, being good Englishmen, hate to see the virtues of America extolled by the living fact, especially since American virtues are the same kind of virtues they would like to have. It's simply that America is pulling ahead and that's a hard fact for any Englishman to swallow.

We woke up Christmas day and found a can of fruit on the hood of each car. It was a wonderful gesture, and though we don't know who gave the fruit, we think it was our lieutenant. . . . For breakfast Christmas day we had two fried eggs each, one fresh orange, toast, bacon, and tea. The eggs and the oranges we bought ourselves from these immortal natives who will outlast them all. How they have lived so far is a mystery no one will ever fathom. You see them in towns which are in absolute ruins. You see them walking across mine fields and you see them coming through the camp. I've only seen one dead one and his camel—he hit a mine.

Tea is worth its weight in gold, and since we don't drink as much tea as the British think is necessary for life, we had some saved up to exchange for eggs. It's interesting that these natives will accept German, Italian, British and Egyptian money. . . .

The only other meal we had on Christmas day was dinner and it was a honey. Here's what we had: punch made of rum (British rationed) and Chianti (left by the Italians and transported in German water cans) plus fruit juice (canned), fresh lemons and canned pineapple; soup (tomato); chicken, pork, squash, turnips, mashed potatoes, fresh lettuce salad, canned fruit for dessert, and cakes and pastry of all sorts. The chickens were bought from the natives. We started out with ten but one got squashed by the others and died so I think we only had nine. The pork was issued to us by the British. The vegetables, except potatoes were purchased from the natives. The fruit came from the canteen and the pastry was the result of foregoing the use of flour for the week in order to have enough for all. The pastry was made of either jam or Palestinian chocolate bars melted up. From this array of food we were allowed to help ourselves to all we wanted, which is somewhat different from being served meagre but adequate portions by our ration-conscious "Tommy" cooks. Furthermore, it was a great deal different from being served bully beef.

Our Christmas table was an interesting affair. It was actually several stretchers placed between the bumpers of a couple of ambulances. The seats were closed up stretchers supported by gas cans. Both the ambulances were decorated, not with holly or the familiar evergreen, but with desert shrub which was quite pretty. The table cloth was made up of several patients' blankets and satisfactorily adorned with bowls of candy and free cigarettes. . . .

All of us are genuinely proud to be Americans, proud that we can take it, and glad to have a wonderful place to go home to. I'm really awfully happy out here and though I haven't done much yet I know that we have a better chance of getting to the front than anyone else and that we'll get more than our share of the breaks.

That about brings me up to date. Tomorrow night is New Year's Eve.

Pvt. David S. Dennison, Jr. [Age 24]

Winter Term: January–March 1943

When the first issue of the *Record* came out at the beginning of the new term, a notice appeared that Nichols and Cranbrook schools found it necessary to withdraw from the Interstate Preparatory School League for the duration of the war due to transportation restrictions. Sports competitions with Shadyside and University School would continue as scheduled.

In January, three senior members of the *Record* staff left to enter college early. A senior could take a test to qualify for a new program that made it possible to complete the first semester of his freshman year while awaiting induction. Postgraduate Bob Hamilton ('42) was off to Yale; Dave Owen ('42), another post-graduate, went to Amherst; and Paul Barstow ('43) entered Williams College. They were to receive credits for their college work as well as credits for graduation from the Academy.

Francis C. Lindeman, newly appointed English master, became assistant field director of the Red Cross in Pearl Harbor. Word was also received by Athletic Director R. J. (Tebbie) Theibert that both of his sons—Jack ('40) and Dick ('42)—were called to the Air Corps. Post-graduate Rowland Congdon ('42x) reported to the army on March 4.

In response to new rationing rules that affected petroleum products of all kinds, Assistant Headmaster McGill announced, "all boarding boys would be required to hand their number one ration books over to the school," where they would be kept in the school safe. "On special occasions, for example when a boy needs a pair of shoes, he may obtain his book."

Camp Crowder, Missouri
January 5, 1943

Dear Mr. Wood:

Enclosed is a money order of five dollars for the Alumni Fund. I wish it could be more; but after the government deducts from my fifty dollars all the necessary items, my pocketbook looks mighty thin. Also, I'm buying an extra war bond a month because this is the most perfect time to save money for a rainy day. . . .

Tell everyone at Reserve for me that this army needs officers desperately; and from the schools such as Reserve and Williams must come the greatest majority. It is the responsibility of every undergraduate and alumnus of Reserve to do everything he can to get those gold bars.

I never realized this to such an extent until I got into the army. After all, I'm a typical Reserve man, not much above the average. But when I get in with these men, the only thing I can think about is the necessity of leadership. For instance, one instructor at basic training did not know the name of the Chief of Staff. Another instructor, after he finished showing us the improvised litter, said, "it is very easily did." Those are very small examples, but it shows you the calibre of man that was teaching me.

In relation to current events, here are three questions that were asked of me by men in the barracks. 1) When was Stalingrad taken? 2) Who are we fighting in New Guinea, Hitler or the Japanese? 3) How can MacArthur lead American troops in both New Guinea and North Africa? Those are actually questions asked by sensible and intelligent-looking Americans. I have no doubts about their ability to fight; but as men with any desire to learn or to understand, I doubt their ability very much.

The average soldier is really a swell guy. He wants to be everybody's friend because he unconsciously realizes that we're all in the same boat. What disappoints me is his lack of ambition to learn and to get ahead. He is perfectly satisfied with what he now knows and where he now is.

I really didn't mean to get up on the soap-box, but the army is the most stimulating experience, not academically, but in the understanding of man. As Pope said, "the proper study of mankind is man." And believe me, you really get it in the army. So many soldiers tell me that they think the army is degrading; and all I can say to that is—tommyrot. . . .

And I'm going to have those gold bars within not so very many months. The red tape getting into O.C.S. [Officer Candidate School] is something terrific. Right now I'm at a Radio Operator School and am waiting on the edge of my seat to get going on my training. . . . If I don't

get it, I really think my mind would rot away. I know I'm capable, and I know my responsibility lies there....
          Sincerely,
          [J.] Spencer Dickerson ['38; Age 22]

                             Somewhere in the Pacific
                                       January 7, 1943

Dear Scotch:

... At the moment I'm sitting on my wash bucket with a life preserver as a guard against getting sore where one usually gets sore after resting injudicially and too long. This is the best seat and only seat available to us of the hoi-poiloi! (Ha! bad spelling.) My writing table is a piece of plywood hooked from the construction and repair shop. Speaking of wood, here's a tale of typical navy logic. As wood splinters badly when hit by high explosives, all wood has been removed from ships (officially). But, as they do need wood (unofficially) for various jobs, it is to be had (unofficially). So, as there's no wood to be used (officially) there's no need for carpenters. Yet, as they do (unofficially) have wood, they must also have carpenters. Still, as there's no ratings to (unofficial) carpenters, these shipfitters (officially) work as (unofficial) carpenters with the (unofficial) wood. Very tidy, what? I'm going to put them to work on that old grievance of mankind's, i.e. not being able to have one's cake and eat it, too, and see if they couldn't reverse that edict. I'll bet they could. But, to get on. By this time you'll no doubt have learned from one of my previous epistles that I'm on the USS *Raleigh*. A hooker of rather a dated vintage, but withal still able to kick up her heels and scoot. Just how fast I can't say, but if equaled today by a motorist would bring reproving frowns to the brow of Rationer Nelson. (I think it's Nelson.)
          A. N. Finlayson ['40; Age 21]

                                    Camp Campbell, Kentucky
                                         January 13, 1943

Dear Dr. Hayden,

Am eagerly keeping up with all Reserve happenings through the *Record* and the *Alumni Record*—forgot that it was just a one way stream. You know, it puts one in a very ticklish position to have graduated from Reserve and taught at University School. Feel a little fickle at times when I cheer Reserve's wins over the maroon and black—but it is nevertheless a hearty cheer! Would have given anything to see those games.

Was shocked to hear the news of Jack and Torrey—Camp Campbell's certainly a far cry from such action as they saw. You may have noticed a change since I last wrote. Am now corporal and company clerk—taking care of all the records and correspondence of the company—which is quite a job in this paper army—and in a casual company of 650 men. Am rid of a bit of the drudgery though, because have I four clerks working under me.

Am not quite so sure about O.C.S. as in the immediate future. Would rather, am quite sure, be a staff sergeant than a second lieutenant—especially as I am still working my way through Yale to the extent of $40 a month paying off a loan. . . .

        Sincerely,
        John Ashton ['38; Age 22]

        Notre Dame, Indiana
        January 13, 1943

Dear Dr. Hayden,

I have been here since early October and have now practically finished the midshipmen's course. The work has seldom been difficult, either mentally or physically, but often seems tedious. There is such a mass of material that we have had time to touch on only a few of the highlights. I never did care much for the superficial, learning-by-rote method, but I suppose it is the only one possible under the circumstances. I only hope that the proverbial "little learning" is not too dangerous a thing in this instance. Some of the boys—a minority, luckily, who think they are "old salts" after three months, are probably in for a deserved chastening when they really get to sea. But I trust that most of us will be able to avoid the dangerous pitfall of this "ninety-day wonder" psychology, and will be able to learn enough as we go along to be of some service.

I don't regret my previous year's service in the navy as an enlisted man, though I could wish that it had been more varied. I was stuck for nearly nine months in Hawaii in a rather tedious and unproductive job. But then, I guess all jobs in the navy seem like that more or less, after the initial glamor has worn off. At least I should be able to understand the sailor's point of view, having been one myself. . . .

        Sincerely yours,
        Dick Hirshberg ['36; Age 23]

Headmaster Hayden wrote the following letter in response to the one written by Mrs. Lesley Morris on November 25.

        January 14, 1943

My dear Mrs. Morris:

We were not exactly surprised when your letter reached us from Cheltenham. The silence of uncertainty had been so extended that we had little hope left that what word came from you would be a happy word.

We are profoundly impressed with the spirit and quality of your letter and we send you our sympathy and our profound respect.

Ted [Edward D. J. Morris '36] was a happy boy while here and he did a good, faithful job, and I am sure that that characteristic performance was his until the very end. It may be hard for you to realize it, as it is for us, but we have eight Gold Stars on our Service Roll now and I think the roll itself from this small school totals close to two-hundred boys. And with the next six months they'll be pouring in, so that the number will mount swiftly.

We feel much encouraged in the U.S.A. I don't think we are over-optimistic, but the sense of growing power in all the branches of war activity is with us. My chief concern is that the English-speaking people keep their ranks closed without a rift for the winning of a decent peace, and I am sure the ethical and spiritual implications of the Atlantic Charter must girdle the globe effectively if we are to have anything but renewed horror for our children, and grandchildren and great-grandchildren. I think that in this stage of the development of the human race, we have at last faced the problem of granting humanity first place and putting provincialism, nationalism, and commercialism—any kind of social or economic imperialism—in its secondary place under the control of a respect for man and human life which is the very heart of the Christian revelation.

    Most sincerely yours,
    Joel B. Hayden

Two of the three Babcox brothers, Reid ('29) and Ed, Jr. ('35), were working side by side in the same location in Hawaii. Their youngest brother, Tom ('37), was serving "somewhere in the Southwest Pacific."

                January 15, 1943

Dear Reid and Ed [Babcox]:

Just had a call from your dad and he told me what you are doing and where you are. I am not revealing this information because I don't give a damn for the comfort of the enemy. I think of you fellows as working together and living together and being in the intelligence division warms the cockles of my heart, and I mean that, believe me! . . .

Reid, I want to thank you for that fine booklet on Hawaii. Mrs. Hayden and I have been going over it and thoroughly enjoying the pictures which have brought everything back to us as we recall the wonderful trip we had in the winter of 1941. I was not too fit, but I really let go and sagged down into the Waikiki sands when I hit Oahu. . . .

Things are moving here at Reserve. I know this is a small village but, boy, the amount of stuff that goes on here is almost unbelievable! The school is full; the faculty, in spite of replacements, is doing a swell job;

news from all fronts from our boys is encouraging and gratifying—and in some cases inspiring—but there are eight Gold Stars on the Service Roll.

> Ever yours,
> Joel B. Hayden

In December the machine shop had once again geared up for production of war-related materials for Bardons and Oliver, setting a goal of 12,000 man-hours for the school year. Jack Yardley ('44) wrote a note to Dr. Hayden with plans for their future profits.

> Western Reserve Academy
> January 20, 1943
>
> Dear Dr. Hayden:
>
> After talking with several boys since I last spoke to you, it has been decided to use the money earned in the machine shop in the following manner. All but $500, which will go into the bank, will be put into government bonds with the interest either going back into additional bonds or replenishing the money in the bank. It has also been decided that a Machine Shop Scholarship Fund shall be inaugurated. This will amount tentatively to $300 to be awarded at each commencement by the headmaster to some worthy boy in the sophomore or junior class who, because of reverses in his family or financial difficulty, needs the money in order to complete his stay at the school.
>
> Sincerely yours,
> Jack Yardley ['44; Age 16]

Jack Yardley, known as "Mr. Tepper's right-hand man," kept meticulous records of the work being done in the machine shop. In January of 1998 I received a note of remembrance from him about his work with Mr. Tepper:

> For me, who has a natural interest in things mechanical and in working with my hands, I couldn't get enough of being with and working in the machine shop with Mr. Tepper. . . . To use an overworked term, Mr. Tepper was a great role model for me as an upstart adolescent. He showed me not only what could be done with well-mastered skills as I watched and assisted him set up and run our "production line"; he also exemplified the very basic virtues of hard work and stick-to-it-tiveness. Although many details of that period in my life are now forgotten, those that are recalled carry a sense of enjoyment and are still important to me.
>
> Jack Yardley [Age 71]

Jack Yardley ('44) in the machine shop. *Courtesy Jack Yardley*

Jack Yardley ('44) in the navy. *Courtesy Jack Yardley*

>Wood's Hole, Mass.
>January 21, 1943

Dear Dr. Hayden:

 Thank you for your last letter, for you know I enjoy so much hearing from you and in hearing how things are at my fondest alma mater. I am happy to hear that Reserve is as strong as ever in mind and spirit during the difficult period it is going through, and know without a doubt that its success will be complete.

 Your letter arrived on the eve of a new experience for me. I have been detached from communications and am now carrying on my work in the Port Directors office, still in Woods Hole. What the immediate future holds in store for me I do not know. I am less secure than I was before and may at any time receive my orders to go to sea. But things like that are unpredictable in the navy, so I am just going to stand by and wait. As a matter of fact I have been expecting my transfer for three months. . . .

>Very sincerely,
>Bill Horner ['39x; Age 22]

 Mrs. Eilbeck, the librarian whose nephew, James Tew, was shot down over Malta over a year before, received a cablegram from one of his buddies and shared it with the school on the front page of the January 21 *Record*. "On that March morning," the letter read, "Jimmy had been up twice; once on patrol and once on an unsuccessful scramble. He was tired, not from this, but from months of incessant air warfare with no quarter. Yet, when the call came for volunteers, Jimmy was among the first."

The cable continued. "Four planes from his group met four other Hurricanes at twenty thousand feet. Soon they met more than thirty 109s and several JU-88s in a terrific series of dog fights. Jimmy dove on one 109 and blasted it from the sky. Climbing again, he was hit and went straight into the drink." Jimmy was remembered by his fellow pilots as a "wizard pilot." He kept the squadron's diary and regaled his pals with stories from the Far East.

Somewhere in Hawaii
January 22, 1943

Dear Dr. Hayden and family:

Have been meaning to answer your several notes and nice letter, but this is the best I can do. Eddie [Reid's brother] is with me here now in the same office and same work and some miracle—at 5500 miles from Akron I'd say—but it has happened, and he is fine and likes this new work very much. . . . Eaton and Gillespie must have been over here in Pearl Harbor recently but we didn't see them. [My brother] Tom knew them better. Tom is all the way down [in the Southwest Pacific] I hear now and I hope he gets in here occasionally and he probably will too.

   Regards,
   Reid Babcox ['29; Age 31]

USNAS Olathe
Somewhere in the Pacific
January 23, 1943

Dear Mr. Hayden,

I can't tell you how much I enjoyed your wonderful letter of the 15th, and must confess that I showed it to several of my closer friends, who were all very interested in that swell paragraph on post-war reconstruction. It seems that you've caught in black and white just what most of us are thinking and discussing these days, but haven't the time nor ability to set down on paper. I want to thank you, too, for your Dec. 28th letter which, because of my overly cavalier methods of keeping track of correspondence, I don't know whether I have acknowledged.

I must admit that I'm beginning to believe, with Freddy Artz of Oberlin, among others, that the only possible working peace we can have after the war is an armed peace, with the so-called United Nations maintaining a sort of police system, using our marines and navy as an international patrol. As soon as a nation can prove that it is democratic (or at least not imperialistic in its intentions) it should be admitted to the United Nations, as states

[are] to the United States. This will mean that we'll have to take the leadership away from England in the peace conferences, and possibly settle her Indian question for her, as we were settling our own Philippine problem.

It will call for plenty of close cooperation, and an unselfish national policy, especially on the part of the U.S., but I think we can do it. We could enlist France, Belgium, Holland, Norway, Greece, and Italy (they're tired of war now) to begin with, and gradually educate and finally set on her own feet a cooperative, if emasculated, Germany. Of Japan, I don't know—though I believe if we can show them they're not the "supermen" they think they are, and that their divine mission is not to rule the world (by striking uncertainty and mistrust into their confidence in their military machine) we might also, eventually, be able to admit them.

Of course, this type of thinking is highly idealistic and may get us nowhere—but we must have a high goal in mind, even during the lean years of an armed, military peace. . . .
Sincerely,
Doug Handyside ['38; Age 22]

A letter from Alan Ward ('36) brought an eyewitness account of the battle in which Torrey Eaton was lost.

Norfolk Navy Yard
Portsmouth, Va.
February 2, 1943

Dear Dr. Hayden,

I have put off writing you for several weeks because I have just been relieved of my place on the ship I was on and was sent down here to await further transfer to another ship, another new one, I hope.

My travels and experiences have most certainly been wide and interesting. I have been through the "big ditch" [Panama Canal] twice and have traveled at least a distance equal to one and a half times around the world, though I never got quite around. I have been well below the equator (consequently a good shell back) and across the international date line several times, so you can see I was pretty far down under.

The ship I was on was the far-famed battleship [the *South Dakota*, known only as "Old Nameless" for security reasons] which shot down thirty-two Jap planes one day, to prove that the battleship is still something with which to be reckoned.

While I was in Pearl Harbor at one of the swimming pools, I ran into Torrey Eaton. When we left, his ship was one of our escorts, so, the world was not so big. We went out, all lashed down for a good fight, and we got it, but Torrey, as you know, did not come back. I can't remember which part of the attack the event took place, but from my lookout station I saw all of it. The Jap plane had been hit, so the pilot jockeyed onto Torrey's ship. It hit the forward mount, and as it did, the forecastle of the destroyer became a flaming gasoline torch. The ready ammunition blew up and the war head of the torpedo the plane was carrying let go. Even while this was going on, the "can" dropped back into our wake, which was very high as we were at top speed, and by staying in the wake and dipping up and down, the fire was put out. There were no fire fighting parties on board, so that was the only method of getting this fire under control. While this was going on, the other two guns kept firing effectively on the attacking planes.

The next morning, when the destroyer came along side for fuel, I inquired for Torrey, and the report came back "missing in action"—his battle station had been on the outside platform of the bridge.

Several weeks later, our ship again saw action—the final phase of the big offensive on Guadalcanal. It occurred after midnight in "iron bottom bay" between Savo Island and Guadalcanal. We claim to have sunk three cruisers, a destroyer, hit several other cruisers and a battleship. Naturally, we took a few hits, but we came out in as good spirits as we went in.

One of the biggest satisfactions I have is the way I reacted under fire. Probably, to most every man, the most serious question in his mind is "Am I going to do the job I have to do?" Because of superior training all along the line, no one on our ship went berserk. On the ship, we were fighting for our captain in whom we placed our faith. Because of him, we claim to be the best ship in the fleet.

For several reasons, the ship came back to the states, so many of us got to go home for Christmas. My brother was home, too, so when I walked into Dad's office, when I spoke, he mistook me for Fred, until he turned around. There certainly was a good answer to that old song "Where is my Wandering Boy Tonight."

The birthday greeting was certainly a grand gesture on your part. That day was rather uneventful—ship's routine went on as usual. Because of the abrupt change of location, some greetings have not caught up with me yet. Someday soon, I am going to have another Christmas, too.

My writing is foul, my spelling and grammar a 1.0, but I hope the content is over 3.0[.]

      Sincerely yours,
      [William] Alan Ward [Age 24]

                February 13, 1943

Dear Doc [Hayden],

Please consider this letter as addressed to Dean Wood as well as yourself. . . . I am now stationed in Alaska, but I may not be more specific. The censor won't let us discuss weather, location, morale, type or strength of units, their armament, where they are going, or what they are doing. There isn't much left to talk about, yet the lads seem to write a tremendous number of letters in spite of the handicap.

I had suspected, Mr. Wood, that the "war unrest" evident in colleges would creep into secondary schools with the advent of the teenage draft. I have also been interested in numerous statements on the moral difficulties of youth in war time. Many people seem to blame the war itself, but such censure of an abstraction seems to me to be foolish, impractical, and bosh, no matter how you view the matter. During peacetime, we young Americans are not constrained into "morality" by any abstract love of codes, it's just that we feel responsibility, security, and we are absorbed by and interested in our work. We have a picture of a certain desirable future based to a great extent on present conduct. Then, too, many of us never before had money enough to cut up in a grand style. Now a private in the army can spend $30–$40 on payday and still live well enough for the rest of the month. The other restraints are weakened by varying degrees or dismissed, and the pattern of alteration is different in each individual.

I do not speak as one above the influence. It has affected me, but I am no more evil than before. I tend to think of evil as being somehow ignorance and somehow opposed to [censored]. I can be enlightened in my own opinion and act in a measured manner most of the time, yet still outrage certain people of frozen moral sensibilities.

That the outrages are more frequent and prominent now is due to coincidence and a change of circumstances, but there has been no alteration of the soul. I submit that this is the general case, and there is no feasible way to change those who haven't changed yet. Peace will not automatically restore our feelings of security and the old picture of the future. "Stability" in youth must wait until a way of life becomes established once again. Meantime, we live. Some of us may never again fall under the influence of the natural restraints; some of us have never escaped them to any great extent. In any case, there is no use throwing stones at the windows of the gods.

My statement is incomplete and possibly a bit unclear. In any event, if it bores or confuses you, merely consider yourselves unfortunates who got into the way of a spontaneous stream of words. My pen has diarrhetic tendencies lately. . . .

          Sincerely,
          Buzz [John U. Anderson, '39; Age 21]

John U. "Buzz" Anderson ('39).
Courtesy Mrs. John Anderson

February 26, 1943

Dear Buzz:

I am sharing your fine letter with Mr. Wood and other members of the faculty whom you mention. 'Tis a grand letter, Buzz.

We are with you and for you lock, stock and barrel and we want to see that searching mind of yours advancing on new frontiers without any let-up. It will be all right.

Joel's a senior in Oberlin, V-7; may be in uniform any time now. Herb Tepper ['39] is in the army, headed toward meteorology. Brooks Shepard, Jr. ['39] has just left. The two Theibert boys have gone into the . . . Air Corps; Dave Varley ['40] left Deep Springs at Christmas and is in the army. "Dek" Miller ['39] graduated from Princeton February 1st; now working with Sikorsky Aeronautical Research. He'll be married the third of April. I'm not going to give you any more chin. This is just a note of acknowledgement. I'll have to write you a real letter when my "breather" comes during the spring holiday.

                      Ever yours,
                      Joel B. Hayden

Dr. and Mrs. Hayden were away for a week during which time they visited with a number of alumni attending Princeton, Yale, and Columbia. They gathered at the Biltmore Hotel in New York City to view eight hundred feet of film based on life at Reserve. The film was being made on the campus during the school year and contained views of the campus, as well as views of the many classes that were part of the war activities program. Stephen B. Lamb ('40) wrote his regrets that he was unable to attend.

Princeton, New Jersey
March 1, 1943

Dear Doctor Hayden,

I feel that I must write and explain my not showing up, or at least acknowledging your very kind invitation of last month. Reserve apparently has my address of freshman year. Since then I have moved several times, and your letter followed me around to several dormitories. By the time I received it, the day had come and gone. I was terribly disappointed, a feeling which is deepened by the fact that we probably won't meet again until after the war.

Princeton, its personnel and its atmosphere, have changed so as to be unrecognizable. The student body has been halved. Navy trainees occupy much of the available living quarters. Those of us in the R.O.T.C. must wear our uniforms every day. The curriculum has been telescoped still further since you were here. In a word, college has gone, and a training camp is in its stead.

Those of us who are left, you might think, would resent and deplore this change. On the contrary, the warlike atmosphere here, coupled with our increased academic load, makes us feel justified in being here. There is doubtless at Reserve a feeling of self reproach, and a desire to leave the books for the gun. But they must learn, as I have, that they are much more valuable to their country at Reserve. We are, even though not in the field, trainees for the big job ahead....

As ever,
Steve Lamb [Age 20]

Torrey Eaton's father wrote to Mr. McGill on March 7, thanking him for his letter of February 23 that included a quote from Alan Ward's letter. Mr. Eaton had received further details from an officer who was aboard the *Mahan*, the ship following the *Smith* during the battle in which Torrey lost his life. "This officer actually saw Torrey and several other officers and men from the *Smith* in the water following the explosion," he wrote. "Torrey waved to him as the *Mahan* went past. The next day, when a search was made of the area, this particular group of survivors was not found. It seems dreadful that the ships had to go on and leave these men to their fate—but of course, that is war, and in the heat of an action no ship can stop to pick up survivors."

Fort Riley, Kansas
March 12, 1943

Dear Dr. Hayden,

I just want to write a quick note to thank you so very much for your birthday card and note. It was really very thoughtful of you and WRA, and I mean it when I say I am deeply touched.

It is so seldom that I hear from any of my old schools—except for a donation of some sort or another. Therefore, it is more than nice to get a small note such as this which means so much.

. . . As you may know, I spent almost two years with Colonel Woods King's 107th Cavalry. It was a great experience, a lot of work, and also a lot of fun. However, just before Christmas my orders came through sending me to O.C.S. at Ft. Riley.

And here I am! The weather here, the cold days especially, reminds me of those cold runs I used to take from North Hall to breakfast. It has been fun here too—one reason being that I have been able to use some of my experience. It is not a tough course, but it does touch the high spots, and it does make you stop and think.

In twelve more days, March 25th, I should board a plane for New York with some gold bars on. To say I am excited is putting it mildly. What is especially nice is that I will be with my wife on our first anniversary.

One of these days I will be seeing you and WRA. In the meantime, don't let it change too much because I liked it the way it was. Remember me to "Scotch," Mr. Parker, and some of the other men I knew—Wally, Tebbie, Roundy and the others. . . .

                Yours,
                Mal Vilas [Jr., '35; Age 25]

At the end of the winter term a military funeral was held in the chapel for Harold "Tug" Hoffman ('41), who, while in the first stage of his army training, contracted spinal meningitis and died at Camp Biloxi in Mississippi. The service was held in the Academy chapel with the entire school in attendance. One of his classmates sent a note to Dr. Hayden; later in the month Dean Wood described the circumstances of Tug's death in a letter to Mr. Price.

                Texas Technical College
                March 16, 1943

Dear Dr. Hayden,

Yesterday I learned the sad news of the passing of Harold Hoffman. To say the least, I was shocked and deeply moved. "Tug" was a wonderful fellow and his passing, I know, is deeply felt by everyone who knew him.

By some strange coincidence, Miss Doyle's [Dorothy Doyle, Secretary] nephew, Edward, is stationed here at Texas Tech. and is taking a course preparatory to entering the Army Air Corps. I met him a week ago and since then I have seen him several times. He gave me the newspaper clipping his aunt sent him that told of Harold's death.

                Earl Christy ['41; Age 21]

Spring Term: March–June 1943

March 23, 1943

Dear Lucien,

...As I look out of the window of my office here in Seymour Hall this morning I see the campus lighted up with the rays of the early morning sun. The paper promises "rising temperature" today and how gladly we shall welcome the warm spring days. I noticed that the tulips and the daffodils were trying hard to prick their way through the hard crust of earth.... This is the last day of the spring vacation. The boys will be returning tomorrow afternoon and the work of the spring term will begin on Thursday. Before we know it another commencement will be upon us. It was forty years ago this coming June that we had to close the doors of the old Academy. A lot can happen in forty years—two world wars, a depression and a new Academy....

The work of the past term was quite successful. Our enrollment keeps right up close to capacity and the outlook for next year is good. Last Saturday sixteen boys were here to take the entrance exams for next fall and Mr. Parker told me that all were acceptable. I believe we shall have a full school unless something happens. It is always wise to insert that proviso these days, for anything can happen within a space of even a month's time....

Two weeks ago tragedy struck in and took one of our boys. His parents live here in Hudson. The boy graduated one year ago last June and had finished three semesters at Amherst. He entered the service, was sent to one of the southern states and in less than a month was stricken with spinal meningitis and died the following day.

The body was brought to Hudson and a military service conducted in the Chapel. He was a boy of a good deal of promise and very popular. I stood out here on the steps of Seymour and watched his classmates and friends carry the casket down the Chapel walk to the street and the war seemed at last to have made its way in reality to the old campus....

When and how will it all end? Perhaps there are some minds somewhere capable of finding a solution but they do not seem to have appeared above the horizon as yet. Perhaps the solution of it all will be made by these boys who today are being deprived of their normal and just rights. And who can think any more clearly than the leaders among these young boys? Our hope rests in them....

Very sincerely,
Harlan N. Wood

March 25, 1943

Dear Earl [Christy]:

Thank you for your good note of March 16th. I can't tell you how appreciative the Hoffman family was to get your message relayed through the school office.

Harold K. "Tug" Hoffman ('41). *Archives*

Mrs. Hayden and I called on Mr. and Mrs. Hoffman the other day. They are extremely brave and they are wonderful people on their own account as well. I cannot tell you what a difficult assignment that was for the whole school.

      Ever yours,
      Joel B. Hayden

              March 26, 1943

My dear Lucien:

 . . . These are busy and, in some ways, confusing times for all schools. But our enrollment situation is first-class and our Trustees are alert and loyal; we've held together a competent staff and our temporary replacements are doing an excellent piece of work. You would be proud of your old school. . . .

 The school reassembled at 9:00 P.M. last evening to get into its spring term. Our physical fitness program comprises some interscholastic athletics, some intramural athletics, and a complete campus maintenance program with all the boys and all the faculty participating in jobs to be done, as well as games to be played. Our own boys are building a first-class 18-hazard commando course on the non-playing sections of the fields along Route 91.

 Blessings on you and expect a really decent sort of letter later on. At present, I am swamped in all kinds of administrative details. I am sending longhand birthday notes to every boy in the armed services and we have more than 230 in that category right now. It is a long-drawn-out enterprise, but a blessed one from the standpoint of a Headmaster who really knows his boys individually. That's the top benefit of a school this size.

      Devotedly yours,
      Joel B. Hayden

March 29, 1943

Dear Mac [Malcolm B. Vilas, Jr.]:

It was certainly good to get your letter and I am delighted to know that you are winding up on your special training and that you are going to have a chance to be with your wife on your first anniversary. That really sounds like a dividend, and between you and me you boys are earning dividends in more ways than one.

WRA is spread like buckshot all over the globe. It keeps me busy trying to verify the latest address. What we do is just shoot a note out in the direction of "the last point from which" and let it go at that. It kind of trails boys around and finally catches up with them and then we can verify, for a few moments at least, the addresses on our mailing list.

We've had a good year so far. Prospects for next year, I guess, are even better. The last chance for stiff, high-grade, formal education seems to be in places like these and many parents are simply insisting on that type of training. That helps us. . . .

                Affectionately yours,
                Joel B. Hayden

Earlier in the spring former *Alumni Record* editor Marvin Walker ('35) visited the campus while on leave before reporting for active duty. Faculty member Charles Mears, who had taken his place as editor, invited him to write a message to the alumni before he left. His letter appeared in the April issue of the magazine and included his observations of the current students.

> The boys still have not heard the expression "uniform of the day." Their hats . . . are not trim, their shoes are not shipshape, they keep their hands in their pockets and in general look quite unmilitary. . . . they are a serious lot and ask intelligent questions . . . For example: not one boy has asked me about liberty, vacations, . . . hitting the sack, or any other activity . . . questions as to the amount of mathematics required, the necessity of foreign languages, the amount of physical work and other practical things have popped up in general conversation, showing a healthy tone of mind.

His message ended with a hopeful closing: "May we all meet again soon." The editorial in the April 1 issue of the *Reserve Record* acknowledged the feeling of discouragement that apparently had struck the boys on the campus with regards to the constant call to do their part: "I'm tired of hearing about it! I'm tired of being told that there's a war going on. I know it already because my draft board says I'm about to start fighting it!" The writer reminded the boys that "men just aren't available to pick up stones on the track or clear an infield. That's not your fault, but it's not the school's either. . . . Remember that you are the only one that can do this. No one else is available. Forget the war effort! Be selfish! Get to work."

Information on the army and navy qualification tests for the seniors appeared in this same issue, along with a notice that "due to the poor returns of the mimeograph sheets which were sent out by the school to the parents of the juniors or near juniors" there would be no summer school, which was to be held "to help those boys who would turn 18 before the middle of next year." Individual help, however, was to be made available to "those eight or ten boys concerned before they enter the army or navy."

U.S. Naval Air Station
Corpus Christi, Texas
April 11, 1943

Dear Mr. Hayden,

I was tickled to death to hear from you and much ashamed of myself for not letting you know my change of address two months ago, when I was transferred to Corpus.

I completed my primary training at Kansas about Feb. 1st. There we flew light yellow biplanes, mostly *Stearmans,* built by Boeing in Wichita. Since I've been here I've been flying the *Vultees,* a plane much like those above and called the "Vibrator" by pilots, rather than by the manufacturer's name, the *Valiant!* About thirty hours of my time has been solo—flying in three-plane military formations. . . .

At the present time I have finished the regular "under-class" ground-school course, which includes navigation (a smothering amount of it!), gunnery, bombing, recognition of aircraft and ships—and other such allied subjects. I am waiting for the weather to clear so that I can take my "check" flight in "radio"—that is, instrument flying—with a hood over me (producing a sensation much like that of driving a car with a blanket over your head, I imagine!)[.]

As soon as I can "check out" of instrument squadron, I'll be a "first-classman" and will be assigned to an advanced squadron—either dive or torpedo—bombers, I hope. I'll spend two to three months in this squadron—maybe not that long. Then, all things going well, I should graduate, with those hard-earned "wings of gold!" After that no one knows. Perhaps I'll be assigned a job instructing, or maybe sent to a transitional base, and then on to an operating squadron. In any case, that is several weeks away—the limit of my knowledge of the future since I have been in this game.

Right now I've become very suddenly homesick! Perhaps it's because of spring—maybe because I've had no "leave" since I've been in the navy. But more likely, I think, it's because I get so little chance to listen to music down here—and almost no chance of playing any. This afternoon I smuggled my little radio into the hangar, disguised as a raincoat—and have been trying to listen to the Philharmonic concert, and at this moment Debussy's "La Mer" as played by Toscannini and the NBC orchestra. However, reception in a steel hangar isn't so good, and there's so much static, it's almost impossible to make sense out of what I can hear (have just discovered it on another station—much better!)[.]

I have a few sets of records with me, but have no machine to play them on—and very little opportunity to use the big machine for that purpose in the station library. I have made up my mind that if and when I get out of the navy, I'll get back into music. I'm convinced that there is where I belong! . . .

        Sincerely yours,
        Doug Handyside ['38; Age 22]

                         April 12, 1943

Dear "Yardbird"[1] [Charles J. Killian]:

Thanks for the letter and thanks for the reminiscences about Hudson, and thanks for the invitation to sit down and have a good "chin" with you somewhere or anywhere!

Tip me off, Chuck, as to what you think you would like to do and be when this show is over. I want to send you one or two things which may be of help to you in thinking and working these things through. Ask Steve Lamb to do the same thing because part of my fun here at the school is trying to keep up with what you fellows are going through—the questions that trouble you. If I can shoot something your way that will be helpful and which will lay the basis for a "jam" session, all well and good. So just think it over and let us see what we can do about it. . . .

        Ever yours,
        Joel B. Hayden

---

1. Yardbird—a new recruit.

Charles Killian ('40), who was known at Reserve as "Boots," was attending Princeton along with his former schoolmate at Reserve, Steve Lamb.

Harry Allchin, Jr. ('39), was preparing to get his wings in Texas after completion of his training in the Army Air Corps. There was much discussion between Dr. Hayden and Harry's father on the subject of his brother, Tom ('46), attending the ceremony. Should he take the time away from his freshman studies to travel with his family to Texas to see Harry receive his wings? Dr. Hayden wrote to Harry about the decision that was made.

April 21, 1943

Dear Harry,

Just had a good talk with your father. I went into [your brother] Tommy's situation with your dad and showed him how serious it would be to Tom, himself, if he should try to take the time out in May which visiting you would entail. It is the very peak of his ninth grade year at the Academy and he might miss-fire so badly at the end that it would literally ruin his year from the academic point of view.

Therefore, your father and I decided that Tom's best contribution to you and to the family would be to finish his job here with a full head of steam and gird up his loins for an interesting summer and an even better year at Reserve starting next fall.

You're going to have a fine family representation anyway. Your two brothers won't be able to make it because they are in training themselves in a very real sense. Your mother and your sister and a neighbor, I believe, will be there and they will give you a royal send off.

Your father let me read your last letter. Landing at 110 miles an hour—that's really something, isn't it? What an experience it must be to gain the mastery of a new element, such as the air.

We are thinking about you and we will be thinking about you right straight through this whole show. You Reserve fellows have a way of burning yourselves into our minds and hearts. I guess that is what it's all about. Am I right? Every letter we get from a boy in the armed forces has that intimate personal note, that sense of responsibility, that clear, heavy determination which we have seen growing and developing with our boys over the last twelve years. You see, I'm speaking from my own experience and Mrs. Hayden's experience because we are winding up our twelfth year in the Village of Hudson.

                    Devotedly yours,
                    Joel B. Hayden

                    Lubbock Army Flying School
                    Lubbock, Texas
                    April 26, 1943

Dear Dr. Hayden,

I think my father was asking a little too much. When he told me Tom was trying to arrange to come I thought it would be quite impossible. I appreciate your position in the matter. I fully agree with the decision, although I would have liked to have had him here. He is very much interested in airplanes and he would have gotten quite a kick out of seeing the place. He is a great little kid. I sure hope he does a good job there at Reserve. Knowing that he is doing all right there does something to me which I just can't quite express or put down on paper. Being able to go to Reserve was just about the most wonderful thing that ever happened to me and I'm hoping that Tom appreciates it as much as I did.

Yes, May 24th should be a big day. After that it won't be long before I'll be able to apply what I have learned. I'm getting anxious to get into the real thing and do my share. We've got a lot to fight for and we've just got to come out on top. Keep that little brother of mine on the ball.

Harry Allchin, Jr. [Age 23]

May 5, 1943

Dear Tom [Babcox]:

Thank you for the beautiful pictures of Brisbane. They are going through the faculty and you are going through our minds continually.

We've had no spring to date. Rain and snow and hail and gray skies and low temperatures. This in May! We've had one ball game, five cancellations; two track meets, two cancellations; no tennis meets, one cancellation. Some record!

We are going to do our best to keep the school going full tilt ahead. Our problem is teaching personnel at present. Enrollment prospects excellent. Faculty and boys are doing a large part in campus maintenance. We are learning plenty and I think the campus will look well.

Faculty, as you remember them, are for the most part here. Stacey Eaton [French master, 1934–42 and 1943–44] has gone by resignation because of a home situation; Fred Waring in the American Field Service for a year; Glenn King in the Army; Ray Burns a Chaplain in the Army. The other six men who have gone would be merely names to you. Have brought six men in.

Haven't seen your family for some time but here's hoping! We have quite a job on our hands in America in terms of real national unity. There are many people who are completely and serenely provincial; they like to crawl into a hole and pull the hole in with them and call it the good old U.S.A. If they get in the saddle, they'll dig graves for their own grandchildren and for your grandchildren—possibly for generations closer to us than that!

I sometimes think, Tom, that the biggest job at Western Reserve Academy is parent and adult education. It is so easy to get into a rut and nurse one's prejudices, and then let the prejudices, the ignorances, the blindness get into the saddle and ride away to the Valley of Destruction. What strength I have left is going to be devoted to the counterchage. I am still a Christian minister and I have found nothing in the world quite so comprehensive and inclusive and dynamic as the underlying assumptions of the Christian point of view. My feeling is let's stand upon this Christian ground and fight it out or else call ourselves what we really are—pagans—

and then maybe we can become reconciled to stewing in our own juice. Here's to you, Tommy, from the gang at Reserve—all of us.

Devotedly yours,
Joel B. Hayden

Kent, Ohio
May 7, 1943

Dear "Big Doc" [Hayden]:

I hope I may take the liberty of calling you that, as I remember very vividly that was the name by which you were endeared to the boys.

. . . It was my good fortune to get back and see the campus the other week, even though there weren't any familiar faces around. The folks came up for Easter which gave us the opportunity to drive through Hudson. The school looks just as beautiful as when I last brought Tien Wei [Yang, '41] up three years ago this fall. One of my friends who is flying tells me he can distinguish the Chapel and the athletic field from his view aloft.

I've been in the Air Corps nearly three months now and feel that our next post will be a regular army primary flight school. Kent State is an ideal place for our purpose—although we're pretty restricted for six days a week, there is little of the real army atmosphere. They're throwing subjects at us right and left and the opportunities for picking up valuable information are great in the little time that we have.

Chuck [Charles F. Kennedy, Jr., '40; Age 23]

Somewhere in England
May 21, 1943

Dear Mr. Hayden:

Your birthday greetings came through yesterday and just beat the deadline by two days. Many thanks for the remembrance.

Your asking to tell about myself would probably take considerable time for since coming over here last September, I have done so much and had so many varied jobs it would take a book to cover them all. Consider myself exceptionally fortunate to be in the branch of service that has enabled me to travel over almost all of England and have driven approximately 15,000 miles since being over. Right now I have all the supply, maintenance and service functions for the base where I am now located and it seems to be hardly enough hours in the day to get done all the things that require doing. Prior to my present job I had charge of an operational training unit for pilots and prior to that was engaged in the movement to North Africa as one of the many small cogs. Hoping this leaves you well, I remain,

Yours,
Joe H. Stewart (Lt. Col.) ['30; Age 32]

May 24, 1943

Dear Mrs. Kendel:

The reply which you sent for Bill [William F. Kendel, '27] to our commencement invitation has come to my attention. You state that he is in a hospital at the present time, seriously wounded. . . .

It is our deep and sincere hope that you may receive some encouraging word and be assured that we want to share with you any word you may receive.

Our boys are scattered over the entire globe. Word came only a day or two ago of the safe landing in Iceland of Carder Welles who was a member of Bill's class. Others are in Australia and various distant points. The number of our graduates now in the service is approaching three hundred.

Again I extend to you our sympathy and our hopes.

Very sincerely yours,
Harlan N. Wood

Throughout the school year, the machine shop continued producing materials for Bardons and Oliver, determined to meet its goal of twelve thousand man-hours. Their efforts did not go unnnoticed. Dr. Hayden received a letter from Washington congratulating the school on their contribution to the war effort.

May 25, 1943

Dear Sir:

It has come to my attention that certain of the students at the Academy have established a unique production record in producing machined parts for turret lathes and other tools. It is further my understanding that these parts have been entirely acceptable to the war contractors for whom they have been produced.

I wish to express my appreciation to the young men who are cooperating so wholeheartedly in the war effort and who are at the same time becoming better trained to continue the battle of production.

It is also apparent that the production record of the Academy could not have been made without careful planning and technical skill contributed by the machine shop instructor and others in the faculty.

I congratulate the Academy on its fine contribution to the war effort.

Sincerely yours,
Donald M. Nelson
Chairman, War Production Board
Washington, D.C.

For the first time in the long history of the school the enrollment was closed by the first day of summer. This curious development was pondered by Ralph McGill in a letter to an alumnus. "Why this remarkable interest?"

Forrest ("Bug," '34) and Hamilton ('37) Kenner made front-page news in the *Cleveland Press* on March 27, 1943. Forrest happened to be in port where he was stationed in Australia when a large group of American troops pulled ashore. Although he had last heard his brother "Ham" was in the States, Forrest thought he saw him among the men. An article in the December *Alumni Record* described their chance meeting. It explained that since, given the crowd, it was impossible "to get near enough to discover whether the face he had glimpsed was his brother's, he whistled the first bar of the violin number 'Souvenir,' with which Mrs. Kenner had called the boys home from their neighborhhod play when they were children. He repeated it and Hamilton, amazed, answered. Then back and forth went the whistle until the two were able to reach each other through the crowd." They "managed to have a few steaks together" before Ham proceeded to New Guinea.

he wrote. "We don't know. . . . In any event, WRA is profiting rather vigorously at the moment."

On May 19 Winston Churchill addressed the U.S. Congress, declaring, "After Hitler's downfall we shall lay the cities of Japan in ashes." At home, a strike by more than fifty thousand Akron rubber workers ended on May 27.

As the class of 1943 received their diplomas, the war in North Africa ended with the German surrender. Of the fifty-two boys who graduated on May 30, 1943, thirty-five went into the service by summer's end. Before Dr. and Mrs. Hayden left for Maine for the summer, the headmaster sent Joe H. Stewart ('30) his reflections on the end-of-year activities.

June 4, 1943

My dear Colonel [Joe H.] Stewart,

Thank you for your newsy letter which brought us up to date on what you are doing. I know that at this minute you are just doing more of the same with more intricate problems all around you. . . .

I want you to know that we had a fine Commencement. We graduated about forty-eight boys, twenty-two of whom will go directly into the armed forces without bothering to be accepted by some specific college because they have all taken their examinations for V-12 and A-12, which means that they will be placed in army or navy colleges as part of their armed forces training. The rest of the boys were accepted by colleges ranging from Oberlin to M.I.T. in geographical distribution, and most of them will quickly find themselves in uniform doing their work under the direction of those in charge of both offense and defense.

Raymond Gram Swing, with whom I spent two years in Oberlin back in 1905–1906, was our commencement speaker. Mrs. Hayden was also a classmate so the three of us had a grand reunion and we "fanned the breeze informally" all around the edges of the commencement program itself.[1]

The interior of the Chapel was even more beautiful than ever, I think, since we have added a chancel with an A-No. 1 organ, a Palladian window to the east and the Christopher gold cross hanging in the center of that window.[2] The Glee Club, supplemented by some of the lower school boys, was our vested choir, and the whole day brought satisfaction and joy to all of us. Yes, we know the days are grim, but youth has a natural protection thrown round about it by Mother Nature herself. They look into the future without a quiver, without a quaver, and, knowing these boys as I do, they are going to give a great account of themselves.

Sincerely,
Joel B. Hayden

1. Dr. and Mrs. Hayden met at Oberlin College, from where they both graduated in 1909.

2. The "Christopher Cross" referred to by Dr. Hayden is an iron one, said to have been knelt before by Christopher Columbus before he left for the new world. The Palladian window was bricked over in 1967 to allow space for the installation of the pipes for the current organ, a gift of Walter H. Holtkamp ('47) of Cleveland, and it is above the organ pipes that the cross still hangs today.

Peyote, Texas
June 10, 1943

Dear Dr. and Mrs. Hayden,

Many thanks for your thoughtfulness in sending me *Flight to Arras*. While waiting to be assigned a crew I've had quite a bit of spare time and was able to sit down and read almost the all of it today. It is about something which isn't too far distant for me. I suppose it is really hard to explain exactly what flashes through a pilot's mind during such a mission but I think he has hit the nail on the head. I've had somewhat the same feelings even while flying with a co-pilot in the pitch darkness of the night. These boys in the Air Force are real boys. After flying with them for awhile you can't help but put a lot of faith in them.

... After my short furlough I was ordered to report at this base for training on the medium bomber B-26. However they have only the *Flying Fortress* at present, and, unless there is a change-over in the next few weeks, I will probably be flying a *Fortress*.

I was quite surprised to find the kind of country they have here. It is very hot and dry. Very sparsely settled. I would hate to estimate the date of the last rainfall. There are quite a few rattlesnakes around. That is how this post got its name of the rattlesnake bomber base.

      Many thanks again,
      Lt. Harry Allchin [Age 23][1]

---

1. This was the first letter from Harry that didn't include "Jr." at the end of his name.

Robert Bluem ('39x) was serving near where Jack Gillespie had been killed in October 1942. In a moment of quiet reflection, he wrote his thoughts to Dr. Hayden.

      Somewhere in the Pacific
      June 12, 1943

Dear Dr. Hayden,

Yes, another one of those infrequent letters from one of your former students, if I may go so far as call myself a student. How true was the saying we so often heard there at WRA, one never reaches the end of schooling. We even now have classes everyday although the real lessons come from our daily contacts with men and nature.

I visited Jack Gillespie today, it seems queer way out here in the Pacific, but this war has brought on many such things.

      Truly yours,
      Bob [Age 22]

The news of the death of another Academy boy came to the school early in June, bringing the number of Gold Stars on the Service Roll to ten. Robert F. Heinrichs ('38) lost his life at age twenty-two in a plane crash near the Pecos, Texas, army air base. A newspaper clipping in Bob's file stated, "Word of the tragedy was received by the youth's parents shortly before they were to entertain a group of teachers from Alexander Graham Bell School for the Deaf at supper. Mrs. Heinrichs [Bob's mother], who had spent most of the day preparing for the supper party, carried on despite the tragic news. It was not until after the supper was over that the guests were informed of the couple's bereavement." Bob's wife of five months wrote to Dr. Hayden. "I still cannot believe he is gone," she said. "I feel that he is

Robert F. Heinrichs ('38), death notice from the *Cleveland Plain Dealer*. Archives

just away completing another phase of his training. The last I saw Bob, he was leaning out the car window waving to me as far down the road as I could see. It is such a nice memory."

June 22, 1943

Dear George:

Perhaps ten times in the last six months I have said to myself, "I must dash off a letter to George Manlove" but here we are, the school year over, and I haven't done so. However, an incident occurred a few days ago which again reminded me—in a very strange way—that I had not yet written that letter.

A week ago yesterday, I was riding the bus over to Akron to spend a portion of the day with my wife at the home of her uncle and aunt. On the bus, I sat down beside a good looking young aviation cadet and struck up a conversation with him. He is attending Western Reserve University, taking the pre-flight course up there. One word led to another, as is the case in such things, and it developed in time that he is a good friend of yours. His name is Ralph Heckett and he attended the Mercersburg Academy while you were one of the professors there. I believe he said you lived right across the hall from him, and he asked that I give you his warm regards when and if I should write to you. It is a small world, isn't it?

There isn't a great deal to tell you about your preparatory "almus pater." I guess we have in the neighborhood of 300 boys in the service now, all told, and our tenth Gold Star appeared a little bit over a week ago—Bob Heinrichs, Class of 1938, flight instructor in the A.A.F.; he was killed in a crash landing down in Texas. I guess Bob came on the scene here shortly after you graduated. You may also have heard that one of our recent graduates passed away with meningitis about three or four months ago, down at Biloxi.

This is the 21st of June—the first day of summer—and Mr. Parker closed the enrollment for the coming school year today—something that has never happened before in the long history of the school. On one or two previous occasions, we were able to close it shortly before September 1st, and on one occasion about the middle of August, but never before during June. Why this remarkable interest? We don't know, but we presume that a good many parents have decided that, since the war will probably make college a very questionable thing for their sons, they had better get busy and do the best they can for them before they reach military age. In any event, WRA is profiting rather vigorously at the moment.

I have talked with [your brother] Bill ['44] now and then about your exploits in the fields of Africa; know that you have the Purple Heart and that you've seen a good deal of action. I know, my boy, that you have the background, the fortitude, the character, the philosophy and the good judgment not to let any experiences you may have turn you "sour" on the world as was the case with so many fellows who went through the other war. I knew of two young fellows who left Ohio Wesleyan to become lieutenants in the army. Before they left they were as fine lads as you could ever meet anywhere. When the war was over, they were a couple of super-sophisticated egotists who believed that selfishness is at the heart of every human action and that life is purely and simply a case of "dog eat dog." I have lost sight of them now and am glad to have done so because I can't conceive of an acquaintanceship with those fellows as ever being of up-lifting benefit to anyone, and I say this in spite of the fact that they and I were fraternity brothers. A thing like this couldn't happen to you, George, and I know it.

. . . I well remember how you and Jerry Forbes ['32] went into seclusion one weekend in your senior year in order, by the eternal, to master the trigonometry you knew you should know up to that point, and, as I well recall, you did just that. . . .

We have lost nine masters, all told—eight of them to the service. However, our replacements have been of good quality, I think, and it begins to look like the old school will weather the storm.

Cordially yours,
Ralph W. McGill

July–August 1943

Although the war in North Africa and the Middle East had ended, J. Fred Waring chose to take another year's leave to teach at the American University in Beirut. He would not return until the fall of 1944. English master W. W. Kirk was called to the navy during the summer months, leaving yet another vacancy on the faculty.

On July 10, Allied forces invaded Sicily. Later in the month Mussolini resigned. On August 17, Sicily was conquered. That same day President Roosevelt and Prime Minister Winston Churchill met with Canadian premier Mackenzie King in Quebec. The main topic of discussion was the timing and the location of the invasion of France under the code name "Operation Overlord." Realizing it would be impossible for the operation to take place in 1943, it was agreed that it should be launched as soon as possible. D day was still a year away.

> W. & B. Flying School
> Chickasha, Oklahoma
> July 2, 1943

Dear Mr. McGill,

Having a wee bit of time for the first time since I hooked up with this outfit, I thought I'd drop you a line. Not that you'd be particularly interested in what I happen to be doing, but I like to think that someone back there is. Not having been one of your model children I guess that is almost too much to expect. But it is true that some of us that leave Reserve have retained many fond memories long after we have been understandably forgotten there. Anyway, if my luck ever changes and I grab a wife up for myself, you can count on the job of trying to educate or should we say restrain my offspring. . . .

You don't get much chance to find out what kind of people really live in this world if you have spent the last few years within the more or less secluded walls of a private school and an eastern college. Here we meet real men who have families at home and a small job waiting for them after the war perhaps and not a large bankroll and a Thomas-like attitude. Personally I like them better. This is not to say that Reserve and the boys there are all this way but you and I know one would never become worldly wise on the "long walks and green aisles" of Reserve. This is an experience I'll never forget. . . .

You'd never recognize me. I went to the classification center at San Antonio and luckily got a pilots rating. From there to pre-flight, which was rough. This particular preflight school is ranked by the army second only to West Point. It was rough. Inspections were hourly it seemed and were made with rulers and white gloves. Collars on the beds had to be measured to six inches and not six and one-eighth and that went for all clothing in the lockers. The officer would come into your bay and rub over all surfaces with a white glove including the floor and if it showed dirt or even the slightest trace you were a dead duck.

Ed Metcalf ('42) carried this photo in an escape kit that included money, maps, and a small compass. The photo, taken of Metcalf in civilian clothes at his air base in England prior to flying combat missions, could be used with a counterfeit passport provided by the French Underground if he were shot down over enemy territory. *Courtesy Ed Metcalf*

That was minor compared with the class system that is a tradition at the so called "West Point of the Air." The upperclassmen had the authority of a commissioned officer over the lower classmen. I stood in a brace, politely called a corrective position of attention, for three hours four different times. This would consist of about ten upperclassmen yelling "hop to mister; suck in that gut; drive those shoulders back and down; reach for Texas and straighten out those arms, change colors mister; how old are you mister—well, I want to see nineteen wrinkles in that chin, you are not even trying mister."

They'd insult you and swear at you and call you every name in the book. They would back you against a locker and sweat your outline on it in a matter of a few minutes. It sounds foolish and childish but I'll never regret it. In my class, however, twenty-five men were permanently injured from it in the first week. It was tough on them but those that get through that, they know really want to fly. You would never appreciate this unless you went through it. Others can't understand why they allow it but I, for one, am a better man for having gone through it.

Then there were academics. We had naval vessels, code, maps and charts, physics, math, and aircraft identification, which I passed well enough. I can take twelve words a minute in code and got a ninety-eight average, wonder of wonders, in math. Tell the boys to stick to it; they'll need it sooner or later. Then there was physical training. Thirty to forty minutes of straight calisthenics every day plus cross country, steeple chase, and various games. Even I could run a two-and-one-half mile cross country up and down real hills in thirteen minutes. Can take forty pushups in stride and can play basketball for hours at a time and never even feel it.

In nine weeks we got out four days and our schedule ran seven days a week. Saturday and Sunday were just the same as any other day. I imagine by now you think I'm spreading it on. However, if you would see and talk to me now for just about five minutes, I feel there would be no doubt in my mind.

At present I'm out of that frying pan and into the fire. I'm at primary flight school. We fly in the morning and get academics and physical training in the afternoon. We do get time after supper, which is a welcome relief and which is also the reason I write this letter. I soloed at eight hours and am fairly good at dives, stalls, turns, spins, and mild aerobatics. The wash out rate is high, but I'm determined to stick around until they pass out the wings in December.

The food here is the best and beds for a change are soft, and best of all, we aren't in Texas anymore. All in all it's the best thing that ever happened to me and I don't regret a day of it. It's tough to get used to, but if you keep yourself doing something every minute, it's not too bad after awhile.

    Sincerely yours,
    Ed Metcalf ['42; Age 20]

                July 6, 1943

Dear old Ed [Metcalf]:

Your long letter of July 2 came yesterday and I have read it with much interest. Naturally, I shall pass it around among the men who are here.

Thanks very much for telling us all these things, and particularly for authorizing us to tell our boys that the sort of things we do with and to them here are very, very, very innocuous compared with what you have gone through and with what they are likely to have imposed on them later in the services. Of course, most of them will think we're just "handing them a game of jolly," but some may take us seriously.

. . . Thanks, also, for telling me how well you've done in your academic work in the service. Of course, Ed, we all know here that what you did here at WRA and especially what you did in some subjects out at Amherst, was no indication of what you could do when you really got down to business. Apparently, you have gotten down to serious business in the Air Corps and the results are about what we and you have always had a right to expect of you.

Enrollment for the coming school year is closed now—something which has never happened hitherto in the history of the school. The reasons seem to be: 1) that more people have more money than has been true for many years, and 2) that many people, seeing the impossibility of sending their sons to college in the predictable future, seem to have decided to do the best they can by their sons before Uncle Sam gets them. . . .

    Cordially yours,
    Ralph W. McGill

LaGrange, Illinois
July 8, 1943

Dear Dr. Hayden:

First, I thank you and your associates again for the very fine influence upon and for the very excellent training that you have given our boys [Paul H. ('42) and H. Douglas Barnes ('43)]. Mrs. Barnes and I shall never cease to be grateful to you.

Bud [Paul] attended the engineering department of the University of Wisconsin this last year, where he was in the Enlisted Reserve Corps. During the latter part of April or the first of May, he was called to active duty and sent to Fort Leonard Wood in Missouri, where he was assigned to the combat engineers. He takes to army life like a duck to water and has been having a wonderful time. He qualified as a sharp shooter and came within one shot of qualifying as an expert rifleman. He has been recommended for further schooling and is at the moment taking examinations at Grinnell College in Iowa. Judging from his latest letter, I think he would rather go back and complete his basic training. He said that he certainly had a good time at Fort Leonard Wood, but I know that he will do the best he can at his examinations.

Doug has been called for induction on Friday of this week. He was admitted to Harvard College and we hoped that he would at least have an opportunity to get started so that he would feel that there was some place to go back to when the war is over, but 125 boys from our village are leaving Friday and he is one of them. . . .

        Sincerely yours,
        John P. Barnes

July 9, 1943

Dear Judge Barnes:

I want to say that we were glad to get your recent information about the whereabouts of Paul and Doug. Seems to me we learned not very long ago something about Bud to the effect that he had been taken into the service or was about to be. Perhaps I am thinking of what Mrs. Barnes told us when she was here for Doug's graduation.

Yes, the boys are slowly being "chucked" into the service. In Doug's case, though, he had the misfortune to fail his physical examination for V-12, I think there is little doubt that he will soon find his way into some type of specialized service. From all we can learn, the services are doing a much better job now than they did twenty-five years ago in the fine art of seeking out and finding boys with specialized ability and training and using them where they, presumably, will most benefit the nation's war interests. . . .

        Cordially yours,
        Ralph W. McGill

Somewhere in Arizona
July 27, 1943

Dear Dr. Hayden:

... I have a rather strong hunch that our present growing pains accompanying our national emergence from this welter of egocentricity may restore us our dignity—with or without equity as our tradition always knew it. At any rate these are the kinds of hunches that keep a guy together while soldiering in 120 degree hot Arizona dust. ...

You had asked me if I thought I was just the kind of alumnus who should be back at the Academy teaching training and leading boys. That is a great big question, Dr. Hayden, and I can only answer it now with a terrifying question mark. It is like, "Do you or do you not take this woman?, etc." in so far as it means the acceptance of a way of life—a voluntary immersion in an aesthetic whole. I'd rather talk to you about it than try to place it on paper. So much of my life so far has just sort of happened (it ain't all been aesthetic, I can tell you) that I am a trifle leery of most everything. Please know that the continuing good will of the very few persons like yourself is a thing that I have come to value. ...

But there is still the strenuous pursuit of idle unanswerables in strange bids for which my physical constitution seems to have endowed me. And further, neither of us can predict the societal frame these years are creating. I am sure that if I do arrive as an educator, there is no place on earth where I could do a better job than in the compact reserve of sane tradition the Academy represents.

For now, however, it is "chow time," and I, "chow hound by expedience," must go to mess. ...

    Sincerely,
    Joseph Millar ['34; Age 28]

August 4, 1943

Dear Dick [Richard P. Edwards, '38]:

... We knew that you have been in the service for a long time, though I didn't presume it was almost two years. Congratulations on becoming a lieutenant; I think we had not heard that yet.

True, we are operating under some difficulties—great scarcity of help, high cost of some materials, inability to get some needed materials, and the loss of some teachers to the draft—but I believe the worst is past for one thing, and for another, we all know that in these times we must expect not to be able to pursue "the even tenor of our ways." The worst hazards that may strike us cannot be compared with the risks that most of you fellows are running or may have to run before this thing is over. So don't worry about us; we'll get along and we'll keep our chins up. ...

    Cordially yours,
    Ralph W. McGill

Somewhere in the Mediterranean
August 7, 1943

Dear Dr. and Mrs. Hayden,

I got Mrs. Hayden's letter yesterday, after it had been forwarded around to very many addresses, and it was certainly pleasant to hear about everyone. My midshipman days ended five months ago, and I'm now pretty far from Chicago. It's hard to remember just what I've said in various letters, with the exchange of correspondence so slow, but anyway Dick [my twin brother] probably told you I'd been assigned to a navy tanker after a couple of weeks of temporary duty in New York.

The duty is not at all arduous, though it gets pretty monotonous. Life is just about the same from day to day, with a turn at deck watches when we're underway, and nothing in particular when we're in port. Being supply and communication officer is not very complicated on a small ship, and most of the work comes when in port. Even then it's mainly a matter of catching boat rides back and forth to shore and thumbing around in jeeps to the different offices at the base. Supplies are very elusive and the amount of referring around you get from one office to another for information and approvals is reminiscent of Washington. However, here it isn't nearly as provoking, since it kills time and provides good exercise and an excuse to see the countryside.

I've run into Hugh Bell ['37] in a couple of different spots, and also have seen a few officers from my midshipman class. Do you know what particular unit Mr. Waring is attached to? Possibly he is in this vicinity.

[My brother] Herbert ['41] got assigned to U.C.L.A. for his V-12 training, which suited him fine. [My brother] Walter ['44] is running a drill press at Thompson Products. The last I heard of Dick he was in New Orleans after being assigned to LST 30, built in Pittsburgh, and sailing with it down the Mississippi. I'm keeping an ear to the ground for convoy movements, as very probably he'll be heading over here fairly soon. Already I've met lots of his midshipman school classmates who mistake me for him.

      Sincerely,
      Bob Hirshberg ['36; Age 24]

Somewhere in the Pacific
August 18, 1943

Dear Dr. Hayden,

I want to thank you for your kind wishes. Due to rapid and distant movement of men, including myself, I was nowhere near Miami—but no one can be expected to keep up with a naval officer's travels. At present I am the engineering, gunnery, and executive officer of the USS *SC-670*. Our address is Fleet Post Office, San Francisco. As you might guess from the variety of duties I have, an SC boat is one of the smaller ships in the navy. In fact, the only combat type ships smaller than ours are the PT boats.

Robert L. Hirshberg ('36). *Courtesy Robert Hirshberg*

So far our duty has been rather dull, though rough. No, Japanese do not seem navally ambitious in these areas. Our main dangers are uncharted waters and very violent weather and thick fogs.

It seems that most all of fighting a war is training and marching. The actual engagements take only a few hours. That is true of the island warfare anyhow....

I would like to say though that while at Reserve I often wondered if I was learning anything useful. I know now that I did. And even though our training there was certainly not for fighting a war, still what I learned on the athletic fields and in my classes and from the other guys subjecting themselves to the same things has come in very handy indeed. After all, it's thinking and seeing that counts. I learned how to do those things.

Dick Silver ['38; Age 23]

Iran or Persia
August 19, 1943

Dear Dr. Hayden,

... Yesterday I got into one of those discussions of the war situation with a couple of fellows, and of course we got onto the subject of war aims, too, the one that has been on my mind so much. They agreed that it would be nice if, contrary to our experience twenty-five years ago, we would get some lasting good out of this war, a really lasting peace and a world really safe for democracy, but knowing human nature and past experience, they were skeptical. However, their attitude could still be called constructive.

Then another fellow chimed in with the opinion all-too-typical of the average American today: "There always has been war, there always will be war. Human nature will never change. You can't stop that sort of thing."

This is what I call, the "It can't be done" attitude. It's what Christ meant, in the Bible, when, in near disgust, he said, "Oh ye of little faith!"

Whenever a guy talks that "never will change" and "can't be done" stuff to me, I feel like clipping him on the jaw, but no one ever convinced anybody by clipping him. You don't win friends and influence people by going around socking people on the jaw. Only dictators and similar pea-brains still believe that. Anyway, that kind of thinking is lack of faith of the worst sort, in an age when lack of faith is less justified than ever. The whole history of America is an unfolding story of doing the impossible. We alone have done the impossible, so many times that nothing should seem impossible anymore, and that leaves out of account what our allies (and our enemies, too, for that matter) have done. England "couldn't" resist, Russia "couldn't," China "couldn't." So many things have happened that "couldn't" happen that our minds and imaginations should be open to any possibility.

If everybody lacked faith as much as your average man in the street does, all progress would stop. The steamboat, the railroad, the automobile, and the airplane would never have replaced the sailboat and the horse and buggy; such things were "impossible." The American experiment in democracy and the Russian experiment in Communism were both "impractical" and "impossible" and "could never work." Before Pearl Harbor, the crepe-hangers, calamity howlers, and isolationists told us that if we got into the war, it would "take us twenty years to win." We "couldn't" ship enough men and equipment over to do it in less. Not only did these people lack faith; they even forgot the lesson of 1917–1918. Even seeing wasn't believing.

Now people who in their blindness can't see that human nature has changed, very slowly of course, in the last 5,000 years (and before that, too, now that we know most of the facts of evolution), say it never will change. The principles for which the greatest teacher of all was crucified 1900 years ago, the Golden Rule, the Sermon on the Mount, faith, etc., are "impractical." The law of the jungle, "kill or be killed," will always prevail; every man will continue to put personal gain above the ideal of service, nations won't learn to live together as good neighbors in decency and common sense, there won't ever be a better world for everybody, etc., because all this "can't be done," they say. Nine out of every ten people still laugh and sneer at these ideas, but they have nothing constructive to offer in their place. "Oh, ye of little faith!" was certainly right. It makes it tough for anybody who does want to see lasting good come out of this war, and who does want to help in a small way to bring about a better world.

I suspect that this mental and spiritual vacuum that so many people live in, this negative defeatist outlook which robs life of all zest for so many people, is the fault of our educational system. Too few people are taught to make a habit of thinking constructively; too few people are taught to think clearly and logically at all. That's why people don't have a long range view of the whole picture but see only their own immediate surroundings; that's why they see only the present and the immediate past. That's why most Americans take crooked politics in place of an ideal democracy for granted, and even joke about it. That's why most people have no faith in a better future. They know too little about the great past, and they don't realize how much improvement has already taken place.

Therefore, I say that nothing is impossible. Anything from raising a vegetable garden to reforming the world can be done if you have the faith, the patience, and the determination. In the great age to come, we're going to need faith and clear thinking as never before.

      Very best regards,
      Johnny [T.] Johnson ['35; Age 26]

Late in the summer, anticipating a school year with record-breaking enrollment, Assistant Headmaster McGill wrote the following to Louis S. Whitaker's ('43) grandfather.

      August 30, 1943

Dear Mr. Whitaker,

. . . We shall open the school in about two weeks with the largest student body in the history of the school. Whatever the reasons for this, we are thankful for it and shall accept the larger challenge with the conviction that we can carry through despite the sundry handicaps under which all such institutions are obliged to work under present conditions. At this moment, I just don't see how we'll be able to feed our boys next winter because it looks like an almost impossible task to secure kitchen labor, but we'll do it somehow even if the masters have to take some time out of their leisure filled days to peel spuds, make applesauce, wash dishes and scrub out the dining hall. . . .

      Cordially yours,
      Ralph W. McGill

THE SCHOOL YEAR 1943–44
Busy and Tired

🍂 FALL TERM: SEPTEMBER–DECEMBER 1943

Of the 224 boys enrolled for the school year, 181 were boarding students. This, indeed, was the largest enrollment the school had seen in its long history. The problem of housing was solved by placing the overflow of boys in the homes of some of the faculty members.

In a normal year the thoughts of the juniors and seniors generally turned to college applications. But this was not a normal year. The seniors were in their third year of living in a world at war. They had seen nine of their faculty masters leave for military duty and several schoolmates called to service before completing their senior years. They were aware of the reasons why everyone had to pitch in around the campus: Most of the campus crew had left to join up as well.

Among his regular duties as dean of students, Harlan Wood was the overseer of the Alumni Scholarship Fund. When he wrote to contributors to thank them, he gave to each a description of the campus's climate. There were, by now, over 350 boys in the service, and news came in from locations around the globe. To quote from one of Dr. Hayden's letters, the boys were "spread like buckshot around the world."

Somewhere in the Pacific
September 5, 1943

Dear Dr. Hayden,

It was sure good to hear from you again. I just returned to my outfit after a month of special duty and your letter of the 29th, that is the 29th of July, was awaiting me.

. . . Lately we have had a bit of action here, perhaps the papers have gotten that fact across. Yes, those two sayings hold true; Sherman's historical "War is hell" and the one from Bataan, "There are no atheists in foxholes." The chaplains have done a yeomans service here, some with the notation KIA [killed in action] following their name. I only wish more of the men could have been as lucky as I, not a scratch.

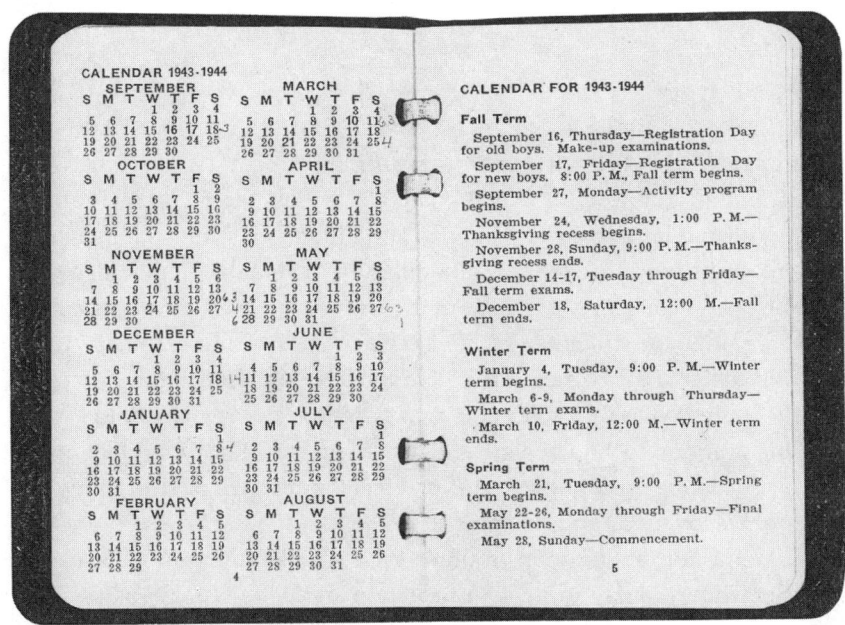

School calendar 1943–44. *Student Handbook*

It is getting dark and no lights are permitted here, for "Charles" [Japanese planes] still visits us quite often.

> Truly yours,
> Bob [Bluem, '39x; Age 23]

> Somewhere in North Africa
> September 8, 1943

Dear Doc,

Certainly appreciated your birthday card which recently caught up with me here in North Africa. Your thoughtfulness recalled many happy memories of the Academy that are most enjoyable to preserve.

I was almost down to see you this commencement past, as I was home on leave, but home ties proved too strong as I was about to go overseas. Landed here amid strange sights and unforgettable odors in June. Since have acclimated myself to the latter and the newness of seeing Arabs, their allergy to clean clothes, their stone and stucco houses, and their terribly overloaded burros has worn away. The scenic views along the coast though are still magnificent. Had a chat with Dave Dennison for a short time while I was in Algiers. Please remember me to your family and to my friends at WRA.

> Sincerely,
> Charles Tillinghast ['35; Age 27]

University of California
September 12, 1943

Dear Dr. Hayden:

Since the last time I wrote to you providence hath turned its shining countenance upon this, its humble servant. The A.S.T.P. [Army Specialized Training Program] for which I had applied last March broke for me last month and by virtue of my French I qualified as a foreign language student. Will you please tell Mr. Kitzmiller for me that he "builded" better than he knew. Thus I am presently at the University of California as a foreign area language student in Chinese. The University offers Chinese, Russian and Italian. I am particularly pleased to have drawn Chinese and completely fascinated at the prospect of what Chinese culture may hold for me.

This program sets up a mighty stiff regimen from both a military and also an academic standpoint; however, I feel that the privilege of living here on this lovely campus in contrast to the lots of other "G.I.s" more than compensates for the strenuous routine. We are given (thirty of us) three hours of Chinese a day—one hour recitation and two hours tutoring. The balance of the day is filled with military and geopolitics (Geography, Geology, Anthropology, etc.) of Asia. I am in pretty fast company I.Q. wise and have no trouble maintaining a healthy fear of being eliminated. And so it goes. I have changed oases. The machinations of government fiat are indeed inscrutable.

Sincerely,
Joseph Millar ['34; Age 28]

George Manlove ('32) wrote to his two brothers: Bill ('44), a senior attending the Academy who was also awaiting the call to the navy, and Ken, serving in the Pacific. His parents passed the letter on to the school.

Somewhere in Sicily
September 18, 1943

Dear Ken and Bill:

It's fall that brings this letter I guess. Of all the months I miss fall the most. Take a good look at it for Ken and me, Billy. There's a sadness about fall with the summer vacation coming to an end and the prospect of a long hard winter ahead, but there is also a colour and beauty to it, a reassembling of old acquaintances and friends, a new beginning with fresh faces and prospects, football season, and the countryside with cider and the rich harvest. In a sense I sort of went back to school for six hard months in Tunisia last year, but there "ain't" too happy a future in shooting and getting shot at.

Here, all goes well. For the moment at least we are getting a brief respite from war, after seven months of it. You grow awfully weary after so long a time. On the front it's go, go, go, with little let up. It's day after day of fighting, of being bombed, of being shelled, of tanks, of "sweating out" your doughboys in every attack and counter-attack. You move up at night, you fire at night, you eat when you can and sleep when you can. You're up at 4:30 every morning to check your camouflage and wait for first light to bring "Jerry" planes and visibility to the OPs. You lose all track of time and of the days of the week. Sundays we always knew because of the distant church bells and the procession of peasants who came out of the hills on their little donkeys to pray at the roadside shrines. Our prayers were always quickly improvised—begun at the first weird whine of a shell coming close and finished just before it landed. The time of the month you know by the moon. You always remember where you were last month when the moon was new, or quarter, or full. We were in Algiers making ready to sail at the new moon last; we landed at Gela, July 10 at 4:30 in the morning under the quarter moon; we were firing just outside of battered Randazzo at the foot of the northern slope of Mt. Etna at the full moon—and so it goes. Now, it's a little past the full moon, and we are bivouacked in a peaceful olive orchard near a "bone yard"—the proud souls of planes rest here, "Jerry" planes, ME 109s most of them. The trees are all scarred, limbs and trunks are lopped off; shell craters big enough to lose a GMC truck, hangars and buildings blown to bits, over a hundred planes riddled and smashed before they could get off the ground, wings and motors and fuselages, propellers, tails with swastikas on them, bits of plastic glass from the windshields strewn about. The GIs gather the glass up and carve out rings which they send to their girls.

But now we are able to temper our work with a little play. We swim in the Mediterranean, which is as calm and blue as ever, and absorb some of its peacefulness into our own bodies. It seems good to have almonds to eat and fresh fruit—prickly pears off the cactus and grapes and tomatoes and melons—and although we sleep on the ground and in the open, at least it is level for a change and as comfortable as the living room floor—after you're used to it. It's a luxury to lie down at night and take off your shoes and wiggle your toes in the night air. Try it sometime—but first keep your shoes on for three weeks.

I think I'd rather be greeted by a hostile populace than a friendly one after Sicily. No matter how soon after you have captured a town, no matter how much you have shelled it previously, a trip through is just like a triumphal procession of old. The people laugh and cheer and dance and hold up two fingers in the sign of victory, throw fruit and flowers, and in their enthusiasm even forget to take the pots off. I got hit in the head with three tomatoes, a bunch of grapes, and a flower pot by one smiling group, who kept throwing kisses and calling out, "Comrade." You can be weary and dusty and soaked with sweat, and even moving up with your guns under fire, but to them you are not soldiers. Just tourists. And everything is "one dollah."

Sicily hasn't changed a bit in the last two thousand years or so, except to go down hill a bit under the Roman empires, both early and late. They live the same, cook the same, travel the same, still sow and harvest their crops by hand, with the help of oxen and women, and the dirt and flies have accumulated over two thousand years. That's what is so picturesque about it here. You often get a mixture of dirt and flies, of pigs and goats and ducks and naked children—all in the same mud puddle. There are some beautiful Greek temples here, still standing in Aggrigentoon, the high bluffs overlooking the sea, and they are as graceful as those in Athens. Here, 500 B.C. was one of the richest and most pleasure loving cities in the world, with temples to Juno, Apollo, Concordia. Juno, Apollo, Concordia—why did you leave this island so soon? Well, the candle burns low and I shall go to wiggle my toes in the night air. All my best wishes to you both and please let me hear from you. From you, Bill, the good news that you made the honor roll; and from you Ken—all about life in the Pacific. And so to bed.

     George [Age 29]

               September 20, 1943

My dear Mr. Barnes,

  When I cut loose from the Academy in June, I really cut loose. The only letters I have written have been concerned with the summer administration and the boys in the service; therefore, the long delay in answering your fine letter of July 8.

  I want to thank you for giving us a chance to know your family so well. Bud ['42] and Doug ['43] were persons of the highest and finest type. They were absolutely dependable; they worked steadily up to their capacity; they never indulged in alibis, and they have an innate sense of honor and decency which made them wonderful boys on this campus. Bud will never know how he affected his generation. He was so quiet and calm and apparently removed from the bustle and turmoil that it will take him years to comprehend what he did for his fellow Reservites. I do hope all the news from him is good. I should appreciate his latest address.

  I am awfully sorry that Doug did not have a chance to "taste" a bit of Harvard but I can assure you that it is there waiting for him whenever he is ready.

  . . . We are holding our first classes this morning. The opening weather has been fine, both from the standpoint of meteorology and from the standpoint of school psychology. The campus vegetation has never looked more lovely, especially the trees and shrubs, but I can assure you that we have lots of rough edges in the sixty acres of grass because of a frightful shortage of manpower. But now we have plenty of boys and faculty power and we'll be having our "face" lifted some.

If Reserve has done anything for Bud and Doug, it has been largely due to the wonderful home into which you brought them and to which they will be unconditionally loyal as long as they shall live. . . .

    Devotedly yours,
    Joel B. Hayden

September 21, 1943

Dear Lucien,

. . . It is now 8:30 A.M. and I have just come to my office from the first Chapel service of the year. It was conducted by Dr. Hayden and was a most impressive service. He is a great master at such a service. He seems to know and understand what is the right thing to do and say and fitting and suitable words seem always available. . . .

We are now entirely under way. There are ninety-five new boys and a total of 224, which goes far beyond any previous enrollment. . . . At the Sunday vesper service Dr. Hayden read excerpts from a number of letters received during the summer from our boys now in the service in various parts of the globe. These boys are doing some thinking and they will come home prepared to help in constructing a better world. I hope and pray that the time may soon come when the blood spilling will come to an end.

As to myself, I am well and have had a quiet, restful summer. I have enjoyed my flowers and in addition have had a vegetable garden from which I have gathered considerable corn, beans, lettuce, tomatoes, etc. Just at present I am facing a domestic problem, for my Annabelle is to be married the last of October. I have no hope of finding anyone who will fill her place. There simply are no more like her. In these times it is difficult to find any domestic help, but she is working hard to find someone for me. I trust this may find you well. Give my kindest regards to your sister and with best wishes to you, I remain,

    Yours,
    Harlan N. Wood[1]

1. This was the last letter from Dean Wood to Lucien Price to be found in the collection discovered by Tom Vince.

A popular phrase used by Dr. Hayden on the state of the school was "short on teachers, long on boys; short on labor, long on jobs." With the extreme shortages of labor in the kitchen, in grounds maintenance, and on the Academy's farm, every boy was called to do his part. The headline of the September 30 issue of the *Record* read "Reserve Manpower is Conscripted for Campus." The "225 healthy, teenage-boys" were put to work on the campus under the guidance of a committee of faculty members led by chemistry master Dr. H. R. Williams. "Beginning at 3:30 in the afternoon," read the article, "two teams, or about 25 boys, will come from both football and soccer to the back of Cutler Hall where they will be put to work. Those having but minor illnesses will also report to the work squad instead of to sports or to their room." No one was exempt. The main projects to be accomplished involved cleaning and repainting the bleachers, repairing the scoreboard on the football field, removing dead trees and, later in the fall, raking the leaves.

And while the physical labor was underway, Hayden continued his correspondence, this time to the parents of Jack Gillespie.

September 30, 1943

My dear Mr. and Mrs. Gillespie:

During the summer I had a V-mail[1] letter from Lieutenant Robert Bluem, a former student of Western Reserve Academy, and now with a battery of some division of the U.S. Army stationed in the Pacific.

He told me that the day he wrote the letter he had visited Jack's grave. This is the way he put it: "Today I went out to see Jack Gillespie." I think that is a beautiful and a profound fact. Both Jack and Bob were members of our school family and, although Bob never knew Jack very well since Bob was a younger boy, the first moment he had, he went out to pay tribute to Jack. It was an experience of profound meaning, with no voice raised. It was just silence and memory and imagination.

Please know that we were thinking about you on Jack's birthday, too; I think that birthday was in April, was it not? Please accept from us the assurance of the loyalty and devotion of this whole school.

Very sincerely yours,
Joel B. Hayden

1. V-Mail was a postal service that provided a speedy dispatch and reduced the weight of mail both to and from armed forces personnel. When it arrived at its FPO or APO address, the message was microfilmed and the negative sent to its destination, where it was reproduced and delivered. Members of the armed forces were able to send V-mail free of charge; civilians paid three cents to send them (six cents for airmail).

United States Naval Academy, Annapolis, Maryland
September 30, 1943

Dear Dr. Hayden:

I thought it best to write you when school resumed at Reserve, since I didn't know whether you would be at Pierce House or not.

The first thing I want to tell you is that I never really appreciated Reserve till I came here. Although this has been the greatest training and the greatest experience that I could ever get, still, I sure miss the real freedom and fraternity that are Reserve's. What I mean by fraternity is the fact that you're allowed to talk and make friends with anyone in the school,

John Jahant, "Bud" Schmahl, and Fred McConky (all '43) on leave in December 1943. *Courtesy John Jahant*

but here about the only persons you can talk to are your roommates, and to them only in the room, for you're not allowed to talk in the halls. . . .

I know you'll be glad to know that I've been writing quite a number of the boys of the class of '43. Doug Barnes is in Texas, [Marvin] Mell in Tennessee, ["Bud"] Schmahl in Indiana, [Ken] Goldsmith in Texas, [Walter] Wood in Cleveland, and [Ken] Zonsius at Harvard, plus many others. But I'd like you to tell the fellows now at Reserve that they should really appreciate what they've got and the fact that they're among classmates. Everyone that has written me says how sorry he is that those days at Reserve among classmates are gone, and they all want to get together if and when this war ends. . . .

               Sincerely,
               John Jahant ['43; Age 18]

                         Somewhere in the Mediterranean
                         October 16, 1943

Dear Dr. Hayden,

Your very welcome letter came yesterday in the middle of work and it wasn't a minute before I was in the third chapter of the Hudson story. I got quite a chuckle out of all the little intrigues and moves and countermoves of our little group as I remembered them. Your letter brought them all back to me vividly. Which reminds me that I haven't heard from "Sad" Sadler ['38] or Johnny Griffin ['38] or George Swan ['37] for almost two years and for "Sad"—not since I graduated. He warned me that he wouldn't write—but, still, I keep hoping that I will get some sort of address to write to. The last time I got some sort of a rumor, he was second or third man in his graduating class at M.I.T. He deserves a "well done." However, your letter makes me feel a part of something (a fellowship) which has come to have a great deal of meaning for me in the five or six years since that last Sunday Chapel.

With a great deal of real humility do I now confess that I used to rail and rant at the things at Reserve which I realize now were only peripheral to the main and important things I was getting. As masters and friends, Mr. Roundy and Fred Waring were tops. Mr. McGill (whom I could never get enough courage to call "Scotch") taught me all the math I think I shall ever know. Mr. Parker and Mr. Kitzmiller, Mr. Jones . . . and Dean Wood. Good old school.

But there is much to tell you and ask you, and I shall do that as soon as I can get a little more time to chaw up a page or two. Your news about Fred Waring was most welcome. Tell Joel that I will get a letter off to him before he leaves for "middie" [mid-shipman school].

Affectionately,
Dick Bliss ['38; Age 23]

Somewhere in the South Pacific
October 20, 1943

Dear Dr. Hayden,

Your birthday greetings arrived yesterday afternoon. Thank you very much.

I see that you were probably summering at your place in Maine when you wrote. I can remember some wonderful summers I spent there during camp days ten to twelve years ago.

[My brother] Reid, as you may have heard, has been home for awhile, partly for further schooling, and partly for a little furlough. He is due back from where he came early in November I hear. Eddie [my brother] should be getting home around Christmas time, I think.

I am just beginning to feel that I have been out of the good old U.S.A. a long time. Actually, it has only been since December, but the months move along quickly, and it will soon be a year. To get home anytime in '44 would suit me fine.

Our location is about as nice a war billet as any soldier or sailor could want. The proximity of a city about one and one-third as big as the one I come from means a lot, and there are plays, movies, tennis, golf, etc. avail-

Tom B. Babcox ('37). *Courtesy Tom Babcox, Jr. ('77)*

able. The production of "Arsenic and Old Lace" put on here the other night was fine, and I am sorry I missed the Boris Karloff version in New York City.

About two months ago I ran into a fellow I used to know at Amherst who served on the same ship with Torrey Eaton. He said Torrey "just disappeared." A tragedy any way you look at it, and I was very sorry to hear the news. There have been several fellows from college who have gone by the board, among whom was my roommate of freshman year—flying for the army somewhere in the South Pacific.

There is much about our situation and function here which I should like to describe to you, but no can do now. I'll save it for Pierce House in post-war days, and may they not be too long in coming. . . .

Tom Babcox ['37; Age 24]

October 25, 1943

My dear Mr. and Mrs. Sprow:

In the Saturday *Plain Dealer* we Academy folk noticed that [your son] Bill ['40] has been missing in action since October 10. We should appreciate more than we can say any word from you because we are profoundly interested in him and in you and in all the members of the Sprow family.

The glimpse I had of you not many months ago as you were going through with Bill, I shall always remember. We all hope that whatever happened, he had a chance to bail out. Two out of three Cleveland friends of mine—boys connected with the church—have, within the last two months, had that experience and I hope that Bill did just that and successfully.

We send you the understanding sympathy of his teachers and his friends here. Blessings on you both and all.

> Very sincerely yours,
> Joel B. Hayden

October 26, 1943

Dear Dave [Owen ('42)],

It was grand to see you even though, temporarily, I was sort of out of the picture. I hope you had a good time. I can't put into words what a visit like that does to me and to all the other men and boys who have known a person like you.

Under separate cover I am sending you a couple of books that have meant very much to me. We've got to live on the globe; we've got to understand our own inheritance; we've got to realize that the greatest frontiers are those which lie ahead. I can assure you that nothing that we do in this war is more important than the development of our minds and our imaginations and our thorough, patient goodwill. We've got to learn to contribute to the common cause which is universal. If we do not, we shall condemn our grandchildren and our great-grandchildren to sudden death!

> Ever yours,
> Joel B. Hayden

Earlier in the term, the machine shop contracted with the Wright Tool and Forge Company to produce ratchet wrenches. Production quotas were put at between twenty thousand and thirty thousand wrenches to be produced by the boys between December 1 and May 1. All work in the shop was on a voluntary basis.

A letter received by Jack Yardley from the Wright Tool & Forge Co. describing the tools appeared in the October 28 issue of the *Record*.

> The ratchet wrench which Mr. Tepper and his gang will machine for us is part of a kit of aviation tools which are used in the repair and maintenance of all fighter planes. . . . A general order was issued last year that all combat planes carry a kit of tools on each mission so that if they were forced down and needed such tools for emergency repairs, it would enable them to save the ship and, in some instances, the lives of the crew. . . . We have trusted you with some of the most difficult precision work we have to do. I want you to feel that you are accepting a grave responsibility; steel is scarce and manpower is short, and your efforts will be of very great material help in winning the war.

Dr. Hayden received an update from Bill Sprow's mother and replied with another note of hope for his safe return.

November 1, 1943

Dear Dr. Hayden,

Received your nice letter and have waited to answer hoping I could give you good news of Bill—but so far we have heard nothing more—only the grim message that he has been missing in action since October 10.

We did have a letter from the War Department that it was the raid on Muenster and Coesfeld from which he did not return and as you maybe remember that was a bad one—I think we lost over thirty bombers on that day.

We have hoped too that he may be safe—somewhere in Germany. Bill was a lucky boy and resourceful and if possible I know he would make it. We received a letter from him since we received the news. It was written on October 8. He was happy—had been on several raids and did say "Mom, if I scare the 'Heinies' 1/10 as much as they scare me, they will soon collapse." He had been in England since the last of August. Had quite an eventful trip over. Their *Fortress* was forced down in Ireland and from the leak he could tell, I think they had quite an experience.

Well, all we can do is pray and hope for his safety. I know he is just one of many fine boys, but when it strikes home it hurts.

[His brother] August ['33] is at the University of Tulsa. He is in petroleum products and thinks they are due to go over seas soon. He finishes there in about ten days, then goes back to Camp Lee, Virginia. He has been in the service a year now and Bill is in the service two years this month. Well, let us hope after this meeting in Moscow that this war will soon be over and all our boys can come home.

My daughter Barbara is married and living in Cuyahoga Falls and if I can get enough gas some day I will drop in and see you on my way over to her. Thank you for your kind letter. Remember me to Mrs. Hayden and to any of Bill's teachers who might inquire.

Sincerely,
Elsie Sprow

November 4, 1943

Dear Mrs. Sprow:

We are very grateful for your fine letter. The only message you could give me was the grim one, as you indicated, but I know of three boys at least who, within the last three months, have been reported as missing and then have been discovered in German prison camps.

Thank you for the news about August, and about your daughter. Please do stop off and see us and have a meal with us in Cutler whenever you can; we should be delighted to see you.

Give our devoted regards to Mr. Sprow and your daughter and Augie and do not forget that this whole school family near and far is thinking of you and hoping and praying for the very best.

    Very sincerely yours,
    Joel B. Hayden

    Williams College
    November 9, 1943

Dear Dr. Hayden,

. . . I am looking forward to life, for the first time, in a completely unselected group—the regular draft army. I think it is a tremendously broadening experience for many of us who have led pretty sheltered lives, whether we will admit it or not. It will also, of course, be a very difficult experience, in many ways. I think, that in this war, the effect of which has been felt so universally, anyone hoping for a position of leadership who has not been through this common experience of our generation will have a distinct handicap, and that those who have been through the mill will have a real asset. . . .

    Most cordially yours,
    Paul Barstow ['43; Age 18]

    Somewhere in England
    November 12, 1943

Dear Dr. Hayden:

At last I find myself in the midst of all the things I learned about from Mr. Waring and the other masters at Reserve, and I find myself at once grateful to them for all their patience with me in those days, and sorry that I didn't pay closer attention to the things they tried to teach me. Everything I see here is interesting, but it would have been more so if I could remember some of the things I should know. . . .

Life here is pretty much hum-drum, with an occasional "Jerry" coming over to keep us on our toes. They are few and far between though—I rather imagine the Eighth Air Force (of which I am now a most tiny cog) is keeping them busy at home. Night life, particularly in London, is exceedingly expensive, though there are some good shows on. Imagine paying anywhere from $.70 to $2.00 for an ordinary movie! Our chief recreation H.Q. is the Red Cross, whose service for the men and women of the armed forces is a thing at which I constantly marvel. Everything the U.S.O. does at home only more of it and better.

    My best to all,
    Bill Newberry ['37; Age 24;]

After nearly a month of waiting, the school received good news about William J. Sprow. Dr. Hayden sent a note to his family on the final day of classes before the Thanksgiving break.

> November 23, 1943
>
> My dear Sprow family:
>
> Three cheers for the fact that Bill is reported a prisoner! We are all delighted and we send you congratulations on the good news.
>
> Can you let us know how we can get in touch with Bill by mail from now on? Thanksgiving greetings in a really big way!
>
> Sincerely yours,
>
> Joel B. Hayden

In another letter from an older brother, Ramon Spooner ('42) sent his thoughts to his younger brother Byron, a member of the class of 1945.

> [Undated] 1943
>
> Dear Gil,
>
> I meant to write sooner, but I just never found time. We shipped from Santa Ana last Monday, and arrived here (about twenty miles from Houston) on Thursday. We had a darn good trip, going through Los Angeles, Phoenix, Tucson, El Paso, San Antonio, and finally Houston. This place is pretty swell. Most of our tough restrictions have been lifted, and it makes this training much easier.
>
> Next weekend we get out Saturday and Sunday. We have a special bus service from here to Houston on weekends, and we never have to wait long for a bus. The city of Houston is the largest in Texas, and there are very few servicemen there. We cadets are treated swell, and the people are always throwing dances and parties for us. The girls are beautiful and they really go for cadets. The fellows say that it is so easy to get a nice girl to go out with you that it's hard to believe.
>
> . . . Since I am now a cadet, I make $105 per month out of which we pay $.70 a day for food. That makes a net income of $84 a month. We will be here for at least nine weeks. This is now called my pre-flight training. There is a good chance that we may stay here for advanced navigation, which lasts about eighteen weeks. I hope so, 'cause I like it here a lot.
>
> . . . I'm going to make a bargain with you. For every term grade you get that is 3+ or better, I'll send you five bucks, and for every test you get 3+ or better in I'll send you one dollar. So, how about working, Gil.
>
> You'll be surprised, Gil, how much your school work means to you later in life. Even here in the cadets it is very evident. These fellows cuss up and down at themselves for not studying and taking their subjects seriously in high school. Here in our classrooms the fellows are so damn

anxious to learn that they wouldn't miss a class for five bucks. If we had school in the middle of the night, we'd all be glad to go. Right at this minute the guy in the bunk next to me is looking for someone to take his place as barracks guard tomorrow so he can go to his classes.

So, Gil, don't be like the rest of the dumb S.O.B.'s. Get down to work even if it is uncomfortable at first. Follow this practice—try to understand everything that you study. Never let anything slip by you, and never say, "Oh, well, I'll never come across that stuff again." You'll never be sorry. Take my word for it, 'cause I've seen too many examples of guys who abused their education, and I don't want my own brother to be like them. Try to be good in everything. I know you can be because you've got everything a boy needs—looks, build, and brains. So, don't let your big brother down.

All this doesn't mean for you to forget about the girls. Just don't let them interfere with your studies or sports. After next weekend I'll tell you about my dates in Houston.

You know, Gil, we cadets really go over big with the girls. You see they look to us as young officers and they know that we are the "cream of the crop" (as the Air Corps is called). Therefore, we have no trouble in getting dates. But, as you know, where there are soldiers of any kind there are always a bunch of girls and women who go around trying to pick up soldiers and take them up to their rooms. We are strictly warned against this because of the danger of diseases. So, even though the girls are beautiful as they usually are, we've got to be careful and use our heads at all times. It's tempting, but we realize the danger. So, here's one boy who is going to look for a nice girl and live a clean life.

I started to smoke a pipe down at Keesler Field, but I found no enjoyment in it at all and now I haven't had a smoke since I left Biloxi, and I don't intend to have any at all anymore. As far as drinking goes, I may have a beer once in a while, but too much is no good. Look, Gil, as a special favor to me I want you to make yourself a promise. Never start smoking or drinking. You will see all or nearly all of your friends smoke and drink and they'll think it is smart or that they are big stuff. Well, you can do as I did—just keep away from it, but don't criticize anyone else for doing it. People, especially girls, will think a hell of a lot of you if you don't smoke or drink. I know you have enough sense to realize that.

It's up to you and I, as Mom and Dad's only sons, to make them proud of us. Just imagine how much it will mean to them to be able to say that their two sons are real gentlemen, who don't smoke or drink and [who] have enough sense to take care of themselves. And [our sister] Phyllis, too. You know how proud we are of her because she is a perfect girl. How about making her more proud of us. So, Gil, how about it? Let's not let them down—do your best. I wish you could see some of our training down here—it would really make you think.

Well, Gil, I didn't mean for this letter to be so full of this kind of stuff, but I hope you understand what I'm trying to do. You'll appreciate it some day. . . .

I think that Mom and Phyllis may come down here to Houston, while I am here. When they do come I'm going to get an overnight pass and we'll stay at a hotel in Houston. From the looks of things now they'll probably send us overseas before we'll get a furlough. But, there is a chance that I'll get a furlough when I get commissioned. Then I'll let you try on my officer's uniform to see how you look. . . .

When you write, keep me posted on your girl friends. Why don't you drop me a few lines about every other night? I'll send you some stamps pretty soon. They don't have to be long letters; just let me hear from you often. If you should run across any gals who would be interested in writing to a cadet—give them my address. I'm always anxious to meet somebody new even though it is by letter. I'll do the same if I meet some girls your age here in Houston, okay?

Before I forget, Gil, if you need any spending money, don't be afraid to ask me for it. I'm making lots more than I can spend, so just tell me when you need it. How much did you make this summer?

Time certainly flies for me. We are always on the go, that's the reason. Pretty soon it will be Christmas and then New Years. I've been in the army about fifteen weeks now. That's a pretty long time when you stop to think about it.

Well, Gil old boy, it's about time I signed off. Write as soon as possible. Remember what I told you about your studies, etc. . . . Work hard and good luck. All my love to everyone at home.

        Your big brother,
        Tex [Age 19]

                Corpus Christi, Texas
                December 11, 1943

Dear Dr. Hayden,

Many thanks for your recent letter—I appreciate your taking the time to drop me a line, because I am sure that you are very busy these days.

It was good to hear some news from Reserve again. It has been quite some time since I was last in Hudson, and I regret that I have not been able to get down there more often. However, the *Record* has been forwarded to me from home regularly, so I have been able to keep up fairly well on the campus "doings."

I have been in the navy just a year now, and am enjoying it very much. For the past eight months I have been attached to a patrol bomber training squadron as an engineering officer. The work is interesting, and is right in line with my training and civilian experience. I have been doing

Merton F. Gerhauser ('35).
Courtesy Mrs. M. Gerhauser

considerable flying on test flights, and I hope to start formal naval flight training around the first of the year. . . .

Occasionally I run across a Reserve graduate who is stationed down here. Ensign Ted Vogel ['39]. . . just checked into this squadron last week. I seem to have lost track of most of my own class, although I know that most of them are in the service. Bob Loughry ['35], as you may know, is flying bombers for the army, and I believe he is still in this country. . . .

                Very sincerely,
                Mert Gerhauser ['35; Age 26]

As the end of the term drew near, Dean Wood prepared a note of thanks to be sent to the boys who had responded to a request for donations to the Alumni Scholarship fund. He added a little something different in each one, but his wish for all of the boys in the service was the same: a safe return to a normal life.

                              December 15, 1943

Dear Carl [Hess, '33]:

. . . It is a pleasure to hear from you and know where you are located. It is very difficult to keep track of the boys, for they change locations frequently and are scattered over the entire globe.

. . . Naturally the war has created many problems for us, but thus far we have been able to carry on and I see no reason why the regular work should not go on until the end of the school year.

The faculty has changed some since you were here but many of the old time standbys are very actively on the job—McGill, Kitzmiller, Jones, Simon, Mickel, Williams, Tilt, Clewell and others whom you may possibly have known before you left.

Carl M. Hess ('33) was pulled out from behind his typewriter in 1941. He was a reporter/editor at the *Portsmouth (Ohio) Times* when he was drafted in early 1941. Carl served fifty-one months in the infantry as a cannon company executive officer with the 313th Regiment, 79th Division. He was in the European theater for fifteen months and was awarded a bronze star. *Courtesy Carl Hess*

My best wishes to you for 1944. I hope the tide will turn for I want to see you boys coming home and entering the normal life again....
                Very sincerely yours,
                Harlan N. Wood

                              Somewhere in Hawaii
                              December 26, 1943

Dear Dr. Hayden,
    Ever since your thoughtful birthday greeting arrived several weeks ago I have wanted to write and thank you for your remembrance. I am glad to hear that all is well at WRA.
    Even a global war has its pleasant surprises. During the last two weeks Ensign Marvin Walker ['35] and Lt. Bob Gulick ['34] dropped in and with each I had the pleasure of a good talk about the folks at home, mutual friends, activities, post-war plans, WRA, etc. Both looked in wonderful condition. As with most of the young fellows these days, their faces had that look of determination which is not only the result of responsibility and a greater maturity, but is also an indication that their every thought and action is based on a determination to get this war over with as quickly as possible.
    Reid and I managed to enjoy a pleasant Christmas together yesterday—in spite of the semi-tropical climate of this place and the difficulty of

conjuring up much festive spirit during these days. Guess like every one else we're saving up for Christmases after the war is over.

Dad has written us that Mother is much improved after her recent illness—which is gratifying news, believe me. That is my chief worry during all this separation and distance—the health and welfare of the folks at home. From all reports, [my brother] Tom and [my brother-in-law] Hugh [Bell '37] are fine, enjoy their work, but, like everyone else, are anxious to get home, if only for a few days, to see family and friends. It will indeed be a great day when Hugh glimpses Hugh, Jr. ['62] for the first time.

I suppose that every alumnus of WRA has written you countless times that Reserve means more and more to him as the years go by. It is doubly so with me. The standards of value, the idealism, the association with inspiring teachers and friends, the emphasis on moral values, the sense of humility and responsibility—all mean so much now. And underneath it all at WRA was your own unique emphasis on the Christian ethic.

    Sincerely,
    Edward S. Babcox, Jr. ['35; Age 27]

    Somewhere in England
    December 31, 1943

Dear Dr. Hayden:

Your V-Mail of December 9 arrived a few days before Christmas, and believe me it was a real treat to hear from you and Reserve. I have rather lost touch with the school in the last few years—an evil situation which your good letter did much to remedy.

Christmas over here was spent pretty quietly. Many of the boys, particularly the enlisted men, were invited to spend the day in English homes, and some were able to do so, though we didn't cease operations on that day. I spent the day here on the base (I am at present with the famous Eighth Air Force) and celebrated in the evening at a small but lively party at the Officer's club. We even managed to concoct an "eggnog" made of rum, coffee and ice cream—the third ingredient being made with powdered milk and powdered eggs. Surprisingly enough it was better than it sounds—or maybe that isn't so surprising, as I don't think it could possibly be as bad as it sounds! . . .

    Sincerely,
    Bill Newberry ['37; Age 24]

The December *Alumni Record* carried the news of a few of the masters in the service. Along with an announcement about English master J. Fred Waring's decision to remain in the Middle East for another year and the location of former history master and wrestling coach Ed Caldwell in the Pacific was word of one of the magazine's former editors, Marvin Walker, who was serving on an aircraft carrier "somewhere in the Pacific." The issue also noted two alumni who were listed as missing in action: Devin H. Gilchrist ('40) in New Guinea, and Harry Allchin, Jr. ('39), over Germany. (Allchin was actually shot down over France.)

Winter Term: January–March 1944

During the Christmas break, E. Mark Worthen, the navigation instructor who was also teaching algebra, Latin, and American history, was commissioned a lieutenant junior grade in the Naval Reserve. He left the school on January 25 for six weeks of training before active sea duty.

Since the beginning of the school year, seniors had been faced with a number of choices from the navy and the army, including the opportunity to further their education while serving their country. The navy offered a variety of programs: The V-5, the aviation cadet program, was designed to procure and train officer pilots. Upon completion of a six-stage training course the cadets were commissioned ensigns in the Naval Reserve or second lieutenants in the marines. The V-7 was an officer training program for volunteers with bachelor's degrees. They were trained as line officers for surface vessels. The V-12 was an officer training program designed so that a volunteer could complete his bachelor's degree while receiving military training. Jack Mooney ('43x), the star of the football team, left in December to enter the Navy V-12 program at Yale; Joel Hayden, Jr. ('39), was in the V-7 program at Oberlin, and Worcester Seely ('41) was in the V-5 program at Colgate.

Some were involved with the Army Specialized Training Program (ASTP). This program was designed to prepare its participants, such as engineering and medical students, for professions that would be needed for postwar reconstruction. The ASTP, as well as the navy college courses, enabled students between the ages of seventeen and twenty-one to continue academic training at government expense.

According to some of the boys already in the ASTP, the program was on its way out, and those who were previously involved in it were eventually assigned to battlefields around the world. "Of course, no one knows when the European phase of the war will end or what the repercussions on our national life will be when the end does come," Mr. McGill wrote in a letter dated January 15 to the mother of a former student. He had learned from a "reliable source" that "plans were being formulated by the army for mustering out some five million men beginning very shortly after Germany surrenders." His letter continued.

> Just when Germany will surrender is anyone's guess, to be sure, but the overwhelming consensus of opinion now seems to be that the end is in sight and that it will quite probably be an event of the coming spring, summer or fall; surely we shall not have to wait until the

summer of 1945 for it. We are distinctly of the opinion here that the army will not continue to draft eighteen-year old lads while at the same time mustering out some four or five million men—the idea contains no logic.

Uncle Sam's plans for the boys were a world away from the plans made by the administrators, the parents, and the boys themselves. "Operation Overlord" was on the verge of becoming a reality.

Miami Beach, Florida
January 1, 1944

Dear Dr. and Mrs. Hayden,

Before being called to active duty with the army, I was able to complete two and one-half years of academic work at Bard College. Perhaps you will be interested in knowing that I have a very high opinion of Bard and its progressive methods, and I fully appreciate your recommendation which decided my choice of colleges when I was in a quandary during my senior year at Reserve. When I left Bard, the student body was depleted to such an extent that closing of the institution was almost inevitable. Since then, however, a detachment of Army Specialized Training men have come to the reserve, and from recent reports, Bard will stay open for the duration.

While pursuing my studies at Bard, I joined the Enlisted Reserve Corps on August 21, 1942. There was a rather hazy guarantee that I would be allowed to graduate connected with this volunteer enlistment. Such was not the case, for I received orders the following year in June to report to Camp Dix, New Jersey for processing and induction.

My stay at Dix was short, and I was herded into a train for points unknown. As it turned out I was destined for the infantry and Fort McClellan, Alabama for my basic training. My morale took a decided dip and memories of stories about the rugged infantry crept through my mind. However, one does not have much choice in the army; so I decided to make the best of what they had to offer.

Then for thirteen weeks of rigorous training 'neath a torturing sun. For the first time in my life I experienced a close unity with Mother Earth (rather, clay). Living in tents, fox holes, or on the nearest rock pile wasn't delightful, but it did build character.

When my basic training was over I was chosen to remain as a drill instructor with a rating. But after two months of barking at poor unfortunate "jeeps," I became restless and generally fed up with the infantry. There were no chances for advancement nor was the work at all stimulating. I was deeply concerned with the rut I had fallen into and worried about a disintegrating mind.

The opportunity arrived one day when the Army Air Force began asking for men in other branches of the service. I literally grabbed the chance and applied for a transfer. After taking several mental and physical tests, I finally received my shipping orders for Miami Beach. Needless to say I was very happy and considered my good fortune a "break" in army slang.

Upon arrival at the "Beach" I was hustled to a spacious hotel and given a room with an ocean front view. This was very definitely not the army, and for the first time in my military career, I enjoyed the luxuries of a real bed, clean linen, excellent food and decent treatment. It was almost too much to comprehend. For awhile I thought I was back in civilian life.

More tests had to be taken here, in fact a whole week was devoted to this maze of screening and processing. Today I have no doubt that the A.A.F. knows more about me than I ever will. The following week I was informed that I had passed successfully and was an aviation cadet. This is all I could ask for and was plenty happy with this news.

Now I am merely marking time until there is an opening in some college or university where I can continue my training.

I wish to add in closing that I thoroughly enjoy receiving the *Record*. It keeps me in contact with the Reserve that meant so much to me. Please give my very best to those whom I knew as a student.
    Sincerely,
    George Blackstone ['41; Age 22]

Dr. Hayden received a note of thanks and hope from the families of Harry Allchin, Jr., and Devin Gilchrist, who were missing in action, as they waited for some word of their being located.

                    January 5, 1944

Dear Mr. and Mrs. Hayden:

Your wish for Harry, Jr.'s safety is greatly appreciated as are all the other expressions received from Hudson and from the many friends he made while at the Academy. He told me while training for the Air Corps he wouldn't trade his training at Hudson for anything and he is so pleased Tom is now getting the same. The other brother, Dick, is training for the Navy Air Corps—located at present at Walla Walla, Wash.

We are anxiously waiting for good news from Harry, Jr. and will let you know as soon as we do.
    Mr. and Mrs. Harry Allchin

                     January 1944

My dear Dr. Hayden,

Your thoughtfulness in writing to us makes our anxiety easier to bear. Until we receive more definite word, we feel Devin will return to his squadron, God willing.

This morning I received a letter from a mother whose son graduated at Luke [Field] with Devin. This boy went into a tail spin, bailed out over

Harry Allchin, Jr. ('39), after his first solo flight, Thanksgiving Day 1942.
Courtesy Betty Linsz

Devin H. Gilchrist ('40), photo taken days before he disappeared over New Guinea.
Courtesy Anne G. Paterson

the ocean and returned to his fighter squadron at Guadalcanal a week later. This gives us renewed hope. For some, though they are young, they have lived a long, long time and they have reached the heights.

    Very sincerely,
    Martha D. Gilchrist

January 7, 1944

Dear Harvey [Tanner]:

. . . We've got a little bit more than 1100 living graduates, Harvey, and at the last count, December 11, there were 422 of them, including former students, in the service and that count is rising. Just heard within the last ten days that Harry Allchin '39, is missing over Germany and Devin Gilchrist, Bill's ['32] younger brother, is missing in the South Pacific. If those losses are confirmed, there will be twelve Gold Stars and that is an unduly high proportion. It just happens that our WRA family is in the thick of it; therefore, when I get a Christmas or New Year's card like yours with best wishes to the faculty and student body, I swing right in with it. That's what's happening to your greetings Sunday afternoon, next, January 9, at our vesper services.

The place looks just about the same. It is fine to have [your brother] Charles here, and if you can tip me off as to what things you'd like me to bear in mind about Charles—things to do, attitudes to take—I shall be very grateful. Brothers sometimes know each other very thoroughly, and if I can fit into the picture, why that is what I want to do.

Joel, Jr. just finished at Oberlin and is awaiting a call to the navy—midshipmen's school. He will go to Columbia, Notre Dame or Northwestern. It is this ninety-day Admiral stuff!

Jean married an American-born Italian who is teaching at Middlebury College. We were with them over the holidays. She has a little two-year-old girl now and our entertainment was largely provided by the youngest generation. Sam, our son-in-law, is waiting for a commission to the navy at the moment; so within a few days, or weeks, both of our sons, you see, will be on their way to some spot of blue. . . .

    Ever yours,
    Joel B. Hayden

                   January 11, 1944

Dear Buzz [John U. Anderson '39]:

. . . Five seniors will get their diplomas January 30 because they are subject to call February 1. Everything is in order for them because they did summer school work so they could be ready for just this possibility.

. . . Joel, Jr., is still here in Hudson with us awaiting orders. Our son-in-law, Sam, has been accepted by the First Naval District, for a commission in the navy. He's awaiting final decision in Washington. Joel is teaching bassoon, studying the Morse Code, and finishing up forty-seven hours of Russian at the Berlitz School in Cleveland. It is tough, just waiting, but I understand from many convincing sources that waiting around is about 95 per cent of any global war even when you have been put into uniform! Check me if I'm wrong. . . .

    Ever yours,
    Joel B. Hayden

                   January 12, 1944

Dear Dr. Hayden:

Am ashamed that I have not written to you, but these busy days, time seems to fly so fast. We still have had no word from Bill, but all reports are that the boys get very good treatment and both Mr. Sprow and I feel we do not have as much to worry about as if he were flying over Germany these days. We have heard that seven of the ten crew in the *Fortress* are prisoners of war—two were killed and the navigator is still reported missing. I have contacted quite a few of the mothers of the boys. I am enclosing an envelope with Bill's address on it if you care to write to him. The family and friends can write—and we can send an eleven pound box every two months—cigarettes and a five pound box of books every thirty days. . . .

>Sincerely,
>Elsie L. Sprow

Dr. Hayden's letters continued to describe the flurry of activity on the campus in light of the shortage of manpower on the maintenance crew. "A high percentage of our sleeves now find their terminus above the human elbow! We are all pitching in one way or another, tightening belts, and whatnot," he wrote in one letter.

The January 13 *Reserve Record* reported that Harry Allchin and Devin Gilchrist were still listed as missing. Devin was piloting a fighter plane over the Southwest Pacific. "It being difficult to bail out of a fighter," the article stated, "it is feared that he was lost." Harry was a co-pilot of a *Fortress* and stationed in England with the Eighth Air Force. It was reported that his parents received a letter on January 8 dated December 11 from a friend of Harry's. At that time it was believed that Harry and the crew parachuted to safety.

Devin Gilchrist's mother received the formal notice from Devin's commanding officer and passed it on to the school. Devin continued to be listed as missing in action.

>January 16, 1944

Dear Mrs. Gilchrist,

It is with the deepest regret and sympathy that I inform you that your son has been missing in action since 26 December 1943.

During a combat mission Devin's plane was observed to be smoking. Fellow pilots saw him bail out but were unable to ascertain as to where he landed.

To adequately inform you that Devin is missing is even more difficult than the realization of it is to those of us who have worked and played with him throughout the past month. Devin was respected and popular with all of his fellow officers for his high personal integrity, intelligence and affability under all circumstances—in addition to being an excellent pilot.

After ninety days Devin's effects will be shipped to the United States. For shipment of his effects write to the Effects Quartermaster, Quartermaster Depot, Kansas City, Missouri.

Judging from the circumstances of Devin's disappearance, we must not arrive at conclusions too hastily. Bear in mind that Devin was flying over a sparsely settled area and that searching such country is a long and arduous process. It is entirely possible that Devin may be located, as many pilots have returned after several months.

Please feel free to call upon me at any time that I may be of any assistance.

> Robert C. Smith
> Captain, Air Corps
> Commanding

On January 18, Dr. Hayden sent a letter to William Klump ('39), who was in the army's ASTP program, asking for his help: "If you could put down briefly, and with a punch, a summary of your three main points on what the army has done for you and to you, I could use it most effectively with boys and families." He sent his observations to the headmaster.

> Indiana University
> January 23, 1944

Dear Mr. Hayden,

You ask me how I like the army. For a number of reasons I am happier in the army than I have ever been before.

With a specific job to be done, and enough perspective to see that job in its relation to the entire endeavor, life is better. My life has meaning and purpose and worth, and that is one of the greatest satisfactions I have yet known.

There is also discipline. Discipline can seem the most petty and annoying insult and injury devised by the cleverly sadistic mind of man. But it is, I believe, rather the most important single factor for excellence in the army, and the best teacher I have met of the necessary concentration of our energy upon considered, desired goals, instead of the dissipation of that energy in futile pursuit of random, passing distractions. To my mind discipline defines the border between sanity and madness, and decides the difference between an existence and a life. I hope I learn its lesson well.

The army, backed by the work of thousands, itself one of the most vast organizations, fighting its way toward a greater unity of nations and of peoples, is, for me, a symbol as well as exemplification of what human beings can accomplish when they work together, a constant joy, courage, and strength. I am not so naive as to have meant the note of perfection implicit in that sentence. But I am sure that the freedom which this united action intends to support and to advance, the freedom which has been shot over our heads and before us by the history of humanity, is too close to us, and too dear, to be obscured by mistakes and miscalculations, or even by willful departure from the path being laid down through the wilderness.

These are not the cliché answers to the cliché questions; they are my answers to your question, which I knew was real.

> Will Klump [Age 22]

On January 30, the first midyear commencement in Reserve's history was held for four seniors who were called to serve in the armed services: Peter S. Hanson to the Navy Air Corps; William F. Manlove, whose brother George had written to him from Sicily during the fall term, the Navy Air Corps; Rudolph Rakowsky, the army; and Richard N. Sisson, Navy V-12. The *Record* described the ceremony as "complete but brief": The congregation sang two hymns, and the glee club sang "Heavenly Light" and "Dona Nobis Pacem." Dr. Hayden gave the commencement address, followed by the presentation of diplomas by Board of Trustees president Robert S. Wilson. Afterward the graduates, their families, and Mr. Wilson were entertained by Dr. and Mrs. Hayden at a dinner held in the Cutler Hall dining room.

February 3, 1944

Dear Bill [Klump]:

. . . You are moving right along; your letter was just what I wanted and I've already used it once or twice with individual families. Some guests were here last Saturday and asked me some questions which I could dodge because I simply turned them over to you and, through your letter, you gave them the answers which they were groping for. You see, in a way, you're a sort of Assistant Headmaster, even though you don't know it!

I do not know just what's going to become of your Russian classes if what I hear is true. I hear that the A.S.T.P. is going to be, like sand, sifted through congressional hands back into the regular army as such. But don't let that disturb you too much. You've got the beginning of an experience which I hope and pray you may be able to follow through. Joel is in the same boat linguistically. He wants to build something upon what little foundation he has in Russian. There are a score of WRA boys from whom I have heard you're being trained to understand the other fellow's lingo. I don't know how we can be decently civilized unless we know not only what we're talking about but what the other fellow's talking about, most of all what his collective experience, as expressed through the greatest minds in literature. [Jan] Masaryk of Czecho-Slovakia was the outstanding statesman of his generation. The top reason was that he read competently fourteen languages, and what is more he read them, he didn't file them away for some far-off future reference!

Joel leaves Sunday and Bernie Tolan ['40], who graduated from Williams the end of October, goes with him. They are headed for Notre Dame.

Devotedly yours,
Joel B. Hayden

Yale University
February 4, 1944

Dear Dr. Hayden,

... My two years at Reserve, which I prize highly, were excellent training for the "rigors" of a wartime education. I suppose there's no need to tell you this—but there it is, from still another source. I thank my "lucky stars" that I not only learned "how" to study but "when" to study. Aside from such habits, the general information which I gathered "there" has given me a background and a foundation as good and as firm as I could have needed, anywhere—at Yale or Franklin & Marshall—in the navy or as a civilian.

But more important, in the long run, than mere book learning, was the "lesson in human relations." I learned that friendship was both a "give and a take" proposition; I had been content to take. I learned that in order to "give", it was necessary to come out of one's "shell"—and I had built up a rather effective shell. Perhaps the most that Reserve did—or could have done for me in 2 years was to get the process of my "extraction" underway. It did, I think, well considering the obstacles I put in its way. Perhaps the prefectship last year did more than anything else to draw me out of myself. For that, I'm eternally grateful.

Speaking of prefects, etc., I had a letter from John Seaman ['43]. As you perhaps know, he finished his "boot" training at Great Lakes last November. He took his pre-radio training in Chicago. . . . John is now a seaman, 1st class at the navy radio school at Texas A & M. He wrote that Paul Barstow is in the army, at Camp Shelby, Miss., taking his "basic" preparatory to entering A.S.T.P. . . .

   Yours very sincerely,
   Lester Shultis ['43; Age 18]

On February 10, the *Cleveland Plain Dealer* listed the names of several area servicemen who had lost their lives or were missing in action. One of the names was that of Calhoun ("Pete") Narten ('38x) from Shaker Heights. A bomber pilot on his twenty-second mission, Pete was listed as missing in the Pacific, where he had been serving since September.

       Princeton
       February 13, 1944

Dear Scotch:

As you know, I'm now in the A.S.T.P. In fact I'm in term five and after term six I would graduate from advanced mechanical engineering. However, this whole program has become quite a mess. Originally we were to get a chance at commissions. Now that is out and it looks as if an A.S.T.P. certificate is just going to be so much paper.

John W. Richey ('36). *Archives*

Scotch, I see a chance to do a little more and to handle some responsibility if I transfer and am accepted into Air Corps ground crew work. If I can get into engineering or armament aviation cadet school and am good enough, I'll have a chance at some gold bars and a more responsible job than I'm at present headed for.

I wondered if you would write me a letter of recommendation as I need three to submit with my application. . . .

Until I hear from you, then, I will of course "get in there and fight" like a true math man.

Sincerely,
R. Bruce Silver ['41; Age 20]

Despite rumors of special programs disbanding, the February 17 *Record* announced that the Army-Navy College Qualifying Test for the ASTP and the Navy College Program (V-12), to be given throughout the country on March 15, was to be administered at the Academy.

The tone of the editorial in this issue was a lamentation from the writer and perhaps suggests the overall tone of the world. The war had been going on for over two years and the boys on the homefront were tiring of the constant call to do their part.

One more Gold Star was added to the growing list of names: John W. Richey ('36) was reported lost in the South Pacific. A lieutenant, junior grade, navy pilot, he left behind his wife and small daughter. Dr. Hayden didn't receive the news about John or Pete Narten until he returned from a two-week trip to the East on February 17. Upon his return, he wrote to their parents.

February 18, 1944

My dear Mr. and Mrs. Richey:

On my desk yesterday when I returned from an eastern trip, I found Mr. Beers' brief note concerning his son and in it there was the confirmed word that John was lost somewhere in the Pacific.

I can't tell you how sick at heart we all feel. Of course, this generation of boys does not know John, but most of our masters do, and any break in this wonderful school family of ours is something which we have to absorb, to gather up and incorporate in our final philosophy and our final faith.

All of us here send you our sympathy, our love, and our assurances that we stand ready to do anything for you that we possibly can. Make this one of your regular stopping places when you come east. We may be able to help one another by seeing one another occasionally. I know that our temporal lives are today on a very precarious basis. The only justification for such loss is eventual decency, fair play, and eternal goodwill.

We shall never forget John and we hope that you, as a family, will never forget us.

    Most sincerely yours,
    Joel B. Hayden

February 18, 1944

Dear Mr. and Mrs. Narten:

I just got back from my trip east to the Headmasters' meeting yesterday morning and found the news about Pete [Calhoun Narten].

Bill Sprow, of the class of 1940, was missing last fall; was missing, in fact, six or eight weeks before it was discovered that he had landed safely and was a prisoner of the Germans. Over the Pacific, it is probably another matter entirely. We just want you to know that the whole school is thinking about you and about Pete and about the whole Narten family.

Pete is a part of our total school life with all its memories of grand boys. Please let us know as soon as you get any definite word. We want you to know that the Academy "stands by" in any and every way whereby we may be of help to the Narten family.

    Very sincerely yours,
    Joel B. Hayden

Neil McPhail ('33) wrote to his mother from Italy, where heavy Allied bombing continued in Cassino. Mrs. McPhail gave his letter to the school.

    Somewhere in Italy
    February 27, 1944

Dear Mother:

In the past no matter what the condition, I've tried to write you rather vague but cheerful letters. I shall not endeavor to change, but thought this time I'd tell you a few serious facts and then skip the subject for good. Firstly, at the moment we're engaged in what you might call total war. One of those nerve racking day and night affairs. We've been able to observe first hand that the Germans still possess great strength and determination. The prisoners we see are horrible specimens of men. Even the unhurt seemingly look more dead than alive. In a battle of this type casualties naturally are high on both sides. You and the people must steel yourselves for a long and costly war. We will win only by hard fighting. . . . I am writing you this so that you will not build up any false hopes.

I am well and feeling fine. Still sleeping warm and eating well. Please don't worry about me.

Love,
Neil [Age 29]

February 29, 1944

Dear Doug [Barnes '43]:

Just a line to say that I had a fine letter from your father. I hear word about you from [Ken] Goldsmith ['43] and, by indirection, around through Marv Mell, Fred McConky, Chubb Barry [all '43] and Dave Owen ['42].

Saw and dined with Jim Stevenson and George Upson [both '43] in Cambridge, Mass. two weeks ago last night. I was on my eastern swing to the Headmasters' meeting and I had quite a fine time with the Harvard group. That is the only place I visited where I had enough time to try to get a WRA gang together and actually "tackle the fatted goose," and that's exactly what we had for dinner when we did have dinner! . . .

We've got a full school but a young school. Fifty-six freshmen form most of the daily diet of Messrs. Theibert, Wallace, Ellis and company, and you know what that means in the long run.

Just had word that Fred Waring will be back, surely, with us next fall. Apparently, he is going to bring odds and ends from the Near East, beginning with bits of the pyramids and winding up with several hundred square yards of oriental rugs. Nothing less than a liberty ship can bring him home adequately.

Exams coming up next week; some 220 boys are slightly pale around the gills. Same old story!! . . .

Best to you from everybody here.

Devotedly yours,
Joel B. Hayden

The Citadel
March 2, 1944

Dear Doctor Hayden:

It seems hard for me to express due appreciation for your wonderful letter of recommendation, for I believe that I have never in all my life received one as good as yours. I only wish that I lived up to about half of what you said about me. I am sorry that I couldn't have written you beforehand. Everything seemed to happen at once here so there was not even time to write home. I had to call.

My fate seems more or less decided for me, for the day after I turned my application in the aviation cadet program was closed to my branch of service. This was in accordance with the army's idea of closing their specialized programs for it was stated that men were needed for the ground forces. Nevertheless, there is a remote chance that I can make Officer Candidate School and again I can use your letter.

Such a scientific training that I have been going through for the last six months has proved very interesting to me and has given me a new confidence that I never thought I had. I find that my entire background for this advanced math was accountable to the Academy and Mr. McGill and Mr. Wallace.

                Sincerely yours,
                Jonathan G. Izant ['41; Age 20]

                                    Hyde Park, New York
                                            March 5, 1944

Dear Dr. Hayden,

Please excuse my tardy reply to your thoughtful birthday card and ever welcome attached note. Although I'm still on this side of the various and sundry oceans and still feel that I've had my share of experiences, and undoubtedly many more in the offing, I never realized that the army could give one such a liberal and unusually varied education. I believe that it has done much to help me find myself, and also realize things—such as—that everything was not always going to be handed to me on a silver platter. It didn't take long to discover that the only person who was going to worry about Bill Glover—was Glover himself. So much for that.

I have been in the Military Police ever since my entry into the army—I like it very much. If the various duties are not exciting, then they are interesting. Always one or the other. I think I've done every type of job an M.P. can be called on to do, and I've gotten a kick out of doing it. Some aren't very pleasant ones—but then they've got to be done. The present army as you well know is made up of everyone—the highest and the lowest. I've certainly come in contact with some plenty low ones too. They teach you all the tricks of the trade at M.P. school—and after a little experience, plus the gaining of self confidence, etc. you're ready for the best or worst of them. I've never come out on the wrong end yet, and I've made quite a few arrests, etc. I've had my fingers crossed a couple of times, though, and I still knock on wood.

Our outfit is a very unusual one—we don't take orders from the army but rather from the U.S. Secret Service. We have been attached to them. Therefore, we handle civilians most of the time now, and seldom soldiers.

One of our main purposes is the protection of the President, his family, and his property. It is naturally at times very interesting. Since I have been here—I have talked to him probably a dozen different times. Other people I have accompanied, escorted, guarded, or watched, include the First Lady and every member of their family. Churchill and his daughter, Madame Chiang Kai Chek, Admiral King, Morgenthau, Knox, Gen. Marshall, the Princess and Queen of the Netherlands and Harry and Mrs. Hopkins.

The outfit is unusual as far as the personnel is concerned also. I am one of the youngest in it. Most of the men are college graduates and of the highest type.

I am in the lower one-third as far as size goes—I am 6'2" and weigh 200 lbs. I am just a Cpl. with a squad of thirteen men under me. Four of them have college degrees—three more were practicing law when they were drafted, one was a federal investigator. All of them had attended college at one time or another—and most were successful business men on the outside. All of them were connected with police work of one sort or another on the outside. There is only one man in the squad smaller than myself. Their ages range from twenty-seven to thirty-four. If they knew their squad leader was only just twenty-one, I don't know what the results would be. I have been accepted for officer's school—Corp. of Military Police—but I don't know when I will be called.

We expect to be overseas by the end of next fall—I only hope it's so. It's about six degrees above zero outside today and plenty of snow—it certainly won't break my heart to see the summer arrive. . . .

Sincerely,
Bill Glover ['42x; Age 21]

Following exam week, the school adjourned for spring break.

Spring Term: March–June 1944

Somewhere in the South Pacific
March 12, 1944

Dear Dr. Hayden,

The Christmas and birthday cards from Reserve, the latter with your very nice note, arrived recently here at my camp in New Guinea. They were as pleasing as they were surprising, and I want to thank you very much. It's a far cry from the Chapel bell of the Academy to the air raid sirens here, but the cards helped recall those "good old days." Incidentally, it's ten years this spring that I graduated—they are "old" days!

I'm just leaving for civilization for my first leave in the army, and the first trip out of the tropics in eighteen months. I'm looking forward anxiously to fifteen days of fresh tomatoes, fresh lettuce, real milk—and maybe a cold beer or two. These jungles can get mighty monotonous in a year and a half!

Sincerely,
Bill Ingraham ['34; Age 27]

Charles "Boots" Killian ['40] was at Princeton in one of the specialized training programs alongside some of his former classmates by the time he received a letter from Dr. Hayden. "Boots" wrote to Dr. Hayden two days later and the letters apparently crossed in the mail.

March 27, 1944

Dear "Boots":

WRA sends its best to you and Bob [Meese '40] and Keith [Carter '43] and Nelson [Sykes '41]. Tell Nelson I had about three-quarters of an hour with [his brother] Carl ['43] yesterday. Carl looks fine. His Corporal is Bob Borden of the Class of 1938. Laugh that one off!

I certainly enjoyed your fine letter, Boots. When you get a chance, shove some more news through to the old home base!

George Montgomery ['41] has been here; Herb Spring ['38] and both the Tebbies [Theiberts] with their wings are on the campus at the moment.[1] Herb Spring has his wings, too.

This is just a note and I am sending it through rapido so that it will get you all together as you put on a Louisiana reunion for WRA. Here's to you all.

Ever yours,
Joel B. Hayden

1. Alumni often visited the campus when home on furlough.

Princeton University
March 29, 1944

Dear Dr. Hayden;

I have been wanting to write to you for some time now to thank you for inviting me to the alumni dinner and to express my regret for not having the chance to talk with you. Somehow whenever I have had talks with you it seems that I leave completely inspired with new feelings of strength.

In this world of rapidly changing events I recognize only too clearly the need for intellectual strength and guidance. There have been two or three times in the past eighteen months that I have felt that I was on the brink of intellectual maturity, but it seems that the feeling was only momentary and I lapse back into a state of intellectual adolescence and impotence.

I suppose the problem is related to the idea that you and I discussed several times while I was at Reserve; that is the question of finding direction and discovering a goal that one must consciously as well as unconsciously strive for twenty-four hours a day, 365 days a year. It is more than life's work. Perhaps it can best be described as life itself, something to accomplish, but what is that something?

It is a difficult feeling to realize that you are merely drifting. Possibly it is merely an extended state of incubation and something may spring forth yet. I hope that the above makes a little sense to you and I suppose that it may.

To catch up to the events, I am now stationed in the barracks here at Princeton under the new specialist training program. It is a cadet system, although we still attend classes in the morning as usual. We are on an active duty basis, but we do have considerable freedom. In June we shall go to either Fort Bragg or Fort Sill for O.C.S.

A great many of the boys have left and are spread all over the country. Bob Meese is playing nursemaid to a mule in the pack artillery at [Ft.] Sill. Paul Fuzy ['40] is at Harvard while Steve Lamb is here with me....

Sincerely yours,
Boots ['40; Age 22]

During the spring break, work in the machine shop continued, with ten "town boys," Academy boys who lived in Hudson, turning out socket wrenches to fulfill the order placed by Wright Tool and Forge. They were paid an hourly wage of fifty cents for their labor. School reconvened on March 21 and the *Record* of March 30 carried a detailed account of the accomplishments of the boys in the shop, as well as a call from Jack Yardley stating the need for more boys to work in the machine shop. "Since production must stop two weeks before the end of the term to allow Mr. Tepper to do outside work, only six more weeks are available for war work," the notice read. Six weeks and nine thousand wrenches to go to fulfill the war contract! Of the twenty-five-thousand-piece order, sixteen thousand had already been produced.

April 5, 1944

Dear Bill[1]:

In these days it is hard to keep track of just where the family really is.... Just what is your status? Is there anything I can do to aid you and give hellfire and brim stone to the enemy?

All's going well here. Our schedule is too crowded, as usual.... Fred Waring will be back, definitely, for the opening of school next fall. Just had a letter from him. He gives us a typical personal summary. I quote:

"Just when I shall be able to get passage back I cannot tell. But I shall be in Hudson for the opening of school next fall—balder than ever, skinnier than ever, and, I regret to say, as irascible as ever. But rearin' to go."

. . . I am holding the fort at Hudson. I am having a series of guests the last of the year, winding up our guest schedule for WRA. It's been pretty complicated business and our labor shortage here has been rather devastating. For the last two days now, it's snowed hard. What do you mean, Easter greetings?! Blessings on you from all of us.

>Devotedly,
>Uncle Joel

1. Wilber I. Newstetter, Jr. ('41), Joel Hayden's nephew.

The April 6 *Record* brought the front-page news that "all boys not participating in varsity sports will spend one day out of each week working on the campus if the weather permits." In the event of inclement weather, the boys were to report to the gym, "where they will be given a physical workout by Mr. Ellis."

Since the manpower shortages on the campus maintenance crew continued, the work program that began in the fall was once again underway. A number of jobs were listed, including preparation of the playing fields and general spring cleanup of the grounds.

On April 13, Dr. Hayden's daughter Jean gave birth to the Haydens' second grandchild, Sam, Jr., in Burlington, Vermont. Jean's husband was stationed at Princeton awaiting orders. Coach Theibert stated that he was eagerly looking forward to the fall of 1961, when he hoped to have young Sam in his backfield. The coach retired in 1959; Sam Jr. was a 1962 graduate of Deerfield Academy.

Of the twenty-four boys who took the Navy V-12 tests in November, twenty-one passed and were in the process of taking their physical exams and holding interviews with navy personnel. The twelve boys who took the army's A-12 exam were waiting to hear of their acceptance or rejection.

>Somewhere in England
>April 14, 1944

My Dear Doctor and Mrs. Hayden,

I have been over here for quite a while now and have seen lots of England already. What I have seen would probably cost thousands of dollars in peace time. I have seen lots more than people that have lived here all their lives. I don't especially like the country—I would much rather be back in the good old U.S.A., but as long as I have to be here I am going to make the best of it and continue to see what I can and do my work the best way I know how.

Just about five weeks ago I came back from my first furlough in over fourteen months and then it had to be over here. Anyway, I had a very good time in Nottingham where I stayed with a swell family. I was glad to get away from the old army routine even though it was for only seven days.

After working hard all day, seven days a week from six A.M. to five P.M., a few other boys and myself either go to a village dance or for a long walk. Even though we do work hard during the day we still like to relax at night by taking a walk.

The weather over here is beautiful now. It gets bright fairly early in the morning and it doesn't get dark until around ten P.M. Instead of just being on daylight saving time, these people are on double daylight saving time.

Things are rough and tough over here and will probably get more so as the war draws to an end, but don't worry about me, for I get the best food and care in the world. Tell all my dear friends around Reserve that I said "hello" and I'm thinking of them. Keep the home fires burning for us and until I return, I remain,

    Yours sincerely,
    W. H[arold]. Kennedy ['42; Age 21]

In his letter to POW William Sprow, Dr. Hayden realized that the letter would be censored; thus he sent general news of the campus.

    2nd Lieut. William J. Sprow
    American Prisoner of War #3204
    Stalag Luft #3
    Germany (Via New York, N.Y.)
    April 19, 1944

Dear Bill,

I just want to send you greetings from the whole crowd at WRA. We are still on the job and when the weather permits I think we'll finally get "out from under" and have ourselves some tennis, baseball and track. Here it is past the middle of April and Old Man Weather has won every round so far. We've had one track meet with Canton Lehman and won that last Friday. Have two letter men back, so it is a brand "new deal" all right! We haven't any idea of what the baseball team will look like outdoors. The campus crew and the fellows released to help on the campus have been able to do nothing to the diamond so far, but I guess their turn will be coming up now. We're supposed to play a ball game today and one tomorrow. . . .

Four hundred seventy-five to eighty fellows of the WRA brand are now serving all around the world. You see, Bill, one of these days a reunion is in order—a reunion of a very unique sort. When I last saw you in front of Pierce House as you were "tootling" along, I had no idea that I would be writing care of your present address.

We just want you to know that "the gang's all here" and we can pledge you our loyalty and affection.

Ever yours,
Joel B. Hayden

Dr. Hayden's letter must have brought a ray of sunshine to Bill in the German POW camp. In letters to other boys Dr. Hayden expressed an interest in what was going through their minds and what their training entailed, and wondered what advice they had to share with the school.

Denver, Colorado
April 20, 1944

Dear Sir:

Today I received your note and I feel as though I more than owe you a letter. First of all I want to thank you for the birthday card which you sent me, it certainly was appreciated.

I go to school from 5:45 A.M. till 11:30 A.M. and then I have lunch; after lunch we have a military indoctrination period and then physical training. From 3:30 P.M. on is our free time, but four A.M. rolls around too quickly, so it is early to bed and early to rise. Our studies are, however, very interesting and different from any I have yet had.

Marvin Mell ['43] is out here also, so you can imagine how that lifts my morale. I only see him about twice a week, for he is over at Lowry Field #1; he is going to a school for the study of electrical turrets, and seems to like it a lot.

The weather here has been very similar to what you have been having, snow one day and sunshine and rain the next. I am looking forward to summer.

Well, sir, lights are about to go out and I must bring this to an end, but first, let me wish you, Mrs. Hayden, faculty, and students the best.

Very sincerely,
Dick Bauer ['43; Age 19]

April 26, 1944

Dear Bill [W. H. Kennedy, '42]:

Just a note of appreciation and acknowledgement for your fine letter which reached me and all the rest of us from "somewhere in England." You're doing the right thing; "cash in" on all the sightseeing you can get ahold of to build up your memories. They'll constitute a very large storehouse for the future.

I can't tell you how much we miss you fellows and how much we depend upon you. If this school is worth the room it occupies, it's only because fellows like you are part of our big family. Feel free to give me any suggestions which I can pass on to masters and students for the better operation of the school and the "upping" of the over-all job.

Affectionately yours,
Joel B. Hayden

Somewhere in England
May 2, 1944

Dear Dr. Hayden,

Thanks very much for your birthday and Easter card, which arrived a week or so ago. Time does not mean much in the kind of existence we have been leading; and answering letters, like a lot of other things, tends to be put off from day to day. Letter writing is quite a chore these days. In the first place, there is very little of interest to write about; and in the second, when something does crop up, in the way of fact or rumor, which might make good reading, it is doomed to a quick death under the censor's scissors. However, it is so long since I have written you (the address of "Midshipman" on your card made me realize about how long), that I can do a little reminiscing and reviewing.

I've been on this *LST* [Landing-Ship Tank] now for ten months, six of them here in England. These ships have received so much general publicity during that time—in newsreels, magazines, and even "the funnies"—that there is little about this one that I could tell you that you do not probably already know. During our first four months, we went through outfitting, training our own crew and other crews, and practice landing operations in Florida and the Chesapeake. Our ocean trip came last October, and is still the biggest thing yet in the life of the "30." It took a long, rough three weeks to get here; but the journey was entirely uneventful as far as enemy action was concerned. Since arriving, we have been marking time and waiting for the "second front." Once in awhile a mock invasion will come along to relieve the monotony. But most of the time, we have been just sitting at anchor. Not a very exciting or a very strenuous existence, to be sure. However, there is not much to be done about it, and I try not to get too restless. Liberty ashore comes often enough, and I suppose we should consider ourselves lucky to be able to see a movie and drink a few beers of an evening. At least it is more than a lot of sailors can do. . . .

The regular arrival of the *Oberlin Review* and *Reserve Record* also helps bridge the distance across the Atlantic. Please give my best to Mrs. Hayden and everyone else at Reserve, and to Jean and Joel when you write them. Let's all hope for a pleasant reunion soon, when all this "unfinished business" is finished.

Sincerely yours,
Dick Hirshberg ['36; Age 25]

In an effort to solve the acute manpower shortage, Dr. Hayden visited schools in the East to learn how they were responding. At Princeton he was able to see his son-in-law Sam, then a lieutenant, junior grade, and a few alumni. Mrs. Hayden was already in Vermont visiting Jean and their grandchildren. Dr. Hayden managed to spend a day with them before he boarded the train home to Hudson. On the train he encountered a father of one of the alumni.

May 3, 1944

My dear "Tim" [J. Scribner Allen, '39]:

I rode with your father from Middlebury, Vermont to Albany last Thursday. We had a grand visit. He brought me up to date on you and your clan. . . .

Your father's proud of everything you have done. That holds for your mother and the rest of the family. You certainly know how to awaken and keep the loyalty and affection of those around about you. Keep it up! That is probably one of the most important things in this business of intelligent and decent living. You've been blessed with a strong and vivid personality and we want you to know that we all have a lot of faith in you and in your capacity to bring the best out of others.

We're "tootling along" here at Reserve. Our chief problem, of course, is holding a strong faculty. I am rather optimistic, however, concerning next fall. In the meantime D-Day will have arrived and so much will depend upon that and all that it means that all present plans may be as feeble as most of those "of mice and men."

All your friends here send you their best. The "old guard" is still with us. We are doing our best to hold our end up, we promise you that.

    Devotedly yours,
    Joel B. Hayden

May 3, 1944

Dear Dr. Hayden:

Two years ago when I was a senior I never dreamed that I would write you from Italy. Somehow the last ten months don't seem at all real. It has been a real education to just wander around the world in this way. At Reserve I wasted too much time, and yet somehow managed to absorb enough to make things very easy. I've met boys from other top prep schools who just didn't seem to have the same stuff in them as our boys. I'm very proud to say I went to WRA and only now am I realizing what you have done to make our lives a bit better. If the present and future graduating classes are equal to those of '41, '42, '43, Reserve will have turned out a generation which will keep America what it is today. I'd like

Russell F. Ashmun ('42), right, on leave from the American Field Service in the Middle East, visited Dick Theibert ('42), an Army Air Corps pilot stationed in Italy. *Courtesy Russell Ashmun*

to hear from you often, so please keep me posted on the whereabouts of my friends and fellow students at Reserve.

Russ Ashmun ['42; Age 19]

The editorial and two articles in the May 4 *Record* were a subtle testimony to the positive side of the grounds work. Even the title of the article, "New Trees Add Beauty to Campus," had a tone of appreciation for the outdoor work that was being done. With so many of the boys pitching in, the campus plantings were being renewed and the boys themselves were taking notice. The editorial talked about the state of the Hockey Pond—not complaining, but, rather, presenting a solution. Not asking, "Why don't *they* (meaning the school) do something about it," but, rather, suggesting how the boys themselves could upgrade the area. They were learning to work together and seeing the results, an experience many would remember as they joined an even larger group of boys when their time came to serve.

On May 4, Dr. Hayden received confirmation of the death of Harry Allchin, Jr. The following day a letter of condolence was sent to his parents from the school, drafted and signed by the presidents of both the senior class and the school council, as well as by Ralph McGill and Dean Wood. The front page of the *Record* of May 11 carried the news about Harry.

May 5, 1944

Dear Mr. and Mrs. Allchin:

On Thursday morning Dr. Hayden announced to the school assembled in chapel the sad news which he had received from you the evening before and which, an hour before, he had communicated to [Harry's brother] Tom.

Under the leadership of Dr. Hayden the service took the form of a memorial service for Harry. He spoke of the days and weeks that have passed during which we have hoped for a favorable word. He referred to Harry's life here at the Academy during which time he was a fine citizen in the school and, although unknown personally to almost the entire present student body, he was a member of the Reserve family and as such is honored and loved by all. . . . Yes, we are all glad that Harry came to Reserve. It was for you, and for us and for others that he died. As long as time shall preserve these walls of old Reserve the name of Harry Allchin will appear on its Roll of Honor.

We sympathize with you in your sorrow and want to say that if we or any others of the Reserve family can help you in any way it will be a glad service on our part. Please accept the sympathy of all those whom we represent at Reserve today.

Very sincerely yours,
Geoffrey Bennett
President of the Senior Class

Bradford Wells
President of the School Council

Ralph W. McGill
Assistant Headmaster

Harlan N. Wood
Dean

Somewhere in England
May 5, 1944

Dear Dr. and Mrs. Hayden,

I got Dr. Hayden's very swell letter this afternoon and am going to answer it right away. I was very glad to hear from my very good friends at "Old Reserve" once more after such a long time. I'm very glad to know that everyone is fine but sorry to hear that you are losing so many of the faculty to the war. They were the best ever and I think you'll have a pretty hard time replacing any of them—at least the ones that taught me during my four year stay with you all.

Harry Allchin, Jr. ('39), on the Academy football field. *Archives*

Dr. Hayden, you ask me if there are any suggestions which I have to give to the faculty and students. Well, there isn't because everything was perfect while I was there. I may not have thought so then, but I sure do now. If there are any big changes let me know about them, but I'll always like to think of old Reserve as it was before we entered the war and while I attended it for just four short years—the shortest years I have ever spent and the best ones, too.

Last Sunday evening we had a church service by our chaplain which was held in the open under the trees and it brought back memories of yesteryear when I attended services in the Chapel. Those days, from every standpoint, I'll never forget. Can you blame me?

. . . I suppose the spring weather in Hudson is just as it always was—very beautiful. It has rained steady here for the past two days and it's very cold even during the day. Will have to close now as space is getting short. Will write an airmail to you soon again. Until then I remain,

[W.] Harold Kennedy ['42; Age 21]

Camp Phillips, Kansas
May 7, 1944

Dear Doctor Hayden,

I was very happy to receive birthday greetings from both you and the Academy. For some time I have intended to write to you, but as we are inclined to do, I have let much of my letter writing slide and now find myself heavily in debt.

As you doubtless know, much of the A.S.T.P. program has been discontinued and as a result I have been assigned to the 44th Division and the 324th Infantry Regiment. This is a very different life than we led in Minneapolis, but as might be expected I find it much more satisfying in some respects and I am very happy to be a member of the ground forces once again. This division has been through very extensive training and the commanding general makes no secret of the fact that we can expect a long trip before many months have passed. Needless to say our preparations require much hard work and long hours, but with the prospect of combat before us we are all putting out to the best of our ability and I am sure we will be ready.

[My younger brother] Doug has just returned to camp after a furlough and when he got there he found that he is now a sergeant. He seems to be making very rapid progress for an outfit such as the combat engineers and I certainly hope he can continue the good work.

It is good to hear that Reserve is carrying on in such a great style during this emergency. I often think of my days spent there and I hope some day to be able to visit all of you again. That day may be far away, but I am sure that Reserve will not be too changed and I will find it much as it was when I left.

Well, I must be getting to work on my rifle to be sure it is in top shape for firing tomorrow. We go to the range at 5:30 A.M. so it appears we will have another full day. . . .

        As ever,
        Paul Barnes ['42; Age 20]

                Somewhere in the South Pacific
                May 8, 1944

Dear Dr. Hayden:

Thought I would drop you a note now that we have a bit of comparative quiet. Regulations prevent my disclosing of my whereabouts or many of the activities of late; however, I suspect you may have better information than I.

We are once more back on a school schedule so our time is rather limited. Two and one-half hours a day in school, an hour working on the area; which, by the way, seems to grow up just as fast as we cut it down, and after dinner till it rains, about three o'clock, try to get the battery out for sports. As yet we haven't been able to get more than half out at a time; seems as though they would rather get that old blanket rash.

Under the conditions everyone is getting along very well. Considerable lumber has been cut here and is available, so our installations are at last a bit more convenient. Rations are more than adequate; however, mostly canned.

The *Record* has been coming in quite regularly lately; does make one feel closer to the things and people from way back when.... Must sign off now, school to teach in the morning you know.

      Truly yours,
      Bob Bluem ['39x; Age 23]

Out in the middle of the Pacific somewhere, A. Neil Finlayson ('40) wrote a letter to Scotch McGill. He had visited the campus while home on leave and observed the work in the machine shop. He also enclosed a letter praising the genius of Mr. Tepper, which was to be passed on to the *Record* editor for publication. It was never published, until now.

           May 11, 1944

Dear Sir:

I have just finished reading an article in the *Record* on the machine shop and the cases for socket wrenches which are now being turned out in large quantities. The data on production figures, discussion of the finished product and the story of the boys who were doing the work interested me. But it seemed to me that the real story behind the shop and its activities had been neglected entirely. I refer, of course, to the leading spirit and genius of Mr. Louis Tepper.

For a long time the shop has been running smoothly and effectively under the guidance of Mr. Tepper. It has turned out trucks, tractors, busses, lawn mowers, reconditioned machinery (sold at an advantage to WRA), as well as more aesthetic adornments to the campus. Take a look at the brass sundial between the Chapel and Seymour Hall next time you pass that way. That came out of the shop. But as the shop is for the most part utilitarian, it takes a machinist to appreciate fully just how much Mr. Tepper has done and is doing for the school. He has become a gadget, like the radio, exceedingly convenient in a variety of different wave lengths. He is taken for granted, tuned in upon, appreciated to a certain extent, but not fully understood.

Mr. Tepper is that rare combination of machinist and engineer who not only can design but also build that which he has designed. Witness the trucks, busses and especially the tractors. The essentials: motors, wheels, gears and connecting members, were furnished at slight extra charge by junkyards; while the connecting framework and all other necessary gears were furnished at no extra cost by Mr. Tepper....

In addition to these talents he is a teacher of the first quality. It was through him that I first learned to do precision machine work. The *Record* article that I mentioned at the beginning of the opus casts aspersions on the pre-production era shop instructions. "Boys came, watched operations, and sometimes touched a lever." This cannot be true, for such was

In the machine shop with Mr. Tepper; Neil Finlayson is third from the left. *Archives*

never Mr. Tepper's method of instructing. He has always assigned the job and then left the student to follow instructions as given. As the work was always chosen with the mechanical knowledge and capabilities of the student in mind, usually nothing came up that the boy couldn't figure out for himself. But, if and when necessary, Mr. Tepper was always willing to go to any lengths to explain that which was not clear. We were not passive onlookers at all, we were operators and for the most part on our own.

In a sense we were more fortunate than the boys who work in the shop today, for we had instruction in a variety of lines besides the basic one of precision machining. Some of these were moulding, pattern making, heat treatment of metals and arc welding—to name but a few. To meet the times, Mr. Tepper has switched the shop from that of jobbing to straight production, which of course will enable the boys to fit more easily into the high production shops that one finds today....

The lathes, completely redesigned and rebuilt by Mr. Tepper himself, have been converted into high speed, mass production machines. And no moss is allowed to grow on the forging between operations. Three snappy operations on the first lathe, then skidded down an incline trough to the side of the operator on the next lathe, three operations there followed by drilling, reaming, tapping and final assembly of case and cover. Then comes the satisfaction of shipping out large quantities of vitally needed hand tools. When I was there they had already shipped out 14,900 and that was in the early part of April.

All jigs and fixtures have been designed by Mr. Tepper so that one operation is automatically checked on the fixture for the next. If the dimensions are out beyond the tolerance specified, the piece will not fit in the next fixture. This makes needed adjustments noticeable immediately, which saves scrapping a number of valuable forgings. He also runs a time study department which is "shop" for efficiency expert. I watched Mr. Tepper single out a new boy who didn't seem to be producing as he should have been. Instead of the usual "get hot," "busy," or "on the ball," Mr. Tepper handed the boy a stop watch and asked to be timed for five pieces. Then he proceeded to give the boy a demonstration of efficient motions. The boy not only learned how to avoid wasted effort and time but also had the challenge to equal Mr. Tepper's output. Together they'll do it, too.

O.K., sez you. All this mechanical omniscience is to be expected in one who was formerly Shop Superintendent of Pierce Arrow. Maybe. But consider for a moment the Academy campus in all its arboreal splendor. Its beautiful landscaping is for the most part of his design, and all of the excellent grooming, which people from far and wide admire so much is the result of his never ceasing efforts. In Mr. Tepper's hands lie many skills and I, for one, am proud to have had him for an instructor and now as a friend.

Sincerely,
Neil Finlayson [Age 23]

Another unexpected reunion of Reservites in the service took place in the Pacific.

Solomon Islands
May 12, 1944

Dear Dr. Hayden:

You'll be very surprised to know that sitting right across the room from me at this minute is Ed Pope ['37]! So far we've run across each other twice in the last three months. The first time was in 'Frisco in February when, without having seen each other, we were assigned to the same BOQ [Bachelor Officers' Quarters] in the Alexander Hamilton Hotel. I left 'Frisco in March, shortly before Ed left, and was happily situated here, with the 12th Special Seabees, when one bright morning I heard somebody yell at me, inquiring about gas for his jeep. I turned around and, of course, it was Ed. He's been staying here with me until he and his men can get further transportation up the line.

Ed is the officer-in-charge of a PT mobile field unit and doing very well. Right now he's in the midst of getting ready to move and wants me to be sure and send you and your family his very best regards, and that he'll write very shortly. . . . Right now it seems an awfully long way to WRA, although talking over a lot of the things that happened while we were with you has made it seem, to Ed and me, as if it were only yesterday that we left.

Paul H. Barnes ('42), on the Academy football field. *WRAA*

We're not doing too badly here; our activity is a stevedore battalion and works seven days a week, but we're beginning to get a few of the comforts of home. We live two officers to a tent built on a raised wooden floor and screened in on all sides, so that actually the only actual tent part is the roof. For washing we use rain water, although we've just completed a shower which has hot water when the sun shines on the water tank in the afternoons. Also, I'm proud to report, we have telephones in our tents and offices, the kind which requires you to turn a crank before and after the call. What's more we've just opened our officer's club and are eating really good food on, more or less, clean linen (made of old sugar sacks) for the first time in a very long while. And, last but not least, we're just now engaged in building a quonset hut for our supply and disbursing offices. Formerly, and still for a few days, we've been working in tents which are not ideal.

        As ever,
        Marv Alexander ['39; Age 23]

                              May 12, 1944

Dear Paul [Barnes]:

   . . . I want to read part of your [May 7] letter to the boys early next week. I want you to know how the seniors this year speak about you, because they regarded you as the "Rock of Gibraltar" of the Class of 1942. Just keep on being a "rock," Paul! We certainly need good anchorages in these troubled days and your fundamental character is just the kind of thing upon which and around which we ought to be able to build something pretty decent. . . .

        Ever yours,
        Joel B. Hayden

Jack McIntosh ('39), right, prepares for the D day Invasion, June 1944. *Courtesy Jack McIntosh*

As Jack McIntosh ('39) made his final preparations for the approaching invasion, which would turn the tide of the war, he wrote a letter to the headmaster.

Warrensburg, Missouri
May 14, 1944

Dear Dr. Hayden,

During a period when things must have been most busy it was gratifying indeed to find a letter from you. In these past two years I have thought of you often there at the Academy, wondering, but with my usual laziness, doing nothing about it.

We have all been equally rushed for time at this end, completing our final few weeks of replacement training in troop carrier before flying overseas. Now that the European war has really begun, our C-47's have at last been given some of the praise they deserve. Despite this thrill of being in an invasion, we all hope that those shipping orders will reach India, or perhaps China, that we might get into a war really our own.

Sometimes the thought of fighting to exterminate a race is difficult to understand, when for so long all of us have been taught to let live, but a few hours in a "session" with the boys who have returned leaves little doubt in our minds as to the job to be done.

. . . Complete crews have been made up at last; most of us are anxious for a little action after these months of training and maneuvers. Just these next two weeks, then, we hope, a very short visit home—and off into the wild blue—or something.

Hoping to make an appointment with you in the chapel with a "friend" after this is over—my best to you all there.

John McIntosh ['39; Age 23]

May 15, 1944

Dear Doug [Barnes, '43]:

... Here we are, starting this morning on the last week of another school year. Final exams begin one week from today. You can imagine how, day by day, as this week advances the blood pressure will rise and the jittery members of the school will get more jittery while those who should get jittery will probably continue to coast along and enjoy life.

The spring weather has not been very favorable for the field sports, but right now everything on the campus looks beautiful and there is plenty of bright sunshine. I judge that the baseball and track teams have had about a fifty-fifty break. They won a ball game on Saturday but lost the track to Canton McKinley by a score of fifty-odd to sixty-odd, not a bad score against such a strong team.

Commencement comes one week from next Sunday and then we scatter. Formerly we used to scatter to different parts of Ohio and a few other states. Now we scatter from Alaska and Texas to China and Borneo, the former home of Barnum and Bailey's wild man. It is no longer a big world. You boys will live to see it a more united world than ever before. I hope this union can be realized without another war, but man has now in his hands many destructive implements, and it all depends upon whether or not he prefers to use them or his head to accomplish a lasting peace. Well, here is hoping that you are in good health and that the day may soon be here when you will be coming home. . . .

Very sincerely yours,
Harlan N. Wood

Robert Bliss, whose brother Dick ('38) was "somewhere in Algiers," stopped by the campus one afternoon hoping to visit Dr. Hayden but didn't find him. Hayden dashed off a note of regret at missing him. "I am so sorry I missed you when you called," he wrote. "One thing I have to do everyday after luncheon is undress and go to bed and just 'unkink' myself and let the 'springs' relax a bit before the necessary tightening up which follows. I'd have given a whole lot to have just looked in your eyes and shaken your hand."

Somewhere in the Atlantic
May 1944

Dear Dr. Hayden,

You may think me not thankful for the birthday card which I got as usual from you and WRA. I repeat that it is awfully nice to know that you

Mr. Tepper and the boys in the machine shop with the fruits of their labor, 1944. *Archives*

still remember me after all these years. Of course, I have a wonderful memory about old Reserve which is a source of joy to me still.

I had planned to write you sooner, but for the last month I have been quite busy! Starting in Georgia on March 1, going to New York, to Kansas, to RLE [Boston point of embarkation] and finally aboard the ship on which I now am. There is a lot of work in preparation for movement overseas.

It will interest you to know that I ran into Tom Sawyer ['36] who, due to some bad luck, is a private in this division. It was fun talking with him about WRA.

> As ever,
> Mal Vilas ['35; Age 26]

The front page of the May 18 *Reserve Record* carried the incredible news: The machine shop completed the order from Wright Tool & Forge. The boys produced a total of 26,400 wrenches valued at $6,600. Production in the fall was behind schedule by 45,000 parts. According to the *Record*, "The heaviest work was done during the winter and spring terms. Even during the Christmas and Spring vacations the work was not slighted, for the town boys completed 5,000 parts during those seasons alone."

William M. Ashley ('40). *Archives*

Bill Ashley ('40) on the football field. *Archives*

Commencement was held on May 28. Three days later it was learned that William M. Ashley ('40) lost his life in an airplane crash in South Hadley, Massachusetts, while in the final stages of his training for combat. Dean Wood wrote to his parents.

May 31, 1944

Dear Mr. and Mrs. Ashley:

On Monday evening of this week our faculty was assembled for its final meeting of this school year. At that time Dr. Hayden called our attention to the item which appeared in the evening paper in which it was stated that your son, Bill, was among those killed in the air plane accident that occurred near South Hadley.

I am writing you this morning to express to you not only my personal sympathy but I am conveying to you the message of sympathy from the entire faculty group.

Between five and six hundred Reserve boys are now in the service. One more Gold Star will now be placed on the Roll of Honor which is hanging in the common room of Cutler Hall.

On Sunday the sun shone bright over the beautiful green campus of Reserve and in the old chapel fifty-three boys were graduated. In former days ninety-five percent of them would have been accepted for admission to some good college next September. In most cases the years beyond college would have been pretty well outlined as to future work.

This year a large majority will go almost immediately into the service of their country. Only a few will be permitted to enter upon their college plans and these plans will be interrupted as soon as they reach eighteen.

We know nothing as to the cause of the plane accident but it seems all the harder to bear when our boys must lose their lives through some accident that might have been avoided except for some defect in machinery.

Bill was the type of a boy who would prefer to give his all in the thick of battle in the front line of action.

Again, may I extend to you the deep sympathy of all the Reserve family of which Bill was a part. If we can be of any help to you in any way it will be a pleasure to have that opportunity.

                Very sincerely,
                Harlan N. Wood

Mrs. Ashley's response included the details of the tragic accident and assured Dean Wood that it was not caused by mechanical defect. The crew was training in simulation of combat conditions in what was known as a "maximum load flight." The weather was unusually hot and the air was light, and the plane failed to gain sufficient altitude.

The June *Alumni Record* carried a message from Dean Wood, now a regular feature in the magazine.

> As I look back over the years and recall commencements of other days, this one was different. Normally nearly every member of the class could have been looking forward to entering college . . . and the plans for life beyond college would have been made. . . . all but two or three . . . have been accepted for admission to twenty-two different colleges and universities. But herein lies the difference. Only sixteen . . . will enter college . . . and their work . . . probably will be interrupted as soon as they pass eighteen. The other thirty-four or thirty-five will this summer enter some branch of the service. . . .

Then came Operation Overlord. D day. On June 6, 1944 American, British, and Canadian troops, aided by thousands of ships and planes, landed in northern France. The long-awaited invasion of German-occupied Europe had begun.

Before Dr. and Mrs. Hayden left to spend the summer in New England, Dr. Hayden caught up on his correspondence.

                                              June 12, 1944

Dear Bob [Bluem]:

Your letter under date of May 8 brought great good cheer to me and to the rest of the faculty family. It is hard for us to realize how much you have gone through. I get bits of news from other fellows about, and your visit to Jack Gillespie's grave has been an outstanding comfort to the Gillespie family.

You now seem to be resting up a bit and getting reconditioned. If we can put the "squeeze play" on Adolph this summer and fall, perhaps the whole job in the Orient will be shortened by reason of power and concentration. Here's hoping.

Yes, being in the "gramps" category is quite something. Mrs. Hayden and I are going to see a good deal of our grandchildren within the next months because our son-in-law has been ordered to the Pacific. He's Lt. (j.g.) with rather vague orders, but those orders will soon clarify. Joel, Jr. becomes an ensign on 19 July by way of the Northwestern University midshipmen's school. All the sons of the older faculty are in the show now and you can imagine how things tighten up inside all of us as we realize that.

Our chief objective is to carry on that fellows like you, Bob, will feel that we have not let you down. That is the primary responsibility. That is where we have to work out our final salvation as a school and our final salvation as a group of men. There are more than 500 WRA boys now in the service, and there are already thirteen Gold Stars shining out so that we can never forget on the one hand and never let down on the other.

       Devotedly,
       Joel B. Hayden

                                  Somewhere in France
                                            June 13, 1944

Dear Dr. Hayden:

Now that I am not so busy as I have been for the past few days, I feel that I must write you a note expressing my sincerest gratitude for an inspiration which I received through Western Reserve Academy during the most critical hour of my life.

D-Day morning the mail orderly handed me a letter from Western Reserve Academy. In it was an invitation to a commencement which had occurred a week before and a picture of the chapel. For a brief moment I forgot the present and was a student again, thinking only of "*Vergil*" and the coming dance. I looked at the Chapel a little more closely and recalled that within its ancient walls there was a cross. Before this cross, Columbus had knelt to pray before his embarkation upon a journey whose end revealed a great new world.

I like to think that in a small and humble way history was repeating itself, and that we of Reserve who have prayed before that cross and are now engaged in the greatest of all conflicts will someday find a better world for those who will follow.

In closing, I want to restate my appreciation for the inspiration from Reserve and assure you that until I can again walk upon the campus in peace, I will carry the little picture of the Chapel, which is the symbol of everything that is fine in the land I love.

       Respectfully yours,
       Alfred L. Rideout ['38; Age 24]

July–August 1944

After serving as dean of students for thirteen years, Harlan Wood retired and was given the title of dean emeritus. Raymond A. Mickel was appointed to replace him. Wood continued tending to the administrative details of the school during the summer.

Dr. and Mrs. Hayden spent the summer in Maine with their daughter and two grandchildren. At summer's end, Jean and the grandchildren returned to Hudson with the Haydens and remained for the duration of the war. Among the losses of many of his boys, Dr. Hayden suffered a personal loss with the death of his father during the summer.

On July 22, the ninety-one-year-old bell in the chapel tower struck the hour of noon for the last time. In the silence that followed, Dean Wood and Harley Kuhn held a brief ceremony outside the front of the chapel. Workers removed the old bell, and the "new-old" one, salvaged from the clock tower of Evamere, the Hudson home of Academy benefactor James W. Ellsworth, took its place.

It was most appropriate that the two men were in attendance. Among his many duties involved with the maintenance of the school, Kuhn was responsible for the ringing of the bell each morning since 1919, calling the Reserve community to morning chapel. Dean Wood had heard the familiar tones of the old bell as a student, as a faculty member in the years before the Academy closed its doors in 1903, and on the day those doors reopened in 1916. For the past twenty-eight years before this day it was Wood who opened the chapel doors each morning to greet Kuhn on his way to ring the morning bell. Their presence on the campus and their years of devotion to the school were as enduring as the old bell itself.

The day before the new bell was installed, Americans landed on Guam. Earlier in the month, after a twenty-five-day struggle, American forces took Saipan in the Marianas. In Washington, D.C., Franklin D. Roosevelt announced his decision to once again run for president, declaring, "I have as little right as a soldier to leave his position on the line."

On August 10, as the three-week battle for Guam ended, Americans launched an air raid over Nagasaki, Japan. On August 19, Lt. Gen. George S. Patton launched a drive on Paris. Three days later, as Allied leaders met at Dumbarton Oaks to discuss world security, Patton's troops crossed the Seine

Harley Kuhn and Harlan Wood solemnize the removal of the old Chapel bell, July 1944. *Archives*

Campus maintenance crew member Bert Kidgell steadies the old bell as it is lowered from the Chapel tower. *Archives*

River north of Paris. On August 25 Paris was liberated to the tune of ringing church bells and resounding voices, as joyous celebrations were held throughout the city.

As the summer months came to a close, an estimated five hundred to six hundred of the eleven hundred alumni were serving in the armed forces. The Gold Stars on the Service Honor Roll numbered just fifteen. But those numbers were about to rise significantly.

Somewhere in Italy
July 9, 1944

Dear Dr. and Mrs. Hayden,

The graduation of [my brother] Brad from WRA prompted me several weeks ago to write this to you, though as you see, I've just now gotten around to doing so. I must say that the Wells family certainly owes you a debt of gratitude for all you've done for Bradford and myself. I know that the experience I got from Reserve is invaluable to me, to say nothing of the great times and fine friends I had there.

Things have very much changed here in Italy in the past few weeks. The further north we go it seems the more beautiful the scenery and the friendlier the people become. It really does one's heart good to see a fine village left completely intact after the terrific destruction and rubble of the villages of the south. So far I've only been able to gather a general impression of Rome by passing through it several times on evacuations, but later I hope to obtain leave so that I can explore the city as it should be.

Very sincerely,
Howard [Wells, '41; Age 20]

Somewhere in France
Summer 1944

Dear Mr. and Mrs. Parker,[1]

I was so very glad to get Mr. Parker's letter yesterday and know you are both well and enjoying your vacation so very much. I know how very much you must look forward to it each summer after being with the boys for nine long months.

As for me, I am still okay and in the best of health. Everything is still going fine, and I hope it won't be too long before we are all back again.

As you had guessed, and you were right, I am now somewhere in France having come over here some time ago. It's rough but could be a lot worse I expect. For the first three weeks we lived on K-rations which, if you know anything about army rations, aren't very much. They consist of a little can of either cheese, egg, or meat, a few dog-biscuits—we call them that because they are so hard—either a fruit or chocolate bar and either powdered coffee or lemon juice. However, now we are getting dehydrated vegetables, canned meats and once in a while white bread. On the whole we are getting just about the same as we got in England.

I was in the hospital for a few days before I left England and thought I would miss the boat over here but luckily I rejoined my outfit a week before D-Day.

The majority of people over here had given up all hope of us ever coming over, but now that we are here they really are thankful. They are very friendly and say to us, "Yanks give, Germans take," whenever we give them candy and other things. However, we don't get too friendly with them and still trust no one.

The people are very poor and seem to have nothing. They are lots worse off than the people of England. Their towns are all beaten up, but they are quickly trying to fix them up, and those we have taken are lots brighter looking now than when we first came. Myself and the boys are trying to pick up some French so we can talk a little to the civilians, but I'm not having much luck progressing. I haven't talked very much to a civilian since I left England. Before we came over the army gave us French books with all the more necessary phrases so everywhere I go my little book goes along too.

Well, I'll have to close now as it's almost time for the movies to start, and I always try to get to them. We have them every two or three days; that is, if the projector doesn't break down. So far it hasn't worked very well. Whenever we are off we can go to the movies and although we have seen most of the movies way back when, we still go in order to have something to do.

     Sincerely yours,
     W. Harold Kennedy ['42; Age 21]

1. Latin master Harlan Parker was also the school's admissions director.

          Ft. Robinson, Nebraska
          July 15, 1944

Dear Dr. Hayden,

Have just finished reading the *Alumni Record* for June '44 and, needless to say, was pleased to catch up on the latest information "along College Street" and from the boys in the service.

. . . I came to Ft. Robinson to train War Dogs and have been here ever since the first of December. If you recall the Dogs for Defense program we had in the gym in the spring of 1943, you have a vague idea of the work I am doing. It's not easy, as a dog has no real brain and only learns by doing the same thing over and over again until he has it in memory. It's funny—no brain but a strong memory. One learns to control himself and have the utmost of patience—for a dog is no machine and learns only after weary hours of repetition.

. . . The army has been an education money can't buy—and one that I hope the next generation won't have to encounter. . . . My very best regards to all of you,

     Sincerely,
     Louis Whitaker ['43; Age 19]

Camp Shelby, Mississippi
July 16, 1944

Dear Dr. Hayden,

I read the "Alumni bull" bulletin with great relish, and it reminded me of my long overdue letter to you.

Naturally I was delighted to hear that things are going so well at Reserve, and I was particularly pleased to learn of the whereabouts and doings of some of my classmates.

I haven't run into Ray Dinsmore ['43] here, but that is only natural in so large a camp, though I have met up with two Williams men. My platoon leader and a man in my section are from Cleveland and know Reserve. . . . My news from Johnny Seaman is frequent and good, and we look forward to happy days together at Williams after the war. I would greatly appreciate any news or addresses of any of my classmates.

I enjoy my work in communications as much as one can enjoy any job in the army. At present I am a code clerk in the message center, and acting assistant section chief. The work is very interesting, and not arduous. Our outfit is tops, and the men are a swell bunch. I have been turned in for corporal twice, but a rating seems out of the question because of the freezing of all ratings.

I am more and more amazed and disgusted by the isolationism and anti-British sentiment which seems to be rampant around here. I didn't realize that it was possible, after all that we have been through, that intelligent (and unintelligent) people could consider America's playing the ostrich again, or feel that we have been sucked into fighting Europe's wars for her, or what do a lot of Chinese matter to us. My sergeant told me tonight that his only objection to Germany's attempt to rule Europe was the means employed to gain the commendable end of unifying Europe. Between this and the "Negro question," I seem to be in arguments half of my free time. "Christians" act as if they thought Christ died on the cross for whites only. I boil. . . .

    Faithfully yours,
    Paul R. Barstow ['43; Age 18]

August 17, 1944

Dear Dr. Hayden,

Thank you so much for your birthday greeting which I received a couple of days ago. It is always a pleasure to hear from you and to be reminded of my brief days at WRA.

At present, I am located in Italy. Contrary to many, I think, I have so far enjoyed the experience and have reveled in the chance to see some of the world. However, we will all be glad to get back to the wives and families. This thing has gone about far enough, and we believe it to be about time to deliver the anticipated knock-out blow.

To date, I haven't had the good fortune to run into any of the old classmates, but it does happen everyday and I wouldn't be a bit surprised if I should. As I look at that above statement, it isn't really accurate as I did run into Hugh Bell ['37] (no relation) in Africa. He was looking fine and seemed to be thriving in the navy. . . . Thank you again for your card.

      Best regards,
      Lawrence Bell ['36x; Age 25]

          U.S. Naval Air Station
          Peru, Indiana
          August 17, 1944

Dear Dr. Hayden,

I wish I had written you much sooner than this late date, for it was such a long time ago that you sent me your nice birthday note back in February, when I was at Colgate. I appreciated your remembering me very much, even though I am just now thanking you.

. . . I am not actively flying here at Peru yet, but am waiting until a new class starts. Frankly, the navy simply does not want any more pilots—and they have been and still are, cutting down in their V-5 cadet program very drastically. The wash-out rate is extremely high, and the morale of the cadets is at rock-bottom because there is absolutely no incentive left. The program is so long and drawn-out—about eight or nine more months for me—and I've been in it (V-5) since November 1943. Fellows are quitting every day—we are frankly told that the chances are against our ever getting through. However, I won't quit. I'll stay in as long as I can, but nothing is certain—nothing. I only hope that this war will be over soon—that's what we all hope. . . .

      Sincerely yours,
      Worcester Seely ['41; Age 20]

          Somewhere in the U.S.A.
          August 23, 1944

Dear Dr. Hayden,

Was so good to get your birthday greeting. It does mean a lot to me that Reserve keeps up with her alumni—am so glad you do. Will be a long time before I see you again, as we will be going overseas in the not too far distant future, but my best wishes will be with you. . . . I keep up a correspondence bull session on all and sundry—but mainly on theory of culture and society—with Norman Rich ['38]. You remember him—roomed with him my junior year.

... It is with great interest that I am following the doings at Dumbarton Oaks, for I agree heartily with Sumner Welles that it is of supreme importance that a working international executive council be set up at this time as a basis for a peace time world commonwealth. Hope you are stressing the importance of and means of a free world commonwealth at Reserve. It is of the essence of both national and world citizenship.

    Sincerely,
    John Ashton ['38; Age 24]

                August 31, 1944

Dear Don [W. D. Richards, '39],

 ... Two weeks from today we shall be getting ready to receive two hundred and twenty boys for the opening of another school year. Some members of the faculty are already back. There will be five new men on the staff. Mr. Mears and Mr. Worthen both received their commissions. Mr. Shepard will take a year's leave of absence. Mr. Wilson[1] goes to Peddie School and Mr. Eaton to the Asheville School in North Carolina. Mr. Waring, who has been in the ambulance service for two years in Africa and Syria, is returning to take up his work again.

 I was sorry to miss seeing you when you were here. I have no idea where you may be when this letter reaches you, for the boys are being moved so frequently now. However, I know that wherever you are you will be rendering splendid service. That is the only kind of service you are acquainted with, for you demonstrated that while with us.

    Very sincerely,
    Harlan N. Wood

1. Donald E. Wilson (History, Publications 1942–44).

THE SCHOOL YEAR 1944–45
The Greatest Loss

Fall Term: September–December 1944

The news of victories on the war front during the summer was encouraging and hopeful. The elation following the liberation of France, however, was overshadowed by news of the death of five more Academy boys.

Dan Hanna ('41x) confirmed killed in action in France; Bill Heyman ('38), killed during the D day invasion; Devin Gilchrist ('40), assumed killed in action in New Guinea; Rod Gillis ('42x), killed in action in France. After surviving heavy action both in Sicily and at the Anzio Beachhead, Neil McPhail ('33) died in France in an airplane crash while training a new pilot. As of November 1944, the Gold Stars on the Service Roll of Honor numbered twenty.

Dr. Hayden's earlier desire to "keep the core of affectionate loyalty going" continued through his correspondence to the alumni. Dean Emeritus Wood, now relieved of his teaching and administrative duties, joined in sending out the birthday greetings to the boys around the world and responding to the letters that arrived on an almost daily basis. He also shared in the melancholy task of sending letters of condolence to the parents of the boys who had been lost. He continued his involvement with the overseeing of the Alumni Scholarship Fund, acting as treasurer. English and history master J. Fred Waring returned to the school after a two-year absence. Five new masters joined the faculty for the duration.

As part of the fall athletic schedule, 108 boys raked and piled leaves to be burned. Thirty-five boys volunteered to help local growers pick the apple harvest. The machine shop underwent a reconversion program and for the first time in three years was used for the production of peacetime materials. However, the machine shop was still listed as a "war activity." In December Mr. Tepper recruited some twenty volunteers to work with him on the revitalization of the Faculty Garden on the corner of College and High Streets. Their assignment during the winter months in the shop included the creation of several garden ornaments designed by Tepper.

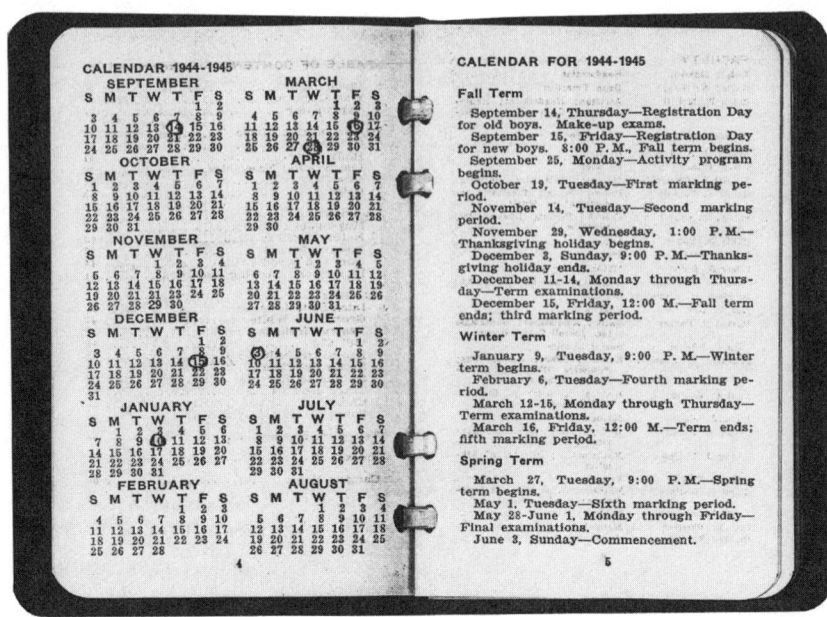

School calendar 1944–45. *Student Handbook*

On October 20, U.S. forces landed on Leyte in the Philippines, fulfilling MacArthur's 1942 promise to return. On November 7, President Roosevelt was elected to his fourth term in office. The Germans launched the massive counteroffensive in the Ardennes, known as the Battle of the Bulge, on December 16. Close to seventy-seven thousand Americans were casualties in the fighting that continued through mid-January.

Dr. Hayden's message in the November 1944 *Alumni Record* included excerpts from some of the letters he had been receiving. Quoted was a letter from Bill Danforth, who was "somewhere in the South Pacific." "When we are not talking about going home, we occasionally discuss postwar problems heatedly," he said.

> Our biggest worry is how to avoid the apathy that afflicted the country before this war, how to keep foremost the attitude which must prevail amongst a people in order to avoid the conditions which made war possible. Unless we have a sound attitude toward other nations and peoples, we shan't be very good at administering peace. A peace-by-force is only temporary and must be superseded by one which at least aims toward liberty and justice for all. Most of our arguments end on the note of education: without a sound background we can never expect our citizens to know what is right and what is wrong.

Bill Danforth ('34) with his bomber in the Southwest Pacific, September 1944. Alumni Record *Fall 1976*

Bill was a marine dive bomber pilot. He returned to his alma mater in 1951 as history teacher, swim coach, and housemaster, and served the school as alumni secretary until his retirement in 1976.

Mr. McGill's message in the same issue of the *Alumni Record* reflected on the past two years, noting, "It is an anomalous thing in a way, that the war by scattering the school family so widely has also brought it closer together." The greeting from Harlan Wood ended with the hope that "it may not be necessary to address future messages to you on the field of battle or in training camps where you are training for war. Meanwhile, all Reserve is with you."

Ft. Belvoir, Virginia
September 3, 1944

Dear Dr. Hayden,

I want to thank you for your card on my birthday. It helped to tie me back in with the Academy. I'm afraid I've lost some contact. Though today that is unavoidable, nevertheless it is a regret.

. . . With the tempo of the war accelerating as it is, we wonder just where we will be used if and when we finally make it through this ordeal and receive our commissions.

With the military situation becoming more encouraging it is likely that Reserve will be less affected by the draft. I hope that becomes the case.

R. Bruce Silver ['41; Age 21]

R. Bruce Silver ('41).
Courtesy R. Bruce Silver

> Rapid City, South Dakota
> September 8, 1944

Dear Dr. Hayden,

. . . I often think of you and the good times that were had at the Academy. I have only run into a couple fellows I knew at the Academy since I left, but have met other people who knew several of the boys.

. . . We have finished our training in the States and are ready for combat. Although most of our preparation has been for the European theater, it seems likely we would be sent to the Pacific. The last we knew there were no B-17's in that area, so we're making many guesses. I am certainly thankful for the training I had with you at Reserve. I think it will help me to keep my equilibrium wherever I go. . . .

> Chuck Kennedy ['40; Age 24]

On August 25 the German commandant had surrendered to French general Jacques LeClerc, officially freeing Paris. Two weeks later George Manlove ('32) wrote to his mother describing the great Liberation Parade that followed on August 26.

> Belgium
> September 8, 1944

Dear Mother:

For the first day in several weeks we didn't move today. We are quite comfortably set in a small Belgian hamlet with hills on all sides. All day the men have been cleaning guns and rifles, bathing in the creek, and boiling clothes. Also, since it's the first day we have seen the sun in five days, blankets and clothes are all out in the open drying, and a steady stream of planes—both heavies and fighters—has been going over-head since daylight this morning. Several mornings ago, about five, while it was still dark, I was awakened by the strangest sound, like an outboard motor that might fail any minute. Soon overhead, not three hundred feet and moving slowly, came a bevy of flying bombs. They had lights in the back as though someone had hung lanterns on them. I guess they must have been on their way to England.

Two weeks ago Barney, who is the battery commander, and Dave, who is the reconnaissance officer and I got unexpectedly into Paris. We weren't the first Americans there, but there were very few before us. We were about thirty miles to the southwest and heard over the radio the night before that General Le Clerc's army had gone in, so we took off, hoping at least to get a look at it from the distance, but the nearer we got the more enticing it got. Signposts read: "Paris 10 Kilometres," then "6 Kilometres," then three and so on. The highway leading in was flat and wide and crowded with people making their way towards the city, some on foot, some pushing baby carriages full of their belongings. Hundreds of them riding bicycles—it looked like a six day bike race. These we passed, then auto-tank guns, tank destroyers, and tanks, French tanks with the names of French cities on them. Finally, when things got rather crowded, we stopped to ask a tank driver where Paris was and he called back "You're in Paris" and held up his two fingers to form a "V".

Another half mile and we entered the city proper, through the Porte d'Orleans, then came to the Seine with the famous magazine racks, across the bridge and headed for the first familiar land-mark—Notre Dame Cathedral. There, a huge crowd had gathered to hear DeGaulle.

The tanks and tank destroyers were coming up on line. The B.B.C. was running wire from a large truck and everywhere people were excited. We stopped, hoping to watch the proceedings, but we were soon mobbed. People cheered, came up to touch us. All through the crowd we could hear them murmur "Americans! Americans!" They shook hands; women old and young, children, came up and insisted on kissing us on both cheeks. "Thank you, thank you for coming!" and "We have waited so long!" they kept repeating over and over. Old people came up who had lost sons, wives whose husbands were prisoners, many with tears in their eyes.

At first we joined in the spirit of the day—we waved, we answered back, we autographed blank pieces of paper; we kissed children, hundreds of them, and women, thousands of them, and we answered their questions. "Where did we live? Where were the English? Would the war soon be over? When would food arrive?" They had not eaten for three days. "Did we

Buildings that housed snipers were destroyed and burned. The Grande Palais was still smoking, destroyed completely by the Germans. Everywhere small bands of men roamed the streets; each band had about a dozen, a leader, tri-colored arm bands; the men were armed with small rifles, little pistols, German hand grenades, clubs, anything. Some groups had uniforms, others had distinguishing berets, green or blue, some had white suits on; each store, each factory seemed to have outfitted its employees with some sort of uniform.

The men were all thin and haggard looking, shirts were torn, some had bloody bandages around their heads or arms. They had knives stuck in their belts. People cheered them wherever they went. The French Revolution must have looked something like this. That was the grand thing about the freeing of Paris. It came from the inside. The people rose up.

I talked with a policeman and told him that I had heard of the good work of the police over the radio the night before. He took me to the station, introduced me to all the Gendarmerie and a band of Patriots. They had German guns, grenades, ammunition; the street was completely barricaded. First the police had gone on a general strike, then the patriots arose; all Paris joined in. I met the underground leader of the district. He was small, about twenty-eight, and wore the uniform of a captain in the French Air Force. He told me of the fighting, how they had attacked a German convoy in the city; others told me of his bravery and his exploits.

I bought a French underground paper, called "D.F.," Defense de la France, founded and published on Bastille Day under enemy occupation, 14 July, 1941. This was the first day it had been sold openly on the newsstands. It summarized the military situation, it praised DeGaulle; it wanted the F.F.I., French Forces of Interior, to be on guard against snipers in the "Guerre des toits," which still was going on, and it warned every Frenchman to seek out the collaborators and fascists.

Between four and five, in front of Notre Dame, just as DeGaulle arrived, there was quite heavy sniper fire. Machine guns took up the challenge, hand grenades went off, the tanks fired. Soon this spread to all parts of the city. Police and patriots moved to points of advantage, the crowd moved for cover; people dropped to the ground and lay close to walls and the pavement for shelter and through it all, and past our jeep whisked DeGaulle, sitting rigidly in the back of an open car, still acknowledging the "Vive's" of the people. Several times we had to stop, wheel about, and retreat as streets were again scenes of small wars. Most of the shooting was the work of the fascists, "millinists", as the French call them. How anyone could have fired from the roof tops, at DeGaulle, or at the patriots, or into the crowds in Paris on that day, I shall never be able to understand. Statues all were heaped with flowers, all buildings were covered with flags, French and American, English and Russian.

"Where did all the American flags come from?" I asked. "We have been saving them four years for this day" came the answer.

Everywhere people tried to get us to come to their homes; they pushed champagne and cognac and wine into our jeep; they stared at our equipment, they put out their hands and touched the jeep reverently and kept saying over and over, "Merci! Merci!"

Towards evening the sniping increased; from all sides came the reports of small arms fire, as little bands of the F.F.I. began to gather to cope with it. So we headed out the Porte d'Orleans and toward our bivouac area.

That afternoon in Paris was the brightest day of my two and a half years away from home. So many people have been concerned trying to define what we are fighting for. I wish they could have been in Paris on the 26 of August.

   Love,
   George [Age 30]

       Somewhere in the Pacific
       September 9, 1944

Dear Dr. and Mrs. Hayden,

Your birthday card and note really came close to hitting the right date. It arrived this morning and my answer will be mailed on my birthday.

Since you last heard from me, my last letter to Reserve must have been six months ago to "Scotch." I have been in the landings in the Marshalls, Saipan, and Tinian. At present I am at a "rest" camp, and anxious to stop resting and get this war over with so that I can get back to my family, and so I can start living again.

I can well imagine how Jean feels having her husband leave her with such a young baby. When he returns home, the baby will have grown into a child. I am missing most of that myself, having to watch the transition through the written words of [my wife] Bea, and the pictures she sends. And I can look forward to having to educate my son into believing that I am his father.

I do have the consolation, though, that I am here doing my bit to provide him with a better world than the one into which he was born. I certainly hope that our statesmen and those of Russia and Britain—I am not afraid of those of China—sincerely endeavor to build a lasting peace, a peace worth the five thousand lives spent for a Mid-Pacific piece of volcanic rock, a bar fifteen miles long and four wide, and the many thousands more on other battlefields. It was no fun to walk past those rows of white crosses and then to look up to see the worthless piece of land they died taking.

Yes, they died, making it possible to advance further over the thousands of miles of water, but the advance made that way can be lost again thirty or forty or more years hence if the peace and the real victory is not properly outlined and set up at the conference table in the months and years to come.

I am sorry for this bit of cynicism, but that is the mood that you catch me in tonight.

Sincerely,
George [Vradenburg, Jr., '37; Age 25]

P.S. . . . You have no idea how much I would like to drop back to Hudson and sit in those chapel seats I pretended to hate; to count checks and get money for Wally; to run errands for Mrs. Cromwell [McGill], and to run just one perfect movie in the gym; or even just to sit in the Chapel, close my eyes, and feel that bit of Utopia that is Western Reserve close over me.

. . . If you have any jobs lying around loose let me know, because I am one of those homeless birds who hasn't a job to return to when this is over. And I am also one of those dissatisfied birds who is not happiest when he is actively serving his country.

Somewhere in Europe
September 10, 1944

Dear Dr. Hayden,

It certainly was nice that you were able to get away for such a swell vacation with your daughter and your grandchild. Here it takes a long time now for our mail to reach us, because we are moving so fast that it is very difficult for the APO's [Army Post Office address] to keep up with us.

We got some time off awhile ago and I was able to take my men to visit some of the larger towns here, and it was the finest morale builder ever. It surprised me because I thought the people would be starving and dressed very poorly, but they were all healthy and dressed beautifully—I have never seen anything to match it. It gave the boys something to talk about all their lives, and if they keep up at the rate they are going now they will talk about nothing else.

Sincerely yours,
Harvey [Tanner, '38; Age 24]

September 12, 1944

Dear Bruce [Silver]:

. . . Hang onto your opportunity at Ft. Belvoir because I think you've got what it takes in this engineering field and I am perfectly sure that you can qualify for your commission. You are absolutely right about the war's tempo. We can't tell "what the heck" at the moment, but right here at Reserve we have our regular job to do and you know what that means well enough to read everything you want to between the lines and what you read will be absolutely correct.

. . . Fred Waring's back and, oh boy, does he look good to us! If you get a chance, drop him a line, Bruce; it will do him good. As a matter of fact, it's a liberal education to talk to Fred about the Near East, the Moslem world, the French and British varying points of view on the Near East.

Dr. Hayden's son, Joel, Jr. ('39); his daughter, Jean Hayden Guarnaccia; and Mr. Tepper's son Herbert ('39), 1944. The three grew up together on the Academy campus. *Courtesy Herbert Tepper*

Dr. Hayden and his granddaughter, Gina. *Archives*

He's got a grasp on the situation that is remarkable but you know how sensitive and keen he is and when I say that he's got an unusual grip on matters, you know just what I mean.

I understand that [your brother] Dick is out on Saipan; a nice quiet place for a summer and fall holiday! Joel, Jr. is at San Diego, Amphibious Division of the navy, being trained to handle combat ships with infantry and marine detachments. Now that's just guess-work on my part from the vague insinuations of his all too infrequent letters. He can't say much; therefore, he doesn't write much; therefore, he thinks it isn't necessary to write much, but that's no news to you.

If there is anything you want me to remember and think about as [your brother] Stu ['45] enters his last year, just drop me a line. Our collective best from the Haydens and the school.

Joel B. Hayden

The first vesper service of the year was held on September 17. Dr. Hayden's talk "called upon all the new boys to find their places in the daily life of the school and begin their contributions as sons of Western Reserve." The new bell was dedicated and tolled at the conclusion of the service with the prayer that it "might ring for many years over a world of peace and concord." Dr.

Hayden used Alfred L. Rideout's letter written shortly after D day, dated June 13, 1944, and quotes from George Vradenburg's recent letter as the basis for his talk. In the days following he wrote to the boys describing the "new-old" bell.

September 18, 1944

Dear George [Vradenburg]:

What do you suppose happened to your letter which was written on 9 September, the very day which is the only natal day which you possess? Well, I got it on Saturday and on Sunday at our first vesper services at 5 P.M. at the old Chapel I quoted some of your final paragraph in the P.P.S., the paragraph about Chapel and "Wallie" and "Scotch" and the business concerning what you called the bit of Utopia that is Western Reserve Academy. Being a good naval man, your figure of speech is entirely of the deep blue sea; you spoke of the whole thing "closing over you." Well, you're in the *Record* now—you and Lester Rideout.

He wrote a beautiful letter concerning the school and the Chapel on 13 June. About an hour before he joined his formation to fly over Normandy on D-Day, he was handed a letter—an invitation to commencement, etc., and the receipt of such a letter of invitation impressed him so that his answer is an imponderable one, just as your birthday letter was an imponderable one.

We dedicated a new bell in the Chapel tower yesterday. The old bell, in service ninety-one years, is badly cracked and the bell which used to be in the water tower at Evamere and which was "founded" in 1611, now calls us to our place of meeting and worship. We dedicated it yesterday; it rang for the first time, and the quotation from your letter is in the dedication service. From the 9th of September in your remote spot to the 17th of September in the Reserve Chapel may represent a great space geographically and quite a space in time, but the spiritual hook-up was incident, I can assure you that.

. . . Two hundred fourteen boys; full faculty with some new blood which looks very good; ten old faculty members 'round the world in service; Fred Waring home again, bless him; Dean Wood, our senior master, unusually well; Mickel, the new Dean; "Scotch," exactly the same if not more so; Mr. Eaton gone to Asheville, and Raymond Burns' best man [Franklyn S. Reardon], a Colgate graduate, now teaching English, running the *Record* and heading the Athenaeum—and so it goes. . . .

                Devotedly yours,
                Joel B. Hayden

The front page of the September 21 *Record* carried Lester Rideout's letter, along with the news of the death of Dan Hanna III ('41x). A *Fortress* pilot, he was believed to have been returning from action in France on May 12. His death was confirmed on September 10.

Daniel R. Hanna ('41x). *Archives*

William H. Heyman ('38). *Archives*

The September 28 issue noted that Bill Heyman was killed at Normandy on June 8; his parents received the confirmation the week of September 21. Dr. Hayden presided over the memorial service held at the Plymouth Church in Cleveland. After the service Bill's mother wrote in a note of gratitude, "How fitting that you were the one to conduct the service for Bill rather than a stranger to him, for you knew him and had him in your charge for three years." Three days later Bill's father sent his thoughts to the headmaster. "While most of those in the congregation present were strangers to us, it made us feel that we are not alone in our sorrow. They stood up with us, and I noticed that the eyes of many were moist, indicating a sympathetic understanding of a loss felt by them as well as by us. People, even strangers are good when you get right down to it and have time to think about really important things."

San Diego, California
Fall 1944

Dear Dr. Hayden,

I was so delighted and touched by your birthday greeting. To think that of the thousands of Reservites, worthy men that you have started on their road with a smile and warm hand, you should think of me. Honestly, Doctor, I could scarcely contain myself for the joy and presence of the goodness in life.

It's not that there is a rareness of it during this war. Actually aboard my ship—I call it my ship but it really isn't; I'm only executive officer (the skipper's right and left hand man)—the warmth of life's problems and passions are constantly brought before me. I hear their stories and laugh

Bernie Tolan ('40) and his fiancée, Marilyn, at his graduation from Williams College. *Courtesy Bernie Tolan*

and cry with them. And, Dr. Hayden, though society would never acquit them for their actions, the men are not bad—they are good. Of course there are exceptions and that's what makes life interesting. . . .
     Bernie [Tolan, '40; Age 23]

             Peru, Indiana
             October 4, 1944

Dear Dr. Hayden,
 . . . At last I have begun active flight training again—have been doing so for the past three weeks. It's great fun and I love it—but the program is still a very tough one—any way you look at it. At the present, about half of our complement are British cadets. They're a good bunch of boys, and I find it very interesting to talk to them and get some of their ideas.
 . . . Mother wrote me last week and mentioned Dan Hanna's death. He was a flyer in the AAF. I'm very grieved to hear of that, for I knew Dan very well. He was a year ahead of me both at Hawken and at WRA. I remember meeting him one day in June '43 in downtown Cleveland in front of the Union Club. He had just come from enlisting in the Air Corps, and the finger print ink was still on his fingers. The tragedy of war is beginning to fall on America—and the only way to obtain peace in one's mind is by faith and prayer. . . .
     Yours sincerely,
     Worcester Seely ['41; Age 20]

 Nine sons of faculty members were serving in the military. The *Record* listed each of them along with their branch of service and general location in the October 5 issue. The following week four more names of faculty sons were added.

A letter from Blaine Rawdon, Jr. ('42), who was serving with the army in France, was later used as a basis for one of Dr. Hayden's chapel talks. Later in the month an excerpt from his letter to his close friend and classmate Lewis Ball would have quite a different tone.

Somewhere in France
October 6, 1944

Dear Dr. Hayden,

Today I suddenly realized that I have not written you in an extremely long time and I am ashamed of my neglect. My thoughts turned towards Reserve, possibly because I haven't been quite so occupied with war in the last few days and Reserve is the direct opposite of war—Reserve is heaven and war hell!

I hope that the war hasn't changed Reserve too much either internally or externally. For me it remains as the most pleasant experience of my life and I don't want to see it change. In that respect I'm a reactionary. There is very little I care to say about this experience. It is wholly distasteful. But I, and I'm sure all the others, are trying to do as good a job and as quick a job as possible.

I feel that I have been extremely fortunate since we have been in combat for a month now and I have not had a scratch. In spite of the seeming ease with which we have sped through France this has been a costly, sickening advance. Of course, this side of the war is not plastered across the front page, but there are many who have fallen and who will not rise again. It seems to us, from the news that we hear that America doesn't realize this. We hear that in the States it is all over. Maybe that is so, but still I thank God everyday that I am alive. I have come too close to being "past-tense" to think that it is all over. Enough war talk. . . .

Blaine [Age 20]

In the process of locating relatives of the deceased correspondents during the summer of 1997, I received a copy of a letter sent to the mother of Devin H. Gilchrist. It is used in this collection with his sister Ann's permission and describes the circumstances surrounding Devin's disappearance on December 26, 1943.

36th Fighter Squadron, 8th Group
APO 926
October 8, 1944

Dear Mrs. Gilchrist,

This is a letter begun in March of this year. Today, much to my distress, I came upon the nearly completed letter deep among my personal effects. The squadron moved to a new base sometime in March and it must have been the attending confusion which caused me to pack it away so deeply. Since it was not among my writing materials, the move once completed, I was under the impression that I had sent the letter. . . .

March 1944

I have purposely delayed writing this letter in the hope that I would be able to announce a more hopeful situation, but the weeks have gone by with no new developments and I know I must write now.

The official squadron account of the circumstances under which Devin was reported missing did not, I am sure, give you much idea of exactly what did happen. I think I can describe to you the situation in clearer detail and still observe the strict limitations set by the censor.

Devin was flying my wing, we making the second of two elements in a four ship flight. The squadron was providing air cover for a beach-head (Cape Gloucester, New Britain) and enemy dive bombers and fighters were reported in the vicinity. An attack was imminent. Our flight leader made a sharp turn to the right, Devin and I following, but Devin necessarily falling in behind me in order to be able to keep up. In that position I could not easily observe him. The order to drop our jettisonable auxiliary gas tanks was given by the squadron leader. As soon as the flight straightened out I looked for Devin on my wing, but as he had not regained his position I maneuvered about and saw him just below and behind me in level flight, but losing altitude.

I left the formation and circled about him to provide protection, as now the "Nips" had been engaged about us and a few were actually in sight. I saw Devin's motor conk out, characterized by the usual couple of tiny black puffs of smoke from the exhaust, but there was no fire and the plane itself appeared undamaged. He was headed for the shore about four miles distant.

When still about three miles from the beach he rolled his ship over and bailed out, making a beautiful delayed jump into the water. His parachute opened at about 1500 feet and he landed in the water without being molested by any marauding "Nip" fighters. I observed his plane to crash and burn about a mile from him. I circled low until I was reasonably sure that he had inflated his life vest and saw that a friendly naval launch had put out for him from a nearby bay. Then I climbed to join combat.

Fifteen minutes later I was overhead to check and see if he had been picked up. The boat was still about a half-mile from him and not headed directly for him, so I dropped low and buzzed back and forth over him in a crisscross pattern in order that the boat would be able to pin-point his position. I observed the launch to turn and head in his exact direction. When buzzing I flew quite close to him, about fifty feet away, and saw that his life vest was inflated and his head above water, but more than that I could not be sure of the speed I was going. I then climbed to a couple of thousand feet, made sure that the launch was headed directly towards him and about 300 yards distant, so I again climbed to join combat. Fifteen minutes later I left the area with the rest of the squadron and returned to our base.

That's all! Since then we have heard nothing. What could be more enigmatic? Arthur Heckerman, who was shot down in the same engagement, was picked up in the water and made his way back to the outfit in a couple of days, but as the days went by Devin did not return. Every effort was made to locate him through the Navy, landing forces and hospitals, but we are still as much in the dark as ever. It seems incredible to me, who thought to see him within a few days, that he did not show up and that we heard no reports of any kind, favorable or otherwise.

What actually did happen is yet a matter for conjecture: whether or not the failure of his plane was due to enemy action; whether or not he was injured before, during, or after parachuting; whether or not he was actually picked up (that he might not have been seems inconceivable to me), and if picked up, where he might have been taken.

The adjoining coastline is now in our hands, though at the time it was not, leaving us open to other conjectures. I am not one to offer hope where there is none, but so many escapes and rescues have been completed only after several months of struggle and evasion of the enemy through the wild and exceedingly difficult terrain that there is always the long chance that a missing man may turn up. A man hiding there may even have to remain in enemy controlled territory until our troops have advanced their position to him. Frankly, in Devin's case I hold no hope in this direction.

October 8, 1944

This is evidently as far as I got in March. Since then there have been no new developments in the situation. . . . If we were to learn anything more we should most certainly have heard by now. I myself have given up hope. . . .

Let me again say how deeply I regret that my original letter was not sent long ago. I am distressed that I could have been so negligent about such a thing. At the same time I hope that this letter may even now serve some of its original purpose: to help put your mind at rest regarding some of the elusive details of the situation, through which you have suffered so great a loss. I offer my sincere and heartfelt condolences. Though not a close personal friend of Devin, I knew and liked him for a fine, affable and reliable man, a capable pilot. As his element leader at the time I cannot

Devin H. Gilchrist ('40). *Archives*

help but feel some measure of responsibility, and at the same time, considering the circumstances, I think of nothing I could have done to better assure his rescue. Please accept my deepest sympathies and be assured of my desire to do anything I can, within my poor powers, for you in your bereavement.

      Most sincerely yours,
      Thomas R. Huff
      Capt., A.C.

An article in the October 12 *Record* contained the results of a schoolwide poll on the military and political views of the student body, complete with predictions of when the war would end. Seventy-five percent of the students favored Governor Thomas E. Dewey in the coming presidential election. "Practically everyone thought that Adolf Hitler would flee to Argentina, Sweden, or some other neutral country," the article stated. Some believed Hitler would commit suicide; others believed he would be taken prisoner. The general belief was that the war in Europe would be over by the end of 1944, and the war in the Pacific by the end of the following year.

      Germany
      October 19, 1944

Dear Dean Wood:

In February, 1941, I volunteered for service in the U.S. Army and became one of the many "G.I.s" at that time . . . in February 1942 I became a buck sergeant. . . . On September 28, 1942, I was married in Baltimore, Md. to,

Arthur J. Saalfield, Jr. ('38).
Courtesy Mrs. Arthur Saalfield

naturally, the most wonderful girl in the world and have lived happily, together or apart, forever after. On November 22, 1943 I became the proud father of a bouncing boy—he is absolutely the cutest baby I have ever seen. . . .

In May, 1944, I shipped overseas. . . . At the moment I am sitting in the midst of several thousand "Krauts" somewhere inside Germany, having left behind me the hedgerows of France, a prolonged period of isolation at Mertain, France, as a member of the "Lost Battalion", the friendly people of Belgium, the locale of the "House of Orange" in the Netherlands, and a number of badly mangled pillboxes here in Germany. Surprisingly, most of the German civilian population seems glad to see us arrive.

Everything is fine here at the front. When we aren't ducking, we keep "Jerry" ducking. In fact, a German prisoner told us the other day that when the British fired, the Germans duck, and vice-versa; but when the Americans fire, everybody ducks.

Seriously, after over three months of slugging it out toe to toe with "Jerry," I am still thankful that I don't hate the enemy as individuals or as a race. I do hate war, more each day. I sincerely hope that there are competent people back home doing a competent job of planning something that is far greater than this war; i.e., the peace that is to follow. I have been ever thankful for the high standards and religious background that Reserve offered me. I pray that the old Academy is still operating on that very same basis. . . . Many thanks once more for remembering me.

                    Most sincerely,
                    Arthur Saalfield ['38; Age 25]

October 19, 1944

Dear "Buckets" [Blaine Rawdon, Jr.]:

Have just read and thoroughly enjoyed your letter from France dated October 6. You certainly put it on the line in your description of your responsibility and the kind of job we are all trying to do. What you say has been confirmed over and over again from every boy who has been in there pitching. . . .

This whole business of trying to keep this school on an even keel so that it will be the same kind of place that you left is our main controlling motive and it always will be, I can assure you that. I like your definition: "Reserve is heaven and war is hell." That is a very effective summary.

And I like what you said about the mass indifference back here. The great difficulty is that we sit on bleachers and regard this as a world series somewhere down in the gas house gang's region! Well, it isn't! This is something beyond the comprehension of any one man or any one generation. We are all trying to survive; it is as simple as that, and when we do survive, we've got to learn that the old business of being at each others' throats, politically and economically, is simply and utterly a complete denial of the sacrifice of youth. It is a cynical partnership with the lazy, homicide technique. You fellows save America and America betrays you in utterly selfish cynicism. If we can't do a better job than that, we should be liquidated once and for all!

                Ever yours,
                Joel B. Hayden

In the spring of 1945, Blaine Rawdon's parents forwarded an excerpt from a letter he had written to Lewis Ball.

EXTRACT FROM LETTER WRITTEN FROM SOMEWHERE IN FRANCE
ON OCTOBER 22ND 1944 BY PFC BLAINE N. RAWDON TO A CLASSMATE

In my last letter I told you to start praying now. I hope you took my advice. Although you have had wonderful training in all respects you will get the biggest shock of your life the first time the lead starts flying. God is the strongest force in the world, Lew, and its kind of nice to have him to hang on to—and you'll need him, believe me. In every fight between "Jerry" and me there have been three guys, and I've had that Guy with me each time. I guess I sound like a preacher, Lew, I don't mean to, but I should have been hit a long time ago. Shrapnel has torn through my shell case and stopped when it hit the shell itself, ripped through my trousers, and bounced off my helmet. I know I alone am not that lucky. He was with me each time. Ask any "Joe" up here, or who has been up here about that guy upstairs. He'll tell you. . . .

This is just a side light before I close: You know that army (and navy) language is pretty rough. Well it gets rougher than ever when an attack is in progress, but of all the cuss words that are used, very, very, seldom do you ever hear the Lord's name used. Get back from the front a ways and you'll hear it—but not up there. When I slip, I think of it, and it bothers me, and the other guys will look at you as if to say "Asking for it, aren't ya? . . ."

U.S. Naval Air Station
Pensacola, Florida
October 24, 1944

My dear Mr. Wood,

I was so happy to receive your letter a few weeks ago which was forwarded to me down here at Pensacola. I've been down here now over two months and have just begun the final stage of my training. If everything goes well I should be able to get my wings in about three months, but that is a long way off; anything can happen!!

. . . What I wanted to tell you in this letter was how much I appreciated hearing from you and receiving the *Records* once again. I remember reading in one of them of how the choir sang "Jubilee" at vespers. It's a beautiful song; I often try to sing it myself, but then I think of how Jim Freeman ['42] used to sing it; he did it proud. Many other things in the *Record* bring back fond memories of a peaceful world, the kind of a world I hope to return to when this mess is over.

I hear from "Buckets" quite often. He is really seeing this war the hard way in France. I hope he comes out of it alright, for I don't think I've ever met a finer man. . . .

Sincerely,
Lewis Ball ['42; Age 20]

A column in the October 26th issue of the *Reserve Record* entitled "Keeping Up With The Masters" became a regular feature throughout the school year. The first to be profiled was history master Edward Caldwell, who was commissioned a lieutenant in the navy. Second in command of an LST, his craft participated in ten landings on the Normandy coast before being sent to the Mediterranean.

Four masters were profiled in November. History master Robert Morse received his commission in the navy and was assigned to the USS *Baltimore*; orchestra and band leader Charles Fehl was a first lieutenant in charge of the Air Force Band in Dayton, Ohio; and French and Spanish master W. W. Kirk was a lieutenant, junior grade, in the Naval Reserve in charge of a convalescent group in a North Carolina hospital. His duties included interviewing those recovering from fatigue and shell shock and counseling them on their post-discharge objectives. Religion and ethics master Raymond Burns had been an army chaplain in the Pacific until he contracted a serious tropical disease in New Guinea and had to return the United States for treatment.

Marvin Walker was serving somewhere in the Pacific as a lieutenant, junior grade, on the aircraft carrier USS *Nassau* as of January 1945. In February the column noted that word had not been received from former English master Francis Lindaman since October 1943; it was assumed he continued as director of the Red Cross in Pearl Harbor. History and English master Lt. (j.g.) E. Mark Worthen was awaiting embarkation for his next assignment—six months on a destroyer studying personnel problems and efficiency, and art teacher Charles Mears was an educational services officer in Hawaii.

There was no word of the location of faculty master Glenn King until January 1946, when he returned to his post with the music department. After two years of training in the United States, he had gone to Europe to join a unit, where he was in charge of supplies immediately behind the front lines in Normandy, across France and Belgium, and eventually into Germany. During the Battle of the Bulge he was within fifteen minutes of being captured by the Germans.

Neil McPhail's ('33) mother enclosed the following notice with a letter she sent to Dean Wood during the Thanksgiving holiday:

HEADQUARTERS 171ST FIELD ARTILLERY BATTALION
APO#45, c/o Postmaster, New York, N.Y.
October 27, 1944

My dear Mrs. McPhail:

By this time you have received formal notification of the death of your son, Neil McPhail, 01165912. There is probably very little that I can say to assuage the grief that this message brought, but it is my sincere hope that what I have to say will prove of help to you.

Neil was killed in action in Southern France on 30 August 1944, and was buried in the American cemetery in the same locality, being given an appropriate military burial, with a Protestant Chaplain officiating. The ceremony was conducted with all of the respect and honor due to one who has given his life for his country.

We who had known Neil so well were shocked and saddened by his death, even as you; it was hard to think of one who had been so full of life as no longer being with us. During the years that he was among us his sunny disposition and keen interest in his work made him a legion of friends and gained for him the respect and admiration of all with whom he came in contact. In spirit, Neil will always be with us, and the thought that he gave his life so bravely and unselfishly in the cause of democracy will make us proud that he was with us.

To you, Mrs. McPhail, all of the officers and enlisted men of the 171st Field Artillery Battalion join me in expressing our grief over the loss of such a fine comrade and soldier as Neil. His memory will be a spur to us as we continue our mission of defeating the enemy, and the resultant freedom in the world will be an imperishable monument to Neil and others who, like him, have lived and died as worthily.

> JOSEPH G. CATHEY
> Lt. Col. FA
> Comdg. 171st FA Bn

> Somewhere in Germany
> October 30, 1944

Dear Dr. Hayden:

... I never knew about Harry Allchin or Dan Hanna and Bill Heyman. That's just the way things come to pass by the Hand above us. I suppose you know that I would give my right arm to be back just for a day. I really expect to do just that, but not for eight or nine months will I be able to even start thinking about it.

I have hit a few rough spots over here, but nothing as bad as the infantry have to put up with day after day. Those boys can really take it. Our food is not bad considering the place and the long supply lines.

People at home, so we hear, seem to think that this terrible struggle is over. And we don't blame them much when the government starts to sell war plants. I know they are probably not necessary anymore, but I also happen to have seen what effects their sale has on an unthinking public. They leap before they sit down and rationalize things. This I suppose is part of the so-called war nerves. This may all sound like so much bosh to you, but it is the general trend of things over here. The fellows in general are getting to the point of sarcastic pity for short sightedness of some people back there.

I should apologize for this preceding paragraph, I imagine, but I won't, for it is true—every word. ...

> Your Ex-Reservite,
> [J.] Led Miller ['42x; Age 21]

A handwritten note from Mr. Wood informed Dr. Hayden that Rod Gillis ('42x) was reported as killed in action over France on October 8, 1944. He had entered the Academy as a sub-freshman in 1937 and left at the end of his sophomore year in 1940. Dr. Hayden wrote a note of condolence to Rod's parents.

> November 1, 1944

My dear Mr. and Mrs. Gillis:

Monday noon a little newspaper clipping was put into my hands. That is the first that any of us knew about Rod.

We, here, were devoted to Rod. During the three happy years together, his smile and his good cheer and his enthusiasm formed sort of a campus tonic for some of us older folk who caught the spirit of the boy and cherished it.

It is not possible to think of him as gone. We did not know about Margaret, his wife, and, through you, we want to send her our love and our very deep sympathy. Getting in touch with Macedonia [Ohio], I found out that you were gone to New York City so I am sending this letter by way of Macedonia that it may follow you and meet you somewhere, assuring you of our understanding love and our continuing sympathy. I am speaking for the whole school, old and young.

Devotedly yours,
Joel B. Hayden

When the news came to the school that Alan A. Moore ('39x), believed to be missing, was found to be a prisoner of war, Dr. Hayden shared his feelings with his parents.

November 2, 1944

My dear Dr. and Mrs. Moore:

We were so delighted to get word that Alan is no longer missing, but found! Of course, it is not easy for anybody to think of their loved ones in a German camp, but he's living and relatively safe, and that is something to warm our hearts. We think of him and of you often. Mr. Wood and I had a little visit about Alan just the other day and here we are with definite news. That is wonderful! . . . Please call on us for anything we can do at any time.

Very sincerely yours,
Joel B. Hayden

A Thanksgiving message from Dean Mickel appeared in the November 16 issue of the *Record*. The long-awaited free day, it was announced, would be "tacked on the end of Thanksgiving vacation." This term's free day was an acknowledgment of the "marvelous school spirit displayed at the U.S.–Reserve rivalry" and honored three alumni who had excellent records in college: Brad Wells ('44) at Princeton; Tony Smith ('44) at Harvard, and Tien Wei Yang ('41) at Oberlin.

During the Thanksgiving holiday Mr. Wood received a letter from Mrs. McPhail about her son Neil, stating that she had received a telegram from the War Department the latter part of September saying that Neil was missing in action in Southern France. Later a message came that confirmed his death in action on August 30, just two weeks after he had been transferred from the Fifth Army in Italy to the Seventh Army in France. He would have been thirty years old on September 16. Mrs. McPhail asked to be remembered to Dr. Hayden and said, "I am sure he too will regret to hear of Neil, as he took such an interest in all his boys."

November 28, 1944

Dear Mr. Kelsey:

It is our earnest desire to keep in as close touch as possible with all our graduates and former students.

A report has come to me that Edward [W. Kelsey III, '40x] was reported as lost in action. This report is unconfirmed and we sincerely hope that it is not true. I am, therefore, writing to ask if you will inform us as to the facts.

Our Roll of Honor now numbers over 500 and as I have already said, we desire to keep in close contact with our boys and be of any possible service to them and to their parents. I shall appreciate very deeply some word from you.

Very sincerely yours,
Harlan N. Wood

The rumor was true. Mr. Kelsey sent a short note on December 13 with confirmation of Ed's death on March 10, 1943. A private in the Marine Corps, he was killed in an accident in New Zealand.

Somewhere in the Pacific
November 30, 1944

Dear Dr. Hayden,

. . . I rather shudder to think of the many Reservites who heard my words about the Utopia that is Reserve. Those who are on the campus, completely surrounded by security and safety, often lose sight of the very thing that makes them so secure. And so a "doddering old alumnus" just doesn't understand all of the trials and tribulations caused by clanging bells, and yelling teachers, and restrictions. Of course, I'm not old, and I know that I am not doddering, although I am often dodging both bullets and problems, but I do remember how I used to hate to crawl out of those sheets when the reveille bell rang. Now I wish I could get back into those sheets, so that I could have some sheets to crawl out of.

At present I am sleeping on a thin pad, with nothing but a couple of Marine Corps blankets, the same pad that I slept on through the Marshalls and Saipan campaign. Unfortunately it is still all there, even though pretty filthy, so that I cannot survey it. Even so, I consider myself pretty lucky, because I know some of my friends who do not have a cot to sleep on. I am one of the select few who has not only a cot to sleep on, but something even better—a steel cot with real honest to goodness wire mesh stretched on springs.

. . . Gosh, but I wish that I could see "Scotch" again, and have him make me eat my asparagus; see Mr. Mickel and have him show me, with those short legs of his, how to make a good corner kick; see Mr. Roundy and have him bawl me out for that awful center shot I made; see Wally and have him send me to the bank for the morning money; see Mrs. Cromwell—excuse me, Mrs. McGill—and have her send me to the post office with $50,000 in endorsed checks and not tell me what is in the package; see Cutler, North Hall, the Gym, and a one-sided game of handball with "Scotch." Oh well, there are a lot of other compensations for living and fighting—a wife, and a swell son—wonderful parents, swell in-laws, and many friends.

      Sincerely yours,
      George [Vradenburg, '37; Age 25]

Jack Mooney ('43x), who was training for radio school at the U.S. Naval Training Center in Bainbridge, Maryland, encountered two former schoolmates within twenty-four hours. He was sitting in his barracks one evening, when in walked Rudy Rakowsky ('44). "I just about fainted, I was so surprised," he said in his letter. Rudy had been in the army and was transferred to the navy. He was attending the Naval Academy prep school in Bainbridge with plans to enter Annapolis in June. "I was sure glad to see him," Jack wrote.

The next day he had just finished dinner and decided to play a little football. He noticed a game going on in the field next to his barracks and went over to join in. "Well you can imagine how I felt when I saw [Irven] "Whitey" Hissom ['43] down on the ground just like he used to be at Reserve." Jack and Whitey were teammates on the football field at Reserve. Jack's letter continued: "I had pictured him out in the Pacific somewhere and I was bewildered when I saw him. . . . We had a swell visit and talked over old times at Reserve." Whitey was also attending the Annapolis prep school. He had been in the barracks next to Jack's for the last eight weeks and it was the first time they had seen each other. "It sure is a small world," he noted.

Director of Studies Paul Roundy completed his study of the whereabouts of members of the class of 1944, which he began early in September. Forty-one of the sixty-three graduates were in training for the military; eighteen were in college, "most of them for a limited period of time." Two were awaiting the call; four "had not been heard from."

Harlan Wood shared the news of Neil McPhail with Dr. Hayden, prompting a response from the headmaster to Neil's parents. Upon his return from a short trip he reiterated his sorrow at their loss.

Neil S. McPhail ('33). Reserve Record, *June 13, 1933*

December 5, 1944

Dear Mrs. McPhail:

Just as I started out for the Mid-western Independent School Meeting in Chicago, Mr. Wood handed me your answer to his note inquiring about Neil.

The Haydens are sick at heart; I, in particular had such a wonderful visit with you last May. You are going through deep waters, and please know that Mrs. Hayden and I are right there with you and we speak for the Academy. If there is anything we can do, command us.

We shall never forget Neil; in fact, he's not going to let us forget him. From the point of view of these boys we have known and loved, "there is no death" and, if there is anything in Christmas at all, it is just that assurance that there is no death. This temporal experience is just a fragment of the real thing which we are going to share and experience beyond mortality.

This is just a note but please read between the lines.

      Affectionately yours,
      Joel B. Hayden

By mid-December the Gold Stars on the Service Roll of Honor numbered nineteen. Five boys were missing. Valentine Fries ('43) was one of them. Dr. Hayden shared his hopeful thoughts with Val's mother.

December 6, 1944

Dear Mrs. Roberts:

Mrs. Hayden and I, our family, and the whole school want you to have this little note of sympathy. Val is missing. I hope and pray that that is the real summary of the case; we hope that before long we shall all hear, with you, that he is safe.

His years with us we shall never forget. He fought a quiet but mighty battle to do his best to hang on and to finish and he succeeded, I think, far beyond his own expectations. We were and we are proud of him; we want you to know that.

May your best Christmas greeting be word, either direct or indirect, from him or about him.

    Devotedly yours,
    Joel B. Hayden

Paul "Bud" Barnes ('42) was killed in France on November 21, where he was serving with the Seventh Army.

December 7, 1944

Dear Judge and Mrs. Barnes:

Mrs. Hayden and I just received the message concerning Paul. We want you to know that we are thinking about you, as we always are, and that you can depend upon the steady loyalty and unfailing affection of the whole school family.

Three boys brought me the clipping which they found in the *Chicago Tribune*. If you could have seen their faces and looked into their eyes, you would have been assured again of what you already know, that Paul won and will always hold the profoundest respect of all the boys in this school.

You can count upon us not only now, but always.

    Devotedly yours,
    Joel B. Hayden

New York, N.Y.
December 11, 1944

Dear Dr. Hayden,

Your very thoughtful birthday note to me reached me at the Normandy beachhead, where I was with my liberty ship in August. It certainly did make me feel happy to hear from you and to know that my very good friends of WRA were thinking of me. Although I haven't been able to keep very close touch with Hudson the past three years, I still think of the Academy often and am eternally grateful for all that was done for me in my three years there. I expect to get back into close touch with the school as soon as I return home to Cleveland after the war.

Up until October, I was a cargo security officer in the Transportation Corps, making trips with army cargo being sent to the European theater. I've had some very interesting experiences in my three trips, my first one being to Naples and North Africa. I was in Naples at the time of the eruption of Mt. Vesuvius, and also visited Pompeii. Then we took a shuttle run to Bizerte, where I had the good fortune to run into Bob Hirshberg ['36], who was stationed on a naval tanker. We spent one afternoon and one evening together, and thoroughly enjoyed swapping our experiences and talking over the good old days.

Then, on my second trip, I went from New York to Glasgow on a short round trip of six weeks. . . . My third trip took me to the Normandy beaches, where I witnessed a great miracle of ship unloading and transportation of supplies. It didn't make any of us feel too happy to see the graves at the top of the hill, which told the story of our landing there on June 6, but it made us all realize how much we all have to do so that they will not have died in vain. . . .

     Cordially,
     Bob Abbey ['35; Age 26]

              M.I.T.
            December 16, 1944

Dear Dr. Hayden,

. . . Today it is rather evident that the war will continue for quite a while, for the rather optimistic outlook of several weeks ago has vanished in a cloud of new restrictions and curtailments of civilian goods. But stronger than that has been first round of the fight for peace.

We who have had regular news here in the states have a good background in the printed history behind the trouble in Greece and Italy, and some of us, myself included, are beginning to question our stand in the peace. For I truly think that after the war we will cease to be an "island," but until we have lost our "island" status we had better let the people who live on the continent settle the peace.

I have seen so many of the mechanical dreams become a reality that distance is soon going to be a minor consideration in transportation. It is too bad that it takes a total war to foster the great mechanical advancements, but these changes must be made faster than the enemy, and my part has been along these lines. I hope, as does every other boy here or overseas, that our part has helped to establish world harmony. But I think that we shall have to give in on a few points at the peace, or we shall be out in the cold. . . .

     Sincerely,
     William W. Galbreath, Jr. ['38; Age 25]

Edward W. Kelsey III ('40x). *Archives*

December 20, 1944

Dear Mr. Kelsey:

I want to add my word of sympathy and understanding. We just heard ten days ago confirmation of the death of your son, Ed, who was with us the year 1938–39.

Boys that age make deep impressions on the school family, even though they are here only a short time. It is a wonderful thing to live with boys; that makes it all the more difficult to comprehend their passing. The age group with whom we are working has the highest mortality rate; we have twenty Gold Stars and five boys are missing, and, at the moment, one tragic crisis after another keeps us wondering almost continually, day and night, as to where the next blow will fall upon our school memories and affections.

... We send you deep and abiding Christmas greetings. This year's Christmas comes, I think, closer to the heart of the reality of the first Christmas.

      Most sincerely,
      Joel B. Hayden

Dr. Hayden was notified of the confirmed death of Val Fries, who had been killed the month before in France while serving with the Seventh Army.

December 23, 1944

My dear Mrs. Roberts:

We send you the love and sympathy of the whole Academy family. We want you to have this note for this season of remembrance. Personally, I want you to know that Val made a contribution to this school which was unique and which we shall never forget.

Richard Barrett ('35) on an Italian street. *Courtesy Phillip Barrett ('61)*

His fine spirit, his generosity, his gentleness in handling younger boys, his courage as over against a job that was very difficult for him, his capacity of "taking it," his unfailing good will all combined to make him a very precious human being.

These are especially difficult days for all of us in this country. Everything has moved along so comfortably for us for many decades that we are bewildered and stunned, sometimes, by the tragic involvements in which we find ourselves. The Academy is at the very heart of this sort of tragic suspense and all of us here want you to realize how deeply we feel your loss. It is our loss, too.

Blessings on you from all of us and may you have the spiritual resources which you need to keep great memories fresh and the future under thoughtful and loving control.

Very sincerely yours,
Joel B. Hayden

Somewhere in Italy
December 25, 1944

My dear Dr. Hayden,

Dad kindly forwarded your nice birthday greetings—it was a real pleasure to hear from you and I sincerely appreciate your thoughtfulness.

I have often thought of you and the Academy and then the memories of those happy days would erase the years and make it seem as yesterday. I consider it a privilege to have been with you and I learned so many things that have held me in good stead since leaving the Academy.

I, too, pray that decency and justice may emerge from the present conflict—a permanent understanding of the former and a permanent practice of the latter. God willing these things shall come to be.

My injuries, as Dad said, have healed normally and there is no need for any further concern. . . .

      Very sincerely yours,
      Dick Barrett ['35; Age 28]

Winter Term: January–March 1945

On January 5, 1945, Dr. Hayden sent a note to John A. Malcolm ('42), who was with the 312th Medical Battalion in Belgium. As fate would have it, that same day John was writing to Dr. Hayden; in addition, three of his schoolmates were "practically fighting alongside" him, though he hadn't seen them in a month. Unbeknownst to John, one of them, Dan Climer ('43), had been reported as missing in action on December 18.

Late in January the Office of Defense Transportation suggested canceling spring vacations at private schools, universities, and colleges to relieve the congestion of railroad transportation. The Academy went ahead with its long-awaited spring vacation in March, as most of its students were near enough to their homes that they could travel on buses or in cars. Their absence from the campus also saved over six tons of coal that would otherwise have been used in the heating plant.

On January 20 the inauguration of President Roosevelt took place in Washington. In the Pacific, B-29s continued to bomb Tokyo and U.S. troops landed on Luzon, located in the Philippines. Early in February General MacArthur reported the fall of Manila. By the end of the month, U.S. Marines raised the American flag on Mount Suribachi. One week later the "stars and stripes" were raised in Corregidor. In Germany, General Eisenhower opened a wide offensive in the Rhineland, and by March 8 the U.S. First Army crossed the Rhine after the fall of Cologne.

In mid-February it was learned that Charles "Boots" Killian ('40), a B-24 bomber navigator, had been missing since January 10 in the Philippines. As the school prepared for exam week and spring break, the names of Charles Kennedy ('40) and William Conrad ('32x) were to be added to the list of Gold Stars. Charles was killed in action over England on November 30, 1944, while piloting a B-17; William lost his life in France six days after D day. Two more Stars were added at the reopening of school, with the confirmation of the death in action of Dan Climer ('43) and the notification of the death of Abner O. McDaniel ('39). Abner was a pilot of a B-24 attached to the Fifteenth Air Force in Italy.

By the end of February, twenty-eight Gold Stars were on the Service Flag. By the end of the school year the number grew to thirty-one. John S.

Knight, Jr. ('41x), was killed in action in Germany; David L. Bennell ('40x) died in the crash of a military transport plane near Sweetwater, Texas. A short time later, James H. Cooper ('41) was also killed in a plane crash in Corpus Christi, Texas. Harrie B. Stewart ('30), who had been a prisoner in the Philippines since the fall of Bataan, died aboard a torpedoed prison ship.

Several boys were listed as missing in action or as prisoners of war: Blaine Rawdon—MIA in Germany since December 18; Forrest Kenner ('34)—MIA in Luzon, Philippines, since May 6 but later reported as killed in action on that same day; and William Wells III ('36)—missing in Germany since April 8. The five known prisoners of war were William Calder ('41), William Sprow ('40x), Philip Holstine ('42), Robert Katz ('34), and Alan Moore ('39x).

Belgium
January 5, 1945

Dear Doctor Hayden,

It has been well over a year since I last wrote you. Since then a great deal has happened to me. When last I wrote, I believe I was still at Harvard trying my best to juggle test tubes and preserved frogs in preparation to entering med. school. That, along with memories of green lawns and a tuneful chapel bell falls into the classification of "the good old days," however.

I received my "greetings" while worrying over an organic chemistry exam. With a shout of delight I cast aside my symbols and formulae and prepared for my entrance into the Army of the United States. At the time I sighed in relief as I sighed that June day in 1942 when I graduated from Reserve. Since then my sigh has changed to one of regret. Now after fourteen months in the army I would give anything to be back with those test tubes I once scorned, or to leap once more up the creaky stairs in North Hall after a last class on Saturday. The latter is forever lost to me, but the former will become a reality again—God willing.

I can't tell you how much I have enjoyed reading the *Record* and various alumni publications from time to time. . . . I also received your birthday greetings. Thank you very much for remembering. . . .

Although I have been overseas only a little over two months, I have seen action in both France and here in Belgium as an ambulance driver with a collecting company of the 312th Medical Battalion. . . .

You may be interested to know that I am practically fighting alongside three other Reservites who were my contemporaries while I was at school. They are: Dan Climer '43, James Stevenson '43, and Benson Tucker '42. I haven't seen them in a month so I cannot advise you as to their present welfare, etc.

As ever,
Johnny Malcolm ['42; Age 20]

George Manlove ('32) was in the thick of the fighting when he found some time to write to Mr. Wood.

> Belgium
> January 6, 1945

Dear Mr. Wood,

Yesterday I received your thoughtful letter, written on the 24th of November just before my birthday. It was good to hear all the news of Hudson. It has been a long time since I have enjoyed a football game or a classroom, and it will be a long time still before I shall have an opportunity to visit Hudson, but I am waiting. So far I have been in the lines ever since D-Day with no rest and none in view, although I have been hoping for a chance to see Paris again. I was there the afternoon of the twenty-sixth of August, before it had been completely liberated. I saw DeGaulle, a lot of shooting, and Paris delirious with joy.

But freedom has bought many new problems, I'm afraid, just as in Africa, Sicily, Italy, Belgium, and France. There are the black markets flourishing, inflation, little food, and the struggle for political power between various factions. Just growing pains I guess. War is always the price the world has to pay for not learning the lessons that are before it. There is certainly no doubt as to the outcome of the struggle in the garden between the weed and the flower if the man with the hoe gives them only freedom with which to solve their problems. We have been too inclined to make a fetish of freedom, I'm afraid, so without discipline it becomes merely the right of each to go to hell as he so chooses, and to drag as many with him as he is able.

The going now has been slow and bitter, and it will be even more so from now on. Recently "Jerry" has thrown in his carefully hoarded Luftwaffe, but they haven't come off so well. We shoot down about a third of those who come over low, and the Air Corps gets even more. Buzz bombs come over day and night, very low, on a twenty minute schedule, but most of them keep on going, which at least is one advantage of being up close. The "Jerries" cut off and surrounded the parachute division in the Bastogne area, and the German commander sent a note demanding that they surrender, since their situation was hopeless. The American commander, General McAuliffe, sent the following note: "24 Dec 44 To the German Commander: N-U-T-S." The French papers were full of praise for the American stand at Bastogne, but it was a little baffled by the word "NUTS." "Vous n'etes que de vielles noix!" ["You're only old nuts!"] was the way the Paris papers finally rendered it.

At the moment I am in a basement. Three times a day I climb out and walk about four hundred yards to the kitchen. I blink a few times in the

J. Scribner Allen ('39).
Courtesy Mrs. J. S. Allen

bright light and feel very much like Dr. Manette, "Recalled to Life." Then I take a deep breath of fresh air, which must last me until my next trip, and go back down in my dungeon and to work. Clear days are always quite busy. All day long in an endless stream the fighters and bombers wheel about overhead, thousands of them, each leaving a long white vapour trail which follows it like a pointing finger across the sky. In fact the heavens look very much like a huge blue schoolboy slate covered with acrostics; the image always quickly fades, however, when the flak appears and the white vapour trail turns black, falters a bit, then heads straight down until it bursts into flame. There are moments of great beauty, even in war, but they are like illusions—quickly shattered. Again, thank you for your letter and please remember me to those in Hudson.

Un vieux noix,
George M. [Age 31]

Yet another coincidence of the Reserve family running into one another —this time a reunion of boy and master.

Somewhere in the Pacific
January 15, 1945

Dear Dr. Hayden,

It has been a long time since last I wrote. (Sounds like a line from one of those songs the Octet used to sing back in '39.) However, there hasn't been much of note to account for during all that time. My work is all on the hush-hush and life is pretty routine and void of excitement, as I guess is true of all service force work. It keeps us pretty busy repairing equipment for and shipping supplies to the boys out front, but you don't hear any sincere complaints. It's sincere because there is always the general run of G.I. gripe, but it is all in the spirit of army life.

I did have one rather pleasant experience while attending a dance at one of the naval stations here on the island. While paying a visit to the place where all men proceed at some time during such a function, I nearly ran over Mr. Mears. I say Mr. Mears because that was how I knew him way back when; now he is Lt. (j.g.) and stationed here at a naval base. You probably know more of his activities than I had opportunity to catch up during our brief meeting, but I hope to have time to join him in a bull session sometime in the near future.

Of other WRA men I know little more than what you write, but I did get John Anderson's annual greeting and reminder of our reunion in '64. I wonder just how many will be there.

Appreciatively and sincerely,
[J.] "Scrib" Allen ['39; Age 25]

Of all of the suffering felt during the school year, none was so devastating to so many as the loss on January 9 of one of Reserve's best known, most respected, and well-loved sons. His death had a major impact on the administration of the school and in the daily lives of the Academy boys. When word of his death reached the boys fighting in theaters of war around the globe, their thoughts turned homeward to the little village of Hudson, Ohio. Dr. Hayden composed and mailed a letter to all alumni to inform them of the tragic news: Dean Wood was gone.

January 16, 1945

Dear Alumnus:

For more than twenty-eight years Academy boys and masters have rung the bell at the north side of the President's House and have always found there a friend. For more than fifty years this friend has moved through the history of Western Reserve, holding it together, giving it strength and foundation, and raising the value of all with whom he lived because of the high quality of his character. This friend was Dean Wood.

On Tuesday, January 9, after working on his annual report as President of the Hudson Library and Historical Society; after presiding at the stockholders meeting of the National Bank of Hudson and delivering his report for the last twelve years, the period of his presidency, Mr. Wood went to the house of a friend to have dinner with the Directors of the bank and their wives. As he entered the side door, which was also the entrance to the basement, in some unaccountable way he fell down the stairs into the

Harlan N. Wood at his desk. *Archives*

basement, fracturing his skull. He never regained consciousness and died shortly after nine o'clock that night.

Harlan Nims Wood was born July 30, 1867, graduated from Reserve in 1888. He received his A.B. from Amherst and M.A. from Harvard. In 1893 he returned to his Academy to become a teacher. Since that time, except when the school was closed (1903–1916) he has devoted his life to this Academy and to this village. Of them he has become a part. His spirit will live and continue to grow so long as there is a Western Reserve Academy or a town of Hudson.

>Joel B. Hayden
>Headmaster

Letters of condolence poured into the Academy from leaders in business and education, community members, and alumni.

>Cleveland, Ohio
>January 10, 1945

Dear Dr. Hayden:

It was a shock to read today of Dean Wood's death. I am, of course, a rank sentimentalist where WRA is concerned but I cannot help expressing to you some of the thoughts that came to me today.

If ever God made anyone in his own image it was Mr. Wood. I cherish the moments I was privileged to spend with him. I cannot help but think, too, that with this wholesale slaughter going on all over the world that the Lord needed a hand with the "boys" and took Mr. Wood unto himself.

His death is a loss to all who knew him but, oh! the rejoicing there must be in Heaven today when the Gold Stars of WRA welcome their Dean.
>Sincerely,
>Jerrie Gressle

Mrs. Jerrie Gressle worked alongside Mr. Wood for two years (1940–42) as switchboard operator, typist, and general receptionist. Her son, Keith ('48), explained their relationship in a letter I received from him in the fall of 1998. When she came to the school, she was in her early thirties, "had never even seen a telephone switchboard before and wasn't a very good typist, either. At first she was very frightened and discouraged. It was Harlan Wood who saw her distress and befriended her. His encouragement and support meant the world to her, and she had a lasting respect for him."

Eulogies from the boys in the military and from those preparing to serve, poured in for months after word of the loss of their beloved dean caught up with them.

> His loss will be keenly felt by all who knew him, and Reserve will seem hardly the same without him. And yet that is not the way he would have wanted it. The only tribute that he would have asked from his fellow men is that we make a part of our daily lives the high ideals and gentlemanly conduct which were synonymous with his name. Yes, I shall truly miss seeing him again. His tall frame and lovable head of snow white hair seemed to be as much a part of Reserve as the Chapel and the beautiful elms. His character was beyond reproach; his face wore a continual smile, his tongue had a kind word for all, and he was never too busy to give advice to the boys who meant so much to him. The world and Reserve are better places because Harlan Wood lived. . . . I truly feel that I am a better person for having known Dean Wood for four enjoyable years.
> —Peter S. Hanson ('44), U.S. Navy

> He was a very fine man, splendid teacher and a wonderful friend to me.
> —Richard P. Lothrop ('44), Oberlin College

> He was certainly one of the finest of the fine. . . . I can remember him so vividly, with his silky white hair, the very distinguished look and warm heart. He always seemed so willing to talk to or help any of the boys.
> —William H. Berman ('42), U.S. Navy

I hope the Academy will always have as strong and understanding masters.

—Herbert J. Tepper ('39), U.S. Army Air Force

Never have I known a finer man. You know, I used to call him "Pop", for that's just what he was to me and to every boy in the school. . . . I recall the little problems I had and how 'Pop' would either straighten them or me out. . . . It is a great loss to Reserve to those who knew him, but a greater loss to those who will come to Reserve in the future.

—James H. Allen ('41), U.S. Navy

Dean Wood was one of the "youngest" elderly men I have ever known. He had that rare knack of taking the best out of his daily contacts with young men and returning it with dividends. I remember that no matter how low one's spirit might have been, the mere meeting of Mr. Wood on the campus with no more than a "hello" would make the world seem bright again.

—Robert Iredell, Jr. ('34)

In a time of so many needless deaths all over the world, his passing seems to me the most needless of all. . . . I shall always consider myself fortunate to have known him, both as a teacher and as a friend.

—C. Lynn McCuskey ('28), U.S. Navy

He was indeed the grand old man of WRA. His character and history remain as tributes to the ideals of all worthwhile education. There are too few like him in the profession.

—Charles H. Winkler ('34), U.S. Army

Those of us of army age are beginning to get hardened to news of death among our friends, but somehow we don't expect tragedy to strike among our friends who are working at home. . . . "All of us" is the term that comes most readily to mind, for certainly all of us who have been connected to Western Reserve Academy or with the Academy feel that the school has suffered a grievous loss, and that the boys yet to come into the school will have been defrauded of the influence which we all came to love.

—Lincoln "Pete" Woodruff ('39), U.S. Army

I shall never forget Mr. Wood for his wisdom, his gracious manners, his ready smile and hearty laugh. He seemed to possess an inbred ability to inspire confidence and better understandings in those with

whom he associated. Western Reserve Academy and the Township of Hudson have lost a true and loyal friend.
—John H. Danforth ('33), U.S. Army

Many teenaged youths, striving for a better education and a chance to live a cleaner and brighter life, both intellectually and spiritually, have already passed through Reserve's 'welcome' portals only to be met by Dean Wood, who started the boy through his long curriculum of studies. Many others will pass through those same gates in future years to come, but will not have the unheralded distinction of chatting with this man.
—Rowland C. Congdon ('42x), USAAF

The news of Dean Wood's death must have been a great shock to every Reserve man, and particularly to those of us who, having lived in Hudson all our lives, had learned to love and respect him since childhood. His passing is a great loss, not only to the school, but with the church, town, and the numerous civic and cultural centers up north to which he was connected. I well remember that when my parents first considered entering me in the Academy, that it was to Mr. Wood that we went for advice.
—Franklin S. Barlow ('30), U.S. Army

I will always remember Dean Wood as a great and kind-hearted man. He always had a good word for everyone.
—Ray P. Dinsmore, Jr. ('43), U.S. Army

Mr. Wood was almost a tradition of the Academy—always present, always available to any and all of his students. He is a man on whom all graduates and students will look back as an example of attainment throughout their Academy days; an example of dignity and intellectual achievement; of personality and interests; of hard work and progress. Throughout my acquaintance with the school, back to the days of Mr. Boothby, through the period preceding Dr. Hayden when Mr. Wood was Acting Headmaster, and through these last ten years of Dr. Hayden, Mr. Wood was always present, his influence ever felt by the students, his Latin classes ever struggling with Cicero and Caesar, his calm personality throwing a pacific blanket over the wild escapades of the student body.
—James L. Pendleton ('34), U.S. Army

The front page of the January 18 *Reserve Record* told of Dean Wood's life and death and the influence he had on generations of boys. The editorial

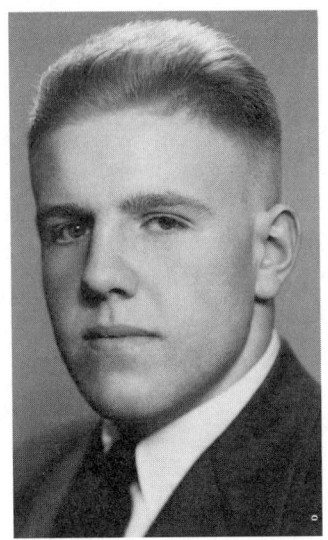
Paul H. Barnes ('42). *Archives*

Valentine A. Fries ('43). *Archives*

Ramon L. Spooner ('42). *Archives*

David A. Read ('43). *Archives*

noted, "His life shall ever remain an inspiration to those who carry on at Reserve and his memory shall be a guiding light to all who study and teach. The words which Edward Markham wrote of Lincoln might with equal truth have been penned for Harlan N. Wood: He went down as when a lordly cedar, green with boughs, goes down with a great shout upon the hills, and leaves a lonesome place against the sky."

The headline on the following page read: "Recent Fury of War Makes Its Sorrowful Mark on Reserve; Four Alumni Killed in Action, One Missing," and profiled the latest casualties: Paul Barnes ('42), Val Fries ('43), Ramon

Blaine Rawdon ('42) on the Academy football field. *Archives*

H. Douglas Barnes ('43). *Archives*

Spooner ('42), and David Read ('43). An Army Air Force lieutenant and navigator of a B-17, Spooner was shot down over Germany in November. Read was killed in Belgium on December 18. Missing was Dan W. Climer ('43).

The following week the *Record* reported two more casualties. Blaine "Buckets" Rawdon ('42) was missing in Luxembourg, and H. Douglas Barnes ('43), Paul's younger brother, was killed during the Battle of the Bulge while serving as an army staff sergeant.

Paul Barnes's parents had only begun absorbing news of their son's death when the War Department notified them of the death of their other son, Doug, on January 3 in France. They were the only set of brothers from WRA to become casualties. Mr. Mickel sent his thoughts to Judge and Mrs. Barnes.

January 19, 1945

Dear Judge and Mrs. Barnes:

We want you to know that all of Paul's and Doug's teachers and friends here are so unspeakably sorry to learn that both have made the supreme sacrifice for their country. But I know of no other way than to frankly face the fact that war is like that. At what terrific cost mankind learns the lessons of unselfishness!

If this war results in some real forward steps in improving human relationships, you can be proud of your share in its purchase.

How proud we are that we were privileged to have Paul and Doug here for part of their training. They were as fine as they come. Both boys

Reid Black ('42). *Courtesy Reid Black, Jr.*

made real contributions to the school, each in his own way, and they left the school better for having been here. My relations with Doug were more direct than with Paul, and I can honestly say that I never had more satisfaction in working with any boy in my twenty-five years of teaching and coaching. It is a treasure of great price, although a poor substitute for life, to have the memories of two such fine lads. . . .

    Sincerely,
    Raymond A. Mickel

    Corry Field
    Pensacola, Florida
    January 19, 1945

Dear Dr. Hayden,

After reading the *Alumni Record*, which was sent to me two days ago, I finally decided to carry out an ambition I have long held and that was to write you a letter.

I have been receiving the *Record* regularly and have enjoyed reading each one immensely. They bring back many pleasant memories of my days at WRA—and I'm not just saying that as a loyal Reserve alumni. I really mean it. I really enjoyed my four years. Besides gaining knowledge, which at this point is a statement that is obviously not being proved, but I gained some very loyal friends which is a great asset these days.

As you may know, I have been stationed in Pensacola for the past eighteen months, so I have had a very dull naval career so far compared to that of some of my classmates. My duties concern radio in aviation. . . .

During my stay in Pensacola I have run into a few ex-Reserve men. Last spring Jimmie Allen ['41] was going through flight class right here at Corry, so we had a grand time during his six weeks stay. He was married here in the navy chapel . . . after which he left for Miami. I received a card from him from Norfolk around Christmas, but no doubt he's at sea now.

Lewie Ball ['42] left Corry Field last week for two weeks additional ground school at another outlying field. He expects to get his wings then. Bill Gregory ['41] was down there for a while, but since November I have lost track of him. He received his wings in October. Lewie Ball informed me that Ade Nussdorfer ['41] was in the area somewhere but as yet I haven't seen him. All in all it was great to see these fellows. . . .

     Best regards to you, sir,
     Reid Black ['42; Age 21]

              Somewhere in Europe
              January 20, 1945

Dear Mr. Wood,

Your letter arrived a few days ago, along with one from Dr. Hayden; after having gone through not a few post offices the address was barely readable. However it did arrive; thanks so much for thinking of me. It is pleasant to be reminded in this way that there are those at home who think of us here. Further, it is well to be reminded that despite present conditions, there are still those schools such as the Academy, trying at least to teach a few the correct way of life. There are many here who regret not having learned, realizing now that it will be all the more difficult, with so many ideas to unlearn, so great a number of new ones to understand.

And yet, you would find viewpoints here most interesting in comparison with what one would suppose, or what some wishful thinkers would have us believe. I was not alone in noticing the apparent pro-Nazi trends of conversations on the continent. Even in places where outwardly there was rejoicing as the Allies marched in, at night it was considered unsafe to go about unarmed or alone. Not so much from fear of hidden Germans who might take pot-shots at you, but from pro-Nazi elements who had lived in the country most of their lives. This certainly speaks of a very thorough Nazi indoctrination during occupation, or perhaps a fear of some sort of retaliation some time in the future.

Naturally there is a certain feeling of wariness among the people as to just what is going to be done; this feeling may explain much of the caution in their association with us. Military censorships keep them as much in the dark as we are, and what little is put out by the English or Americans, coupled with the constant jabber of German propaganda must have them confused indeed as to the policies of the "Big Three." We cannot understand most of it; how can we expect those who know so very little of us to be able to figure anything out. It's no wonder they throw up their hands in despair, much in the way we have been inclined to do of late.

Frequent letters have come to me of late asking an explanation of events, the writers obviously believing that in my nearness to the scene I should be an authority of the true situation. How I wish I did know what was happening, but such knowledge is sadly lacking. It is laughable that we should rely for the bulk of our information, not on intelligence reports, or up to the minute war communiques—of which there is no such animal—but instead on back issues of *Time* magazine.

Thanks to the Russians we are, this week anyway, somewhat optimistic as to our stay here, and, as usual, wild rumors formulate at the slightest excuse. Discounting these, the fact remains that they are making encouraging gains in the right direction; we can but hope for a continuance....

Sincerely,
John McIntosh ['39; Age 24]

January 22, 1945

Dear Mr. and Mrs. Spooner:

We want you to know how unspeakably sorry all of Ray's teachers and friends here at the Academy are that the grim hand of war has taken its toll in your home. You have our deepest and sincerest sympathy.

As one of Ray's teachers and coaches, I had the highest respect for him. His willingness, cooperativeness, fine spirit, and good sense of the fitness of things made it a pleasure to work with him. And he was such an excellent competitor. He was at his best when the going was hardest. Our recollections of him as a guest in our home are only those of a real gentleman. How fortunate you are to have the memories of such a fine son, even though that is a poor substitute for having him return.

Sincerely,
Raymond A. Mickel

January 22, 1945

Dear Dr. Hayden,

I wonder if you have had the word about Blaine Rawdon, who has been reported missing. Lewis, who graduates tomorrow at Pensacola, says Mrs. Rawdon has written him the sad news.... That was terrible news about Ray Spooner, who was such a fine friend of both Blaine and Lewis.

We all hope and pray this war may soon be over. We hope this finds you well.

Sincerely,
Fred L. Ball [Father of Lewis Ball ('42)]

think the Germans would try to return to Paris?" But soon it grew to such proportions that we decided to keep moving, so we moved up to the square in front of the Hotel de Ville near the American Embassy.

Here a large crowd had gathered. When they let out a mighty roar and began cheering wildly, I looked around and expected to see DeGaulle, but it was us they were cheering. We did our best but felt very much embarrassed at so much attention; we had come as spectators, but to them we were Americans; we had been a symbol and a hope for five years. Now Paris was free and there was too much gratefulness pent up inside of each Parisian to hold back. One grand looking young woman made her way through the crowd, took hold of my arm, kissed me on both cheeks. "Thank you, oh, thank you so much!" she said. She was in black. Her husband had been killed three days before fighting for the underground.

Everywhere the story was the same—very little food for four years, something like a pound of meat a month, a loaf of bread a week, butter at $20 a pound; no eggs, no green vegetables, no clothes, a package of tobacco a month, which was part sawdust, twenty-one cigarettes a month and the Germans had taken everything. We had just come from Normandy where vegetables, eggs, milk, butter, even meat was plentiful, but there was no gas, no transportation, and most of the products from Normandy were bought up by the Germans. People had not eaten for three days. One man said, "I have not had anything to eat for the last three days, I have lost sixty pounds in the last three years, but if there had been a feast, none of us could have eaten; we were too excited, too choked up inside with emotion. You have no idea."

"Words cannot describe how the people have fought inside the city. They were like lions; little pistols, a rifle they had taken from the Germans over the bodies of their comerades. With clubs and rocks they stormed machine guns. They had to take the rifles and then take the ammunition to fire, and they had to capture food in order to eat. Oh, I cannot possibly describe it." He said, "Words are not good enough. And the Germans! They mowed them down like flies; they fired into crowds with tanks; the people were just like lions. Four days and nights they fought."

All over Paris we could see signs of heroic battles. There were road blocks at street ends made of sand bags, car tracks, paving bricks. The streets were torn up, trees were cut down to give protection. Bullet holes pock-marked store fronts. Notre Dame Cathedral was spattered all over the front, windows were broken and hundreds of small chips were nicked in the Louvre from small arms fire. The Regent Hotel was shot up, but outside in a small square the statue of Joan of Arc had just been gilded in bright gold by the patriots. Balustrades were shot out of the rail along the banks of the Seine. German tanks were at strategic corners in the heart of the city. They had been set on fire. One had a sign—"For Sale Cheap."

January 23, 1945

Dear Mr. Ball:

Mrs. Rawdon wrote Mrs. Hayden and me just as soon as she had the news, so we are fully aware of what is going on. I am going to be in New York the end of this week and I am going to be with the Rawdons some way or other and bring them all the encouragement and comfort and devotion of the Academy. It is a large order but I shall do my best to fill said order.

Yes, the toll is mounting. A letter yesterday from Reid Black spoke much about Lewis and Jimmie Allen and other boys who have been with him or near him in training.

Just had two messages from Ed Pope, Jr. ['37], who is in charge of a PT squadron in the Pacific. He's been in the Philippine scramble and is now apparently on his way back to the states on a special mission for further preparation with more action ahead upon his return.

Congratulations on the splendid job that Lewis has been doing. May God bless him and keep him and all our other boys everywhere. The boys will take care of supporting all that is significant in our Gold Stars, but only if we older people, with courage, make every sacrifice to see to it that the kind of world which follows will have justice and far-sighted cooperation and great patience at its very heart. . . . If we can't put man first and property second, in the long run we shall simply contribute to the collective destruction which will be suffered by our oncoming generation or our own children and grandchildren. . . .

    Sincerely yours,
    Joel B. Hayden

    Belgium
    January 24, 1945

Dear Mother:

Your latest letter of early January arrived tonight, and news is much better these days. We're almost back to normal now and the Russians are going great guns. Things may happen fast from now on. I certainly hope so.

Last night I got out the crackers, the pickles, the salami, the cheese, and opened a bottle of champagne for the occasion. Was it ever wonderful. Send me some more "Ritz" crackers and a few cans of oysters. We can get milk and a little butter from the kitchen and make oyster stew. Pretty good these cold winter nights.

We have over two feet of snow with the temperature down around zero. The doughboys have to move through snow up to their waists and often they must remain exposed for two and three days without sleep, without blankets, without warm clothes, since they must travel lightly. No reporting or book written has ever done justice to their task.

Ken [my brother] looks fine in his picture. Perhaps the army is agreeing with him. The Pacific War is quite different than ours. With the exception that the "Jap" must be dug out and never surrenders, there is no comparison. The "Jap" hasn't the air force and he hasn't the artillery that the "Jerry" has, nor the tanks. Our pilots over here don't average any ten to one victories in the air, and our ground forces don't average any ten to one over the "Jerry"—and the "Jap" has no Siegfried Line. Jungle fighting is tough, but not tougher than sub-zero weather fighting.

. . . I am glad you liked your perfume. It was a fairly good brand and is probably worth fifteen dollars in the states.

Each day I marvel at the ingenuity of soldiers, making something out of nothing. In our last position the men couldn't put their pup tents up because of the blizzard and because the snow was too heavy for them. Some of them dug holes; others crawled under the ammunition tarps. One gun crew didn't answer a fire mission in the middle of the night, and the chief of the section found them buried under two feet of snow. They were dug out none the worse for wear. After the first two days they dug down deep, made log roofs, and some of them had put together stoves and bunks. About two weeks ago one of our observers spotted some "Jerries" go into a house, which they were using as headquarters. We put a round right through the roof the first round and got eight more direct hits out of fourteen shots—not bad when you're shooting at a target miles away. Later the doughs took the ground, and we found it full of dead "Jerries." One was eating dinner on the second floor, and one was cutting meat in the basement. They were still at their jobs.

George [Manlove,'32; Age 31]

Somewhere in Germany
January 29, 1945

Dear Dr. Hayden,

You say I haven't written for some two and a half months. That's only too true; but during that time we have been having it rough. We came down from Eindhoven, Holland after Thanksgiving, and they sent me with some men to act as front lines litter bearers in the Hurtgen forest, and there wasn't a one of us that thought we would get out of there alive. We came out of there just in time to go to work with the forces trying to stop the Germans on their break through. Now that we have them going back, there is no time for resting. I wish I could say that things look good, but won't be able to say that until it is all over and they have sent us back home. Hope everything is well with you and yours, and thank you very much for thinking of me.

Harvey [Tanner '38x; Age 25]

Somewhere in France
January 31, 1945

Dear Dr. Hayden:

... As for myself I'm in pretty fair shape and have every intention of staying that way. I've had a quick glimpse of France—enough to satisfy my "wondering" appetite. Our outfit has seen a good bit of combat since arrival in France. Its first mission was to help drive the "Jerry's" from the Vosges Mountains and we came through in flying, though slightly soiled, colors. Jon Izant ['41] is in the same regiment as I and, although I haven't seen Jon for some time, I've heard that all goes well with Jon, too. By the way, Jon still seems to be the same jolly fat man we knew at Reserve. Wonderful guy.

My father enclosed a clipping concerning Dean Wood's death. It's strange but it's hard for me to remember the Academy without Dean Wood and "Doc Frew."[1] They were as much a part of the school as were the dorms, the Chapel, or the U.S. games to me. I don't believe I'll ever forget some of the chats I've had with the Dean. I owe him a huge amount which can never be repaid, but I think that is the way he wanted it. If he could help you, he did and expected nothing in return except your willingness to listen and to ask questions. A great man whom none of us will ever forget.

Sincerely yours,
Bob Boyer ['42; Age 21]

1. Angus M. Frew, director of Physical Education 1926–41.

In February a midyear graduation was held for four of the seniors. The Sunday afternoon ceremony in the chapel began with the glee club singing the national anthem, followed by an address by Dr. Hayden. "Commencement is actually a beginning," he said, "a beginning of life away from one's family. Although graduation means the end of education in schools, it is the beginning of a different life. School is just a conditioner for what lies ahead."

February 2, 1945

Dear Mr. and Mrs. Kennedy:

I am enclosing a birthday greeting which was sent by Dr. Hayden to Chuck last fall. It has just been returned to us. The inscriptions on the outside tell their own story.

I am writing to ask if what this implies is true. We have had no word and this comes as a distinct shock. We are hoping that there must be some mistake. Will you please let us know?

Sincerely,
Raymond A. Mickel

(Left and right) Charles F. Kennedy, Jr. ('40). *Archives*

February 5, 1945

Dear Dean Mickel:

We are sorry indeed that the tragic news about Chuck had to come to you with such a shock. We, too, are having mail returned to us almost daily and it has its own peculiar unwelcomeness.

Ruth, Chuck's wife, who is with her parents in Benton Harbor, received a telegram on December 17, telling her that Chuck was killed in action over England on November 30, 1944. Later a letter of confirmation came from Washington, and Ruth also heard from the wives of the other officers in the crew. Letters from General Arnold and General Marshall have also been received, and there seems now no faint hope that the news may have been a mistake.

We knew it would be Chuck's wish that grief for him should not shadow the Christmas season for those dear to him, so we waited until after the holidays to write to those from whom we had not already heard. I say "we" rather inaccurately for Charles, my husband, is still not writing to anyone. As you know, Chuck was his "second self" and the adjustment to his loss is going to take much time and courage. I had the good fortune to be brought up in a minister's family, where belief in a rich and useful future life some way took firm hold on me. So now I have no heckling mind to assail me with questions and doubts about our boy's present happiness and well-being. And I had a special mandate from Chuck which called for courage and a great pride in his undimmed ideals—as his mother.

... Will you tell Dr. Hayden that his name is at the top of the list on my desk and that sometime this week I shall write him more fully about Chuck's overseas experience. . . .

We shall never stop being grateful to all of Chuck's teachers and friends who did so very much for him during his year at the Academy.

Yours sincerely,
Lillian S. Kennedy

The Kennedy family sent the program from the memorial service for Charles to the school.

A Memorial—Charles F. Kennedy, Jr., '40

A wave of sympathy and understanding has broken upon us and filled our souls to overflowing. Without it the loss of one so dear to us would have been immeasurably harder to bear. This burst of feeling from hundreds of our friends was more than sympathy for us in our grief. It was a unison of voices which we believe will join millions of other voices heard above the din of battle proclaiming that this time our fine young men must not have died in vain.

We can only say that we are grateful—deeply grateful for the goodness of our friends in this hour of our great trial. Now we know what countless others have suffered and our hearts go out to them. We contemplate in sadness what must still come to thousands of homes before the wicked blight which infests this earth is purged. May we all carry on in unity and with fervent devotion to our boys who are fighting and dying for us. These boys have asked nothing of us. What a great debt we owe them!

We should like to share with our friends part of a letter from Bud's older brother, Edward, now serving with the infantry in France:

"If I could only be with you, and we could share our grief! My first reaction—as I know yours was—was to ask God why it had to be Bud, and it isn't much comfort to know that a million other hearts have cried out the same question about an individual dear to them.

However, I think I have a little better answer now than I did when I was still in the States or even in England. Over here I've had some first hand impressions of cruelty and brutality that can hardly be conceived—material evidences of a spirit and a way of thinking that can't be permitted in any kind of a decent world. This spirit is the very antithesis of Bud's and his kind is the only kind that will defeat it. From Bud's last letter to me I believe he realized, too, what depended on him and a lot of others like him, and I know he went out smiling and unafraid and believing that any sacrifice he might make was worthwhile. It's up to those who stay behind to see to it that he's justified. He didn't let us down, and we can't let him down by allowing our personal grief to overcloud the vision he gave his life for. Moreover, his spirit isn't dead—it's more alive than it ever was in our hearts, and we know it.

You must help each other, now, as never before, because it means so much to you . . . and myself. For Bud's sake don't lose sight of the vision for which he fought. For our sakes, remember that we still have a tendency to look to our parents for strength and comfort, as well as a desire to give these things back to them. With God's help and the memory of Bud, I'll do my best to do a better job over here, and I want you to do the same. . . . Keep your chins up, my dears. Bud could fight with a smile, and we, his own family, can do the same. (Edward Kennedy)

                        Lillian and Charles Kennedy

The father of Paul and Doug Barnes sent a note to "Scotch" McGill and enclosed with it information on Paul, from the army commander.

                                              February 6, 1945

Dear Mr. McGill:

Herewith are copies of papers which tell us all we know of Paul [Barnes]'s last days.

Paul was a private in Company A of the 324th Infantry, which is a part of the 44th Infantry Division. He was killed in action on November 21, 1944.

Paul's last letter to us was written on November 17, 1944. In it he said they had been taken "back" and given opportunity to take baths "out of their helmets" and changes of clothing. He never said anything about being at the front or in action.

General Patch's order of November 23, 1944, and Captain Bardini's letter of January 13, 1945, tell the rest of the story.

You held a very high and special place in Paul's affections, and I think you will be interested.

                Sincerely,
                John P. Barnes

                                                      France
                                          January 13, 1945

Dear Judge Barnes:

In reply to your letter of 30 Dec. 1944, I will attempt to answer your questions to the best of my knowledge.

I feel that I know as much as anyone at present here with the company as to the circumstances of your son's death, as he was about thirty yards from me at the time.

Your son Paul was instantaneously killed at Avricourt, France, by fragments from a mortar shell that hit near the edge of his hole. The man who was occupying the same hole with your son escaped unharmed. This man has since been killed in action.

The day your son died, this unit plus others, after a night march, scored a breakthrough. We were dug in outside of Avricourt, and all day were under heavy mortar and artillery, plus small arms, fire. Late that afternoon your son was killed.

Paul in my estimation was an excellent soldier, and a credit to both his country and parents. It is most regrettable that he had to die, but this is one of the tragedies of war which may happen to any one of us.

I do not at present know where your son is buried but am endeavoring to find out, through our Graves Registration Officer. It may take some time for me to find out as I am at the front. A letter from you to our Personnel Section will probably get you these details sooner than I am able to find out. . . .

If you still have any questions or doubts in your mind do not hesitate to write and I will endeavor to clear it up for you to the best of my knowledge.
    Sincerely yours,
    Peter Bardini, Capt. Inf.
    Comdg. Co. A

                    Luxembourg
                    February 8, 1945

Dear Dr. Hayden,

So often here in the midst of blasting chaos I find myself thinking with unutterable longing of the peace and quiet that hung over Reserve. I can remember Sunday breakfasts of waffles and sausage, the rush and bristle of recess with the faculty room bellowing friendly clouds of smoke and the stampede at Mr. Wallace's bookstore window. Strange but true—one never appreciates what he has, but always desires to be somewhere else doing something else. The war is going to give us all a new appreciation of the simple things that made up a happy life.

There is a surprising dearth of news of Reservites over here. I haven't met one since I left the states, although I have had several letters from Brian Brough ['39], the Scottish exchange student. He is in the RAF still in England the last I heard. I saw G. G. Grant ['39] in New York on my honeymoon. A handsome Lt.(j.g.).

. . . Paris is dingy on the outside, demoralized in its heart. This winter is being very hard for them to bear. Very philosophical about it but conditions had better improve this summer, otherwise, look for trouble there.

. . . There isn't much to tell about myself. I'm in the 5th Division, the XII Corps and the Third Army. I'm a forward observer, which merely means I adjust artillery fire from a position well forward with the rifle companies. In

fact there isn't anything but Krauts ahead of us. My brother Kay ['43] is due to graduate from Ft. Benning Infantry OCS sometime this month—a brand new second lieutenant in the infantry. Can't say I envy him. In fact it worries me because their casualty rate is very high, and despite all the War Department spokesmen, this war is a long way from being won. The Krauts we are fighting are just as fanatical as ever. They seem to be a little short on artillery, but they certainly know how to organize terrain for defense.
    Sincerely,
    Jim McKay ['39; Age 23;]

                February 9, 1945

Dear Judge Barnes:

  Thank you very much, indeed, for your letter of February 6 in which were enclosed copies of papers which were so interesting and informative in connection with Paul's last days.

  I have read these copies with much interest and appreciation, I assure you, and am sending them around among those faculty members who knew Paul best and who worked with him when he was here. They will all be interested, you may be sure.

  I well remember a statement you made to me in the letter shortly after you learned of Paul's death—that he had been permitted to play a man's role in this life, if only for a short time. Captain Bardini's letter makes it quite apparent that the boy was, indeed, playing a man's role in the fullest conceivable sense when death came upon him. We feel so grateful for the fact that if he had to go it could be instantaneously. I am very fearful that many of our boys will come back to us at the end of the war doomed to a type of life that is not much better than death. . . .

  We have now twenty-five Gold Stars on our Honor Roll. For quite a while we felt rather lucky because only an occasional WRA "son" was reported missing or killed. However, they've come thick upon us during recent months and the number is now twenty-five. Doug and Paul are the only pair of brothers lost to date. . . .
    Cordially yours,
    Joel B. Hayden

           Somewhere in the Southwest Pacific
                February 11, 1945

Dear Dr. Hayden,

  Received both your V-mail letters during the past week, and I now look forward with anxiety to any other letters you may send my way, for they always seem to bring news of the deaths of some of my best friends.

  Dean Wood's death is, indeed, a deep tragedy to the town of Hudson and to the Academy. He will be missed, whether they realize it or not, by all those future "new" boys. During that first fall term of mine when things were strange and difficult, I knew that he was always there with his quiet encouragement and calm advice. He was the embodiment of the spirit of Western Reserve Academy, and his passing is a great loss to the school.

It does not seem possible that happy-go-lucky Val is gone. He was one of my best friends, and one of whom I thought about most often. It is difficult to get used to the fact that he, with his ready wit, will no longer be heard. I did not know Paul Barnes very well, but did realize that he was one of Reserve's stalwarts. Whoever said that war was a blessing in disguise because it purged the race of men of its weaklings and misfits was indeed, snowing. The accomplishments of both these fellows refutes that statement to the nth degree.

That ham that we demolished at Pierce House one night would come in very nicely on this rock. . . . Thumbs down on all post-war picnics where the hostess passes out cold-cuts and Spam sandwiches. However, ("Scotch" may have his doubts) my appetite has tapered off quite a bit since I came overseas. Either I am no longer "a growing boy" or the tropical heat has shriveled the cavity in my hollow leg, for I no longer down those enormous quantities of food. I look back now, and wondered how in the hell I did it.

Hoping to hear from you again, but under less tragic circumstances, I remain,

Sincerely yours,
Dwight V. Peabody ['43; Age 20]

February 16, 1945

Dear Mr. and Mrs. Kennedy:

We thank you most sincerely, indeed, for your recent, wonderful letter, and for the beautiful formal message which came to us yesterday.

The attitude and sustaining thought expressed in your letter, Mrs. Kennedy, is magnificent. What a blessing is our religious faith in times like these. And what a blessing yours must be to you and those dear to you now!

The printed message was one of the most beautiful things I have seen. Dr. Hayden will be most pleased to see it when he returns from his trip east. How proud you must be of Edward!

Charles is the twenty-fifth of our boys on the Gold Star list. And we want to assure you that our sympathy is with you and the deeply poignant feeling over the sacrifice you and Bud have made is just that much greater.

He was a fine lad and we came to love him extraordinarily, considering the short time he was with us. I had him in class and on the track team and was tremendously proud of the way he developed that year. In the spring he broke the school shot-put record and also set a new Interstate League record in the discus in the big meet of the year. You will be interested in

Charles F. Kennedy, Jr. ('40). *Archives*

Charles J. Killian, Jr. ('40). *Archives*

this quotation from the report which went from the school to the University of Michigan:

"He is outstanding in his soundness of character, persistence, earnestness, and desire to achieve."

May God fire us all with a burning determination that these sacrifices will not have been made in vain and that they shall not be repeated.

      Sincerely,
      Raymond A. Mickel

The school received news that Charles Killian had been missing in action in the Philippines since January 10. He and Charles Kennedy were both postgraduates at the Academy, receiving their diplomas with the class of 1940. Their photographs appeared next to each other in the 1940 senior annual.

             February 16, 1945

Dear Mr. Mickel:

Your letter of encouragement was greatly appreciated by Mrs. Killian and myself.

There is very little we can tell you regarding Boots. On Feb. 6 we received word from the Secretary of War stating: "Second Lt. Charles J. Killian has been reported missing in action over the Philippine Islands since 10 January 1945." A week later we received a letter confirming the telegram also advising us that any further information would be given us as soon as possible.

A letter from Boots, dated January 5 was the last we heard from him. He seemed very cheerful, wrote of just returning from a mission, and commented on living on a partially occupied island. Wrote of a nuisance bombing every night which seemed to interfere with his sleep. I might add Boots was a navigator on a B-24 bomber.

This sudden turn of events has been quite a shock to us, still we are very hopeful and look forward to encouraging news in the near future.

Permit me to thank you again for your kind and deep interest. We will advise you of any additional information we receive, hoping for the best.
  Very respectfully,
  Charles Killian, Sr.

           Somewhere in Germany
           February 16, 1945

Dear Dr. Hayden:

I'm writing you to tell you what an awful shock it was to learn of Dean Wood's death as I don't know any of his own family—other than his whole Reserve family. It seems impossible that he will no longer walk that lovely campus, but he and his ways left a mark and a tradition with that place that never could be erased. He will always be one of the best loved men in the lives of everyone who knew him. I know how badly you and the entire school family feel at the same time, and along with the thousands of others who knew him, I wish to send you my sympathy. He certainly was a favorite with the entire Dickerson family for the many years we knew him.

As I write this in an infantry battalion command post in Germany, I can hear the constant shelling that is gradually pounding Germany into a country of total ruin. I'm the artillery liaison officer with the infantry battalion, and the work we are all doing is so foreign to everything that men like Dean Wood wanted for his boys. But soon, God willing, this awful mess will be over and we can return to a better life again.
  Sincerely yours,
  Bill [Willard D.] Dickerson ['36; Age 28]

           Germany
           February 16, 1945

Dear "Mrs. Haydie",

It's been hard trying to find time to write these days, but I have had you all in my mind many times. Your cheeses arrived just before Christmas. We had one for Christmas and one on New Years and I am still lugging two of them about in my bed roll waiting for a special occasion. I often laugh at myself for waiting for special occasions. I carried a can of popcorn around for six months in the African campaign and each time an occasion looked right I would put it away and wait just a little longer. I finally lost it—like so many of our hopes.

Well, we are still in the lines, still no rest, no leaves and going into our ninth straight month, but outside of being a little groggy, all goes well. Until Christmas we were around Aachen, where we were the first to breach the Siegfried Lines. We took Aachen in hard fighting and then went all through the bitter battles of Attrition around Stolberg, Eschweiler, and Weisweiler.

We almost got a rest once, though. We were in position near Rotgen just north of the breakthrough and were to be relieved. Our dreams of showers and sleep and a little while in some place that was warm and dry away from mud and noise were brought to an end about five o'clock in the morning when Jerry began to shell the town, all crossroads, and our positions. All our wire was shot up, several vehicles were put out of commission, but we got through without casualties. The mess was about four hundred yards away and I remember waiting for the shelling to subside until hunger overcame caution and we ran for it, much as you would run to escape a shower. We would go along a ways until we heard a shell whistle and then dive into the ditch. The windows were all shot out of the mess and fragments had scattered the dishes about, but that was ten minutes before we arrived.

About noon we pulled out, reached our rest area that night only to hear about the breakthrough and to be put on an hour's alert. The next afternoon we moved out. Paratroopers had cut the roads and the doughboys who preceded us had to fight their way through, but our column wasn't battered. Buzz bombs came over in pairs at five minute intervals. "Jerry" bombers were all over. We could see the flashes of bombs in the towns we had just passed through and several times our column was lit up by flares, but the bombers passed over to catch others. You feel awfully naked and helpless in a column on the road under the light of flares. It's a peculiar feeling to be moving up when everyone else is moving back.

Going the other way were the remnants of hospital units, ack-ack outfits, engineer units—all that was left of those that were caught without warning. We had experienced the same thing often before at Tabourba, Medjey el Bab, Kasserine Pass, Gela, and now again in Belgium. It's a good feeling, though, to be moving up in perfect order and with confidence when all around things are in confusion. Our confidence is always in our doughboys. I can think of no situation that we wouldn't go into calmly, knowing that our own division doughboys were ahead of us. They have never failed to take an objective; they have never retreated.

We worked all night and were set just before dawn when "Jerry" struck with the 12th Panzer, a Volkogrenedien Division and a parachute division. For eight days he hammered away and for eight days the doughboys held, destroying the better part of four divisions with armour and vehicles.

The stand at Bastogne was played up in the papers. It was dramatic and it was heroic, but strategically [von] Rundstedt failed when he failed to break through to the north, for this would have eventually cut supply routes, captured Liege and other cities, and he would have been able to attack the northern armies from the rear. At best he might have delayed us from six to eight months. As it was he delayed us perhaps four months and got caught on the Russian front without enough reserves. You can draw a circle around the bulge and know that in that whole area few houses and few towns remain standing.

Nothing you read about the conduct of the SS troops is exaggerated. Why anyone takes any of them prisoners I don't know. One CP we had we occupied in four feet of snow. It was part of a building with walls still standing and surrounded by a score of "Jerries," all dead of course, but it was two days before we had time to move them. And so it goes in an endless procession of hours and days until you realize that you are a thousand years old. All my best wishes and my thanks for your thoughtfulness—*Fortune, PM, Christianity and Crisis* all come through in good order.

Best,
George [Manlove, '32; Age 31]

The Philippines
February 18, 1945

Dear Dr. Hayden:

I received the V-mail letter sent out by the Academy about the death of Dean Wood. My parents also sent me clippings from the local press. The school has suffered a great loss in his death and I am sure that every graduate is sorry to hear of it.

It doesn't seem so very long ago that I was at WRA, but in two years so much has happened. I have traveled all over the states and over large areas of the Pacific. The outfit I am with now is one of the B-24 outfits of the Fifth Air Force. I joined the squadron in British New Guinea; moved to Dutch New Guinea, then to Palau and now in the Philippines. Our progress has been very rapid since I landed overseas last May.

I haven't run across any Reserve classmates in the army, but I have run across several of my Harvard classmates. Father forwarded me a copy of the alumni bulletin. I was very much amazed to see how the class of '42 had spread all over the world.

Mark Worthen has written me several very interesting letters since he joined the Pacific Fleet. I believe he was one of my closest friends I had while I was at WRA. I hope to meet him after the war and make a cruise with him along the New England Coast. Incidentally, whatever became of the Snipe sailboat we had during my last years at school? Last I heard of it was when we parked it in Evamere Hall.

My job at present is cryptographic technician—which means sitting behind a typewriter a large part of the time. The work itself is interesting, though.

Yours,
John R. Williams ['42; Age 20]

Somewhere in Germany
February 18, 1945

Dear Dr. Hayden:

. . . I have received two V-mail letters from you. The last concerned the unfortunate death of my friend (every Reservite's, for that matter), Dean Wood. It was quite a shock to me. I was looking forward to seeing him on my next visit to Reserve.

We are having a short rest right now in this German village. Our duties consist of treating and evacuating bad colds and severe diarrhea. It is a refreshing change from treating and evacuating casualties. I have given up my ambulance driving for a job in our station platoon where I can actually be of use in the treatment of casualties. It is a wonderful break for me because of the experience which will come in handy in medical school some day.

Johnny Malcolm ['42; Age 20]

February 21, 1945

Dear Dr. and Mrs. Hayden:

Yes, indeed! Don [my son] and I have suffered a great loss. It is so hard for me to reconcile myself to the way Neil ['33] lost his life. After all the hardships he endured in Sicily, Italy and Anzio Beachhead and then to be killed in a plane accident that looks like carelessness to me. One of the boys from S. France wrote that Neil had to go up with a new pilot and spoke of him as being "raw." The wind was strong and rough and the aileron clamp was on and they spun in. Many of the boys who have been to see me say it is the ground crew's work to check the plane, and also the pilot's.

I can't help but feel if he could have had the pilot he had a year in Italy it wouldn't have happened. Of course, we don't know. Well it did happen, so as hard as it is, I guess there is nothing for me to do but carry on as best I can for my mother and Don, as they need me.

Don was home for a week in October and was leaving for Great Lakes just as the messenger came with the telegram telling of Neil. The poor boy was so heartbroken and yet he had to go. He was twenty years old the 11th of February and Neil would have been thirty the 16th of September.

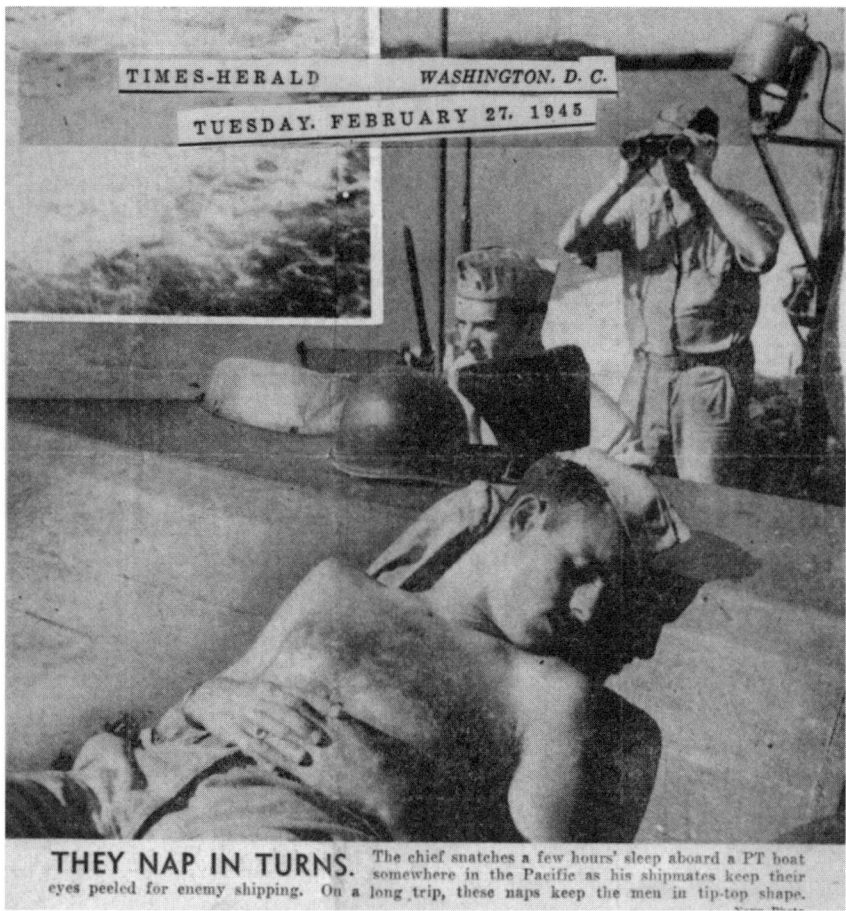

Edward J. Pope ('37) takes a front-page nap, in this Washington D.C. *Times-Herald* photo of February 27, 1945. *Archives*

I am grateful that in his short life he had the privilege of having a happy year at Western Reserve and four years at Ohio Wesleyan. He made the most of his experiences in the war and always wrote cheerful letters.

> Very sincerely,
> Anna S. McPhail [mother]

The February 22 issue of the *Reserve Record* listed the names of the Gold Stars to date. One of them represented Robert S. Prior ('41x), who entered the school in February 1935 as a sub-freshman and transferred to another school at the end of his freshman year. The only information available in his file stated that he was on active duty at the time of his death but the circumstances were unknown.

March 3, 1945

Dear Dr. Hayden:

The other day we received additional information regarding Boots from his commanding officer. According to his letter, Boots' bomber, one of a group, had successfully bombed enemy installations on Luzon Island.

His plane was contacted several times by radio during the return trip and then nothing more was heard from them. A searching party was sent out at once and every effort has been made since to locate the missing plane.

Captain Rowe stressed the possibility of the crew being safe on one of the many islands in the vicinity. If this is the case, he feels it may be some time before the crew will be able to reach friendly troops and contact their base. Naturally we are very much encouraged and look forward to favorable news.

In closing I wish to thank you for your kind letter and deep interest in Boots' welfare. Rest assured I will advise you of any additional news we receive.

        Very respectfully,
        Mr. and Mrs. Charles Killian, Sr.

March 5, 1945

Dear Bill [Peace, '41],

Thank you for your grand letter from the Phillipines area, bringing us all up to date. I am going to tell you frankly that it is a wonderful pleasure, as far as I am concerned, to write these cards for the birthday of each of the 634 boys in the service. The only drawback is the lack of time. I just don't have the time to do it justice and very often the cards are very late. If our thoughts could find some radio beam to travel directly to each boy those thoughts would not only arrive in time for birthdates but you'd get the right kind of a message from us every day in the year.

The news of your operations to date is just what we need to try to understand what your fellows are up against. Just had word, Bill, that Abner McDaniel ['39], based on Foggia, Italy, died of his injuries after an air raid on February 18th. That makes 27 Gold Stars. You remember Abner, don't you? He was a year ahead of you; he had to go back to graduate at U.S. because he couldn't finish here in time, but, of course, he's part of our family and that's that. . . .

        Devotedly yours,
        Joel B. Hayden

March 5, 1945

Dear Mr. and Mrs. McDaniel:

I just had word this morning on my return from a school trip of the tragic loss which is yours. The Hayden family has known Abner since he

Abner O. McDaniel ('39). *Archives*

was a little boy and we have known all of you for longer than that. . . . There are twenty-seven Gold Stars on our little school Service Flag; there are seven boys missing; there are three prisoners of war in Germany—and we are a small school. The total loss is tragic and it is so close to your heart that each day takes a little bit more out of you in a hundred different ways.

I shall never forget the light and the fire and the generosity in the eyes of Abner. They always shown with something that came from the very core of him. He was gay; he loved competition; he was devoted to his friends; he was loyal and fearless. We were very proud of him.

Devotedly yours,
Joel B. Hayden

Somewhere in Belgium
March 6, 1945

Dear Ray [Mickel]:

Thanks for remembering my birthday. The fact that it was a little late is unimportant, for most of my birthday greetings were slightly delayed this year. You shorted me one year in your computation, but I don't feel that young anyway, except in the morning when I arise from my downy concrete couch.

Things are pretty rough here for the doughboys, but we rear echelon people don't have it too bad. We're ordinarily ten to twenty miles behind the front lines and, so far at least, have managed to find buildings in which we set up our headquarters and often times eat and sleep. On one occasion we were well quartered in a civilian home and were treated like favorite sons. The Belgians are very hospitable and can't do enough for us. At that time particularly there was a slight epidemic of buzz bombs and the civilians were more than willing to turn over their beds to us, while they slept in their cellars. Their logic didn't particularly impress me, as I'd as soon be hit by the bomb as have one of these stone houses cave in on me. In either case one is likely to be very dead.

      Sincerely,
      Franklin Barlow ['30; Age 33]

              March 6, 1945

Dear Dr. Hayden:

 . . . Your birthday greeting reached me in the Philippine Islands. After a year's duty in navy yards in the States, I have since amassed ten months' duty overseas in New Guinea and this area. In so far as war necessitates my being separated from wife and family, I have enjoyed to the fullest every moment this trek through the SWPA [South West Pacific]. But, were I to be offered transportation home. . . .

 Return to wife and family, to the work which I'm fortunate to enjoy so much and to all that our country holds for us is constantly in my thoughts, yet my most sincere prayers are that when it is over, just punishment where necessary, unselfish cooperation and understanding, and a strengthening in our will to live as our hearts tell us we should will end world strife and needless suffering. Such a result is certainly plausible and well worth any amount of work or sacrifice to make it possible.

      My best to you,
      Don Lightner ['35; Age 27]

 The front page of the March 8 *Reserve Record* reported that Jonathan G. Izant ('41) was commissioned a second lieutenant on February 22 at Sarrebourg in Alsace, near the German border. He received his gold bars from his commanding general "on the battlefield before the One Hundredth Division."

              March 9, 1945

Dear Jonnie:

 We were all very much thrilled to hear the good news of your recent promotion. This in itself, combined with the circumstances under which it came, makes us all extremely proud of you. We wish we might see you personally to shake your hand and extend congratulations. It is certainly something to know that you have received this reward the hard way and that you unquestionably earned it. All of your friends here join in sending congratulations and best wishes.

 . . . It won't be long until the baseball season will be here. We sure wish you were back to play on the team.

      Sincerely,
      Raymond A. Mickel

At left: Jonathan G. Izant ('41) receiving his lieutenant's commission on the field of battle. *Courtesy Molly I. White*

Below: Cleveland Plain Dealer baseball writer–turned–war correspondent Gordon Cobbledick was sent on assignment to Pearl Harbor, where his son, SFC Bill ('43) was serving with the Seabees, having been at sea for seventeen months. The two enjoyed a forty-eight-hour reunion before Gordon went on to Guam. Both at a loss for words when they first met, Gordon said, "Hi!" Bill said, "Hi! Gee, Dad, I still don't believe it," as they looked at each other and grinned for this photo in the front page of the March 6, 1945 *Plain Dealer. Archives*

Somewhere in the Pacific
March 13, 1945

Dear Dr. Hayden,

Let me say first how sorry I was to hear of Mr. Wood's death. It was indeed a shock. Reserve has lost a loyal friend that will never be forgotten as long as the Academy or her friends shall live. I'm afraid that men like Mr. Wood grow to be so much a part of their surroundings that they are not fully appreciated, at least by some of us younger men, until the intricate part they played in those surroundings appears as a gap, left by their departure. There is little more I can say that has not already been said, or felt, by the many generations of men who knew Mr. Wood. He was loved by all. My only regret in knowing him was that I did not know him better; not take better advantage of his vast wealth of knowledge and kindly understanding. May God rest his soul.

. . . The *Alumni Record* seems to follow me like a faithful dog in my travels about the world, and is very eagerly received, I assure you. Occasionally I get a few copies of the *Reserve Record,* and of course your unfailing Christmas and birthday greetings. The news in the publications is devoured with relish, but it is your personal notes and cards that make me feel a still active and remembered member; part of the Reserve Family. I don't know how you keep up with us, or ever have the time to think about us, but I shall leave well enough alone and merely say how very much I appreciate your remembrance. It is certainly nice to be remembered.

. . . There's a whale of a war going on out here, although to look at some of the scenery you'd never think so. Right now I can look out the port and see a beautiful, peaceful-looking island with its green palm trees against the background of the purple mountains that rise in the distance. The calm royal blue water is broken in its serenity only by the graceful breaking of a wave across a reef and against the broad sandy beach, or perhaps by the quick darting of a sleek azure winged flying fish, or the thrashing of a silver sail fish as it stands on its tail in playful defiance of the world about him. Beyond the mountains one of those fantastic Pacific sunsets lights the scene with a blaze of color. You stand and gaze in awe until the spell is broken by the drone of a plane or the shrill note of a bosun's pipe.

I didn't mean to wax poetic on you, but some of these sights would bring out the poetry in any man, especially when it is such a contrast to some of the reality and sordidness of what may also be seen close at hand. Maybe I should be writing to my girl with such inspiration.

I have been most fortunate in seeing innumerable friends in my travels, among them several Academy classmates and friends. In Boston, Paul Fuzy ('40) . . . on a brief stop at Wesleyan I saw Joe Weitz ['40] . . . at Pearl Harbor "Coach" Bob Morse (Lt. j.g.), Henry Ferris '37 (a j.g.), Bob Wallace ['39] and Ned Brouse ['38] . . . in Miami I saw Jimmy Allen ['41] . . . and so

Dan W. Climer ('43). *Archives*

it goes. Reserve seems to be stretched around the world. No matter where you go, you can't get away from the ties—nor should I want to . . .

    Sincerely and gratefully,
    John H. Noyes ['40; Age 22]

    March 20, 1945

Dear Mr. and Mrs. Climer:

I have just heard the shocking news that Dan has been reported killed in action. We want you to know that we are thinking of you and that you have our deepest and sincerest sympathy. You are fortunate in having such wonderful memories of a truly fine son. His many friends here on the campus remember him very well and very kindly for his good nature and his constant friendly smile and good humor. I remember him particularly well for the contribution he made to the soccer team in his last year.

It is nothing short of criminal that so many of our very best young men must be sacrificed on the altar of war, but that is war. The best thing we can do about it is to unite our efforts in seeing that this does not occur again.

    Sincerely,
    Raymond A. Mickel

Spring Term: March–June 1945

Blaine Rawdon ('42) sent a note to his parents from an army hospital in Germany that brought good news and a sigh of relief: He was no longer missing in action; he was alive and recovering after three months as a prisoner of war. Mr. Rawdon wrote a letter to the school on April 12, in which he enclosed a copy of his son's note.

April 2, 1945

Dear Mom & Pop:

I'm using this means of letting you know that I'm O.K.—all O.K.—because it is supposed to be as fast as anything else and because I have no access to cable.

I hope that you have not been too worried these past three months, but of course they must have had their bad moments. I hoped and prayed that some way word would get to you that I was a prisoner in Germany, but that was the slimmest of chances. I had to rely on your faith—and my own. I am in this hospital in order to fatten up and get some rest. I have no broken bones or anything like that. I should be back to normal before long.

After censorship eases up a little there will be more to say. You write and let me know how everybody and everything is around the Village. Inform Charles, Lewis, Marge and Jeanne that I've turned up O.K. I'll write again when I can. I have no idea what happens after the hospital puts its stamp of approval on me. Be good and write!!

All my love,
Blaine [Age 21]

Word came to the school that John S. Knight, Jr. ('41x), was killed in Muenster, Germany, while leading a reconnaissance unit. A first lieutenant in the army, he died just two weeks before the birth of his son, John III.

April 9, 1945

Dear Mr. and Mrs. Knight:

We have just received the news of the untimely demise of your son, John, while fighting for his country overseas.

Speaking for Dr. Hayden and our entire faculty family, I hasten to extend to you the sincere condolences of Western Reserve Academy. In cases like these, we all know that words seem empty and futile but we do want you to know that we are thinking about you and are hoping, with you, that John's death, like that of thousands of other American boys in the prime of life will, somehow, contribute to a future in which boys do not have to give their lives in this way.

Sincerely yours,
Ralph W. McGill

On April 12, 1945, while in Warm Springs, Georgia, President Franklin D. Roosevelt suffered a cerebral hemorrhage and died a short time later. As

John S. Knight, Jr., ('41x). His death was reported in the April 21, 1945, *Cleveland Plain Dealer. Archives*

the nation mourned his loss, Blaine Rawdon's father wrote to Dr. Hayden and enclosed a copy of Blaine's April 2 letter from the army hospital.

April 12, 1945

Dear Joel:

Here is a copy of the letter we received from Blaine, which brought happiness to us again, and to you and many others, too. Life is again worth living. Now if we can just get him home.

. . . The imprint of Western Reserve character building under your wonderful leadership appears in every word, and I know you will be touched, as are we, by this evidence of the power of the teachings you believe should be a part of the education of each youth, if he is to face all problems everywhere at all times.

It was wonderful that you were here when the news broke and I am so happy that you talked with [my wife] Marie. We shall hope to see you and yours at the earliest opportunity. Remember to take most excellent care of yourself.

Sincerely, to all of you,
Blaine Rawdon, Sr.

Germany
April 18, 1945

Dear Dr. Hayden:

Thank you very much for your letter which I am sorry to admit I am slow in answering. There just doesn't seem to be enough hours in the day to do the things I want to do. I have been terribly busy the past few months, but I keep going with the faith that my small contribution will in some little way help for the goal we are all driving for. Some day not too far off we will be together again and can start off a new life which we can be sure won't see my sons or your grandsons in another war.

I don't know quite how to thank you for your praises of me. There isn't much at all to be said, for after the thought and ceremony has died down I have returned as just one of the boys. This country is certainly beautiful. It reminds me a little of Vermont, but there are many more small towns and of course many bigger ones. The larger ones have been bombed quite badly as everyone has said. The people at first can't understand us because the Germans have given them many false ideas, but soon they go about their business as usual.

I am very sorry to hear of Mr. Wood's death. It was a great loss to the Academy as well as to the people of Hudson. I will always carry a picture of him in my mind as one of the most understanding teachers and friends I have ever had.

Mother has sent several Western Reserve Academy "T" shirts which I have been wearing around under my O.D.'s [olive drabs]. I'll bet it's one of the few that has ever been worn so long and still the green came through.

Jon Izant ['41; Age 21]

Two days later, four days before his twenty-second birthday, Jonathan was reported missing in action in Germany. In the meantime, the father of Paul and Doug Barnes described the details of Doug's demise to Dr. Hayden and enclosed a letter that was sent to Mrs. Barnes.

April 19, 1945

Dear Friend:

Herewith is a copy of a letter dated April 9, 1945, which Mrs. Barnes has received from Lieutenant William D. Maxwell relating to the death of our son Douglas. . . .

Until the receipt of this letter the day before yesterday, we were without details of Douglas's passing. All that we knew was that he had died on January 3, 1945, of wounds received in action in the Department of Bas Rhin and that his body was buried in the Department of the Vosges.

Doug was called for induction under the Selective Service Act of 1940 and was inducted into the armed forces of the United States on July 9, 1943. He did not ask for the three week's furlough which he might have had for the asking, because he was anxious to get in and help finish up the war as speedily as possible. He asked for assignment to the combat engineers because his brother Bud [Paul] was assigned to that branch of the service, and he was assigned to the combat engineers and sent to

Camp Bowie, Texas, where he trained. Doug's company spent the winter of 1943–44 on maneuvers in Louisiana. The company was later returned to Camp Bowie, and during the month of May 1944, Doug had his only furlough, which he spent with us at La Grange. Shortly thereafter, his outfit went overseas.

They spent some time in England, we think southern England, and went into Normandy within a week after D-Day. His outfit crossed France with Patton's Third Army. Douglas later told us that they had built bridges at Avranches, Laval and Sens. About the first of December he had a pass and spent a day or two in Paris. He wrote us of his visit and said that he enjoyed it very much; particularly he enjoyed the opportunity to clean up and sleep in a real bed. Doug told us, in a general way, of various movements, but never mentioned any other towns or places than those I have indicated above.

Early in December 1944 Doug mentioned that he had not seen Bud for almost two years (Christmas in 1942), that he had an idea that he and Bud were in the same neighborhood, and that he thought he would take a jeep some day and go out on a bit of personal reconnaissance. The fact is that Bud was dead at the time of the writing; he was killed in action on November 21, 1944. We cabled Doug, but he did not receive our cablegram until sometime after he had written us above.

. . . We heard of Doug's death on January 16, 1945, and about the same time heard from the parents of a boy in Doug's platoon who was killed on January 3 that their son had written them on January 1, 1945 to the effect that his platoon had been laying a mine field during that day; that they had been under shell fire all day, and that they had to go out again soon. We were fearful, accordingly, that Doug had been wounded on January 1, 1945 and that he had suffered until his death on January 3, 1945. We are glad to know that he did not suffer.

Saar Union, where Doug was wounded and where apparently he died of his wounds, is only twenty-four miles from Avricourt, where Bud was killed in action. Bud was in the Forty-Fourth Infantry Division, which was on the left wing of the Seventh Army. Doug's outfit was on the right wing of the Third Army. Lieutenant Maxwell's letter indicates that the outfit was transferred to the Seventh Army. Whether this transfer took place before or after Doug's death, we do not know.

We have not yet heard where Bud's body is buried, but Avricourt, where Bud was killed, is nearer to the Department of the Vosges than is Saar Union, where Doug was killed, so we think it probable that the boys are buried in the same cemetery.

Doug's first promotion was to that of Technician Fifth Class. Shortly thereafter, he was made a corporal. He went overseas as a sergeant. He was known as Heavy Weapons Sergeant for his company or platoon. That is, he had charge of the squad which operated the machine guns, bazookas and light mortars (when they had mortars). He was promoted to staff sergeant sometime in the fall of 1944 and was platoon sergeant of the Second Platoon.

I am giving you all these details because I know you were fond of the boys.

Sincerely,
John P. Barnes

April 9, 1945

Dear Mrs. Barnes:

I hope that I can be of some help. I received your letter of March 8 yesterday and I'll give you all the details that I think will help you.

First of all let me say that your son, Doug, was one of the best liked men in our company. His men looked up to him as their leader in spite of his youth and the company officers admired him because of his clean cut appearance and excellent morals.

On behalf of us all please accept our regret and condolences for both your sons as we knew, through Doug, of the death of his brother.

We were in Saar Union, France, billeted in some buildings when the event took place. The Germans were methodically shelling all the larger towns in the Saar area with their 380mm railroad guns and Saar Union was one of them. The early morning of January 3 was the third day we were subjected to it and was our unlucky day. At about 0600 a shell scored a direct hit on the building in which the Second Platoon was sleeping and Doug was one of the twenty-five casualties. Lt. Maurer, his platoon leader, was very seriously injured and is now probably back in the States. He took Doug's death quite hard, as they were much closer than the usual platoon leader-platoon sergeant association.

Doug did not suffer at all, Mrs. Barnes. We and the medics did all that was humanly possible for him but he died without regaining consciousness from the explosion. He was killed by shell fragments that cause internal bleeding which could not be stopped. You might say he died in his sleep.

There isn't anything that I can say, I know, that will help to ease your grief but I would like to say that Doug and "B" Company have done more than their part in this war. . . .

We hope with all our hearts that his death has not been in vain. If there is anything else that I can possibly do for you please feel free to ask it.

Sincerely,
Lt. William D. Maxwell

April 19, 1945

Dear Pete [Edgar S. Bowerfind '42]:

... We've just heard from Blaine Rawdon via his family; in fact it was a week ago this very morning that first word came through from him since the 16 of December. He had escaped from a German prisoner's column deep in Germany somewhere. He and another boy hid in an old barn and in an old church, quietly foraging at night managing to keep body and soul together, and then Patton's boys came tearing through and Blaine and company, when last heard from April 2, were in an emergency hospital trying to get some meat on their bones.

Fine letter from Bob Fornshell ['43] from Germany. In fact, there are many letters coming through all the time and it is almost impossible to keep up with them all. I hope you're getting the *Records* right along. If you're not, let me know immediately. I suppose the most difficult job we have on our hands is the WRA mailing list, past, present, and probable future! ...

Devotedly yours,
Joel B. Hayden

David H. Bennell ('40x) had recently returned to the United States after completing sixty air missions in Europe, when he was one of twenty-five military personnel killed in a military transport crash in Texas.

April 21, 1945

My dear Mr. and Mrs. Bennell:

It just came to our attention this morning that David lost his life near Sweetwater, Texas yesterday. All of us at Reserve want you to know how deeply we feel about David and your loss. We shall never forget his charm, his joy in games, his good spirits, and the life he gave to all the boys with whom he associated here at the Academy.

In times like these we all need our friends, even though we may not see them very often. The fact that they are there ready to be called upon, gives us a sense of support and is the very heart of inner courage. I want to send you a little book[1] written by one of our alumni, Lucien Price, of the Class of 1901.... Mr. Price has been speaking to us across the years. He now speaks to us again in terms of war and death and immortality and the final triumphs of the just and decent man, the just and decent people of the world. May it bring you comfort and the assurance that your friends here at Reserve will stand by you through thick and thin.

Most sincerely yours,
Joel B. Hayden

1. *Litany for All Souls.*

David H. Bennell ('40x). *Archives*

April 23, 1945

My dear Mr. Mickel:

... Whenever I read of the death of any of the Academy boys, I am very sad. So many have been lost even from Lester's 1943 group. My heart aches for Mrs. Barnes. I sometimes wonder how she can go on. Lester wrote me this winter after he heard of Doug's death and his comment was "The best always seem to go first...."

Over and over again, I am so grateful for the two years Lester had at WRA. He loved the place and everything in it and it has helped him to grow up so gracefully. He really is a very satisfactory son and seems to do us all credit wherever he goes. We hope it keeps up. He will get his commission in October if the navy continues as planned....

        Very sincerely yours,
        Agnes Dunlap Shultis [mother of Lester Shultis '43]

Somewhere in Germany
April 24, 1945

Dear Ray [Mickel]:

I've had my first look at the Rhine by moonlight and must confess that I was impressed. As most American soldiers, I suppose, I came into this country determined not to be impressed and thoroughly disgusted and angry at everything German. While I still don't like them, I must admit a grudging respect for their industry and there is no doubt left in my mind that they have a lovely country—what I've seen at least. It is difficult to reconcile the peaceful, busy populace with the new atrocities which are

Franklin S. Barlow ('30).
Courtesy Donald S. Barlow

uncovered daily by our advancing armies. They seem so determined to be friendly and it is difficult for many of us who haven't actually been up there slugging it out with them to feel any real hate for them.

We are set up in a beautiful little town nestled down in a valley surrounded by mountains which look as though they've been cut from a scenic postcard. One of them even had the ruins of an old castle—Schloss, I guess, isn't it—at the top. It is still fairly cool up here but as beautiful as it could be anywhere in springtime. As I walked over to mess this morning with the sun shining brightly, birds singing, an old cart drawn by two oxen rumbling along the street, and the populace bustling about their business, the atmosphere was more that of a story book than war.

> Sincerely,
> Franklin Barlow ['30; Age 33]

Dear Mr. Mickel: This is a copy of a portion of a letter received from Blaine—thought it might interest you.

> Sincerely,
> Marie Rawdon

April 29, 1945

About noon of 24 December, Bill Kenneth and I walked into an SS patrol of six men. We were taken to their Commanding Officer (a captain) and given the usual (not then, but they proved to be in the following months) questions. "What are you doing here (meaning Americans)?" "Are you prepared for gas warfare?" "How many tanks have you?" And more of the same, asked in English with an Oxford twang.

From there I was taken to the nearest town, a mile or so away, named Echdorf (better get a good map out), in northern Luxembourg near the Belgian border. We remained there for an hour or so and left when the town started to crumble from our artillery and planes. From this point on all transportation was on foot. I was taken by an officer to Esch—a very lovely ancient village along a river and bounded by mountains where "Heinie" had positions which helped me decide not to escape there. I was put in an attic with other Americans, several of whom I knew. Later that evening we were taken to a safer place.

The next day, Christmas, we were interrogated again, and not fed. In the evening a German aid man came in to brush up on his English and see what he could get out of us. We got tea and marmalade from him, but carried dead "Heinies" to the morgue for him. They had been killed by our P-47's and our artillery. For the next two days we marched, joining other groups of Americans from time to time, without any food save two boiled spuds, a cup of "ersatz" coffee, and a quarter of a loaf of bread. When we arrived at Nachmanderschied, Luxembourg, we became part of a labor gang of 150 (approx.) "Yanks." We worked in the forests chopping trees, dragging logs, and building winter huts. (They were over confident of their limited success in Belgium and Luxembourg.)

We ate one hot meal a day then—spuds, meat or meat sauce. Occasionally sauerkraut. It wasn't too bad. Once in awhile we got a kitchen detail peeling spuds and carrying water, which was a break. We learned how to steal loaves of bread, marmalade and sugar from them with a professional —to be caught was undesirable. They cut off your food entirely.

Twenty-five of us lived in a room 10' x 16' (we measured it) unheated, but clean. We slept on straw cuddled up "S" shape just as close as we could get and kept warm enough. The wounded and sick were given no medical aid and no consideration. They had to work too. One died in March. In our spare time we played rummy and read. We had one, no, two pieces of literature—The Bible and a pamphlet of one page sermons by Dr. and Mrs. Clements[1] which he sent me. I still have the Bible and pamphlet. It was read over and over again by all twenty-five men. I could write a thesis on that phase alone.

We stayed there until the 20 of January when we walked out and away from the approaching Americans. I later learned they arrived two hours after we left. Just before we left, an artillery shell hit the farm house all 150 of us were in. It killed eight Germans—no "Yanks"; wounded many Germans and not a "Yank."

On February 1 we arrived at a transient prison camp at Limbourg, Germany, between Colburg and Giessen. There were many nationalities. I'll list them in order of the treatment they received from good (?) on down. French, British Indian Troops (Hindus), British, Italians, Poles, and lastly the "Yanks" and Russians. The food was non-existent practically; bread, potato soup, and once in a very great while some Argentine beef from Red Cross. Many "Yanks" died from wounds, malnutrition, dysentery, and diphtheria. My guess is about four a week. The Russians had typhus, too, in addition to all the other maladies and died like flies. I'd guess conservatively about thirty a week. We seldom worked here. When we did it was on the railroad in Limbourg. The first day I narrowly missed getting hit by machine gun fire and bombs from our own airplanes.

On the 22nd of March we were moved out again. This time in boxcars—forty to fifty in each car. Same old story. In four days we moved about twenty-five kilometers. Our fighters strafed the train and killed seven officers, four enlisted men, and wounded twenty-four more. They hit some "Jerries" and blew up another train loaded with ammunition. The officers were in the car next to ours. We ate 1/4 of a loaf of "brot" and a cake of limburger cheese (I liked the cheese at the time).

Finally they gave up and started walking us. I walked until they gave out the reserve rations (Red Cross packages) and split them with Henry.[2] We planned to get away separately and meet in a church which could be seen from a great distance just in case we had to have a guide back. A German civilian promised us protection until the "Yanks" got there. [Bill] Kenneth and another guy followed me as I walked out of the formation. A guard came chasing down the path and got them; I dropped in the grass. I went to the church and waited until midnight for Henry. We had planned to wait in order to make certain the German civilian was to be trusted. Finally I went by myself and hid in his barn. Hank showed up at six the next morning. That evening we heard jeeps and tanks and left the barn as fast as we could. The Americans fed us so much, I got sick, but I never felt better in my life. The name of the town was Braunfels.

We flew (C-47) back to France. The end Thank God!

All my love,
Blaine ['42; Age 21]

1. The pastor—and his wife—at Blaine's church in Long Island, New York.

2. According to a notation in a margin of the letter, Blaine met Henry "in Alabama while taking exams for A.S.T.P. Later found him in a Nazi prison camp."

James H. Cooper ('41) was stationed in Corpus Christi, Texas, when he died in a navy plane crash while on a routine training flight.

James H. Cooper, Jr. ('41). *Archives*

April 30, 1945

Dear Mr. and Mrs. Cooper:

We have just heard through Mrs. R. C. Allen that Jimmy was killed yesterday. This is a great shock to us and we want you to know that we are thinking of you and that you have our deepest sympathy.

Jimmy was with us only a short time, but in that period we came to like and respect him a great deal. Considering the fact that he was here for only one year, he was unusually successful in adjusting himself and creating an affectionate place in the hearts of those about him on the campus. We hope that your grief may be lightened by the memories of such a fine son and the thought that he gave his life for a great ideal.

          Sincerely,
          Raymond A. Mickel

On April 30, Hitler committed suicide in Berlin. That same day thirty-three thousand prisoners of the concentration camp at Dachau were liberated. Berlin fell to the Russians on May 2. The Grand Admiral Karl Doenitz, Hitler's successor, surrendered four days later, ordering U-boats to return to their bases and armies to cease fighting.

          Czechoslovakia
          May 7, 1945

Dear Mother:

Oh, the God damn vicissitudes of war! Today is as miserable as the day before was fine. We have left our chalet and trout pond. The past two days have brought cold and miserable penetrating rain. At the moment I have my shoes and socks drying by the fire and I have time for a short note before turning in, for tomorrow we move early.

We moved today in the rain—the tracks bogged down and we had to wench the guns in. All the men worked without a word in the pouring rain, soaked to the skin. After the guns were in, armor stacked, nets up, foxholes dug, they put up their pup tents. There is a long trail of straw from a nearby barn to each tent. I have seen it over and over for years, but each time I marvel and worship these soldiers who make so much of so little. Soon fires will spring up and they will run their wire lines into the generator. Socks and shoes will be drying, radios will be going full blast, and in the midst of the most wretched conditions they will become fairly comfortable—then they will talk of home.

They haven't been home for three years and they haven't been out of the lines for just eleven months now. Each section has a keg of beer, which I went back forty miles for. The thing that hurt most was I had to leave most of our liquor stock—no room. Also everyone else and his brother is out of the war, but one German army fights on and, as usual, we have to be taking care of it. Our last hard fighting was cleaning out the Hartz Mountains. That was where the shells destroyed our house and burst in the room where I was sleeping.

We treated a group of prisoners today—French, English, Russian, Serbian. They had typhus, malnutrition, bronchitis, T.B.—everything imaginable. They had been forced to walk all the way from Silisia on foot. Those who faltered were shot. Often they would go five and six days without food. Some in frenzy would snatch food, gobble it down and fall over dead. Nothing, however horrible, you hear about the Germans is exaggerated. I cannot describe our scorn and hatred for them. Under the Nazis they have lost all humane attributes and should be treated as beasts —and these are strong words from one who has never hated anyone. This will be over in a couple of days, though, and tomorrow the sun will shine. Meanwhile, I look forward to seeing you this summer.

    Love,
    George [Manlove, '32; Age 31]

As George Manlove wrote his letter home to his mother on May 7, 1945, the Germans surrendered unconditionally to the Allies at Rheim, France, and the war in Europe came to an end. In his V-E (Victory over Europe) Day speech on May 8, President Harry S. Truman reminded the nation, "The war is but half won." Four days later George wrote in a letter to his father, "All goes well—and all is over."

In Hudson, after listening to the president's armistice speech on the radio set up on the chapel stage, the entire student body, the faculty and several of their wives, and the administrators of the school joined in singing "The Star Spangled Banner."

Czechoslovakia
May 12, 1945

Dear Dad:

All goes well—and all is over. We were fighting up to the last and were just about to move up when the good news came, "cease all forward movement." The men were too tired to celebrate much and they went quietly about their work cleaning guns and trucks and getting equipment in shape. Inwardly they were happy, but outwardly, regardless of how good or bad the news, they show nothing. They have been disillusioned too many times and they have seen too much, so that by now they accept conditions as facts.

For the first few days you are out of the lines after so long in, the let-up is more like a hangover. You feel terrible; things just don't seem natural. And lights or vehicles or houses lit up seem wrong and you feel uneasy with it. We have been in complete darkness now for three years. This wears off, however, after a week or so and you gradually return to normal. This is what we are doing now, sort of returning to life. It would do your heart good to see the thousands of allied prisoners that have been turned loose and the thousands of "Jerry" prisoners coming in. It will take twenty years to get Europe back to normal.

I would like two things: two sets of good barber tools and some overseas stripes. They are gold embroidered on a brown "OD" [olive drab] background. I would like them in bulk—a roll of about 1,000—enough for the battery. We can't very well get them here. If the roll costs more than, say, twenty-five dollars, let it go.

My best,
George [Manlove, '32; Age 31]

Tien Wei Yang ('41) was an exchange student from China who attended the school from 1938 through his graduation in 1941. A 1991 recipient of the Waring Prize, he returned to the school as a faculty member, where he taught biology from 1952 to 1966. Charles Kennedy ('40) was a good friend, and Tien Wei spent time at the Kennedy home in Van Wert, Ohio. When he read the news in the *Record* that his friend was killed in action, he expressed his sorrow in a letter to Charles's mother.

May 19, 1945

My dear Mrs. Kennedy:

I learned about Chuck's death in the *Reserve Record* shortly after I had received words from my uncle in China about the death of my second brother, Tien Hsiung. Tien Hsiung was killed on the 7 of June last year on a mission over Central China. He was the leader of a squadron of American Mitchell bombers [B-25] stationed near Chungking.

The weather was extremely bad for flying that day—bad even for that part of the country, but the orders were that he was to proceed with his assignment in spite of the weather. Shortly after he took off he ran into trouble which led to his death. The radio silence which followed caused the two other sections of his squadron to remain grounded; twice the number of planes and lives were thus saved from needless sacrifice to fight for China another day.

All that we now know of what happened is that his plane and two others with him crashed into one of the numerous mountains not far from Chungking. After the accident, there was hardly anything to be found at the scene—only pieces of charred remains of what were once the men and the planes. When I received the news I was dealt a stunning blow as if I did not know what had hit me. I did not exactly feel sad; I only felt sort of strange and unreal. I could not believe that Tien Hsiung, my closest brother, was no more, yet I knew it was true. But despite everything, even now whenever I think about him I feel that he is not dead. I suppose I am beginning to realize and understand what people mean when they say that the spirit of a man never dies but lives on in the mind of men.

Shortly afterwards, I read the news about Chuck. After the initial shock was over, I felt exactly the same way about him as I had felt about Tien Hsiung. Looking at both their pictures standing on my dresser now gives me a strange feeling of calm. Both soldiers of their respective countries fighting for what they believed and treasured and both had found fulfillment by giving their lives in more or less similar circumstances. They were both very close to me and dear to me; close and dear in the sense that even as they are dead, to me they can never die. I think of both Tien Hsiung and Chuck very often and in my hours of solitude they afford me companionship and consolation as only the truly living can afford. . . .

   Affectionately yours,
   Tien Wei Yang [Age 23]

            Somewhere in the Pacific
            May 24, 1945

Dear Dr. Hayden:

Approximately fifteen years ago I stood on the speaker's rostrum of the Chapel and asked my classmates to move from their places in the student body to the alumni section. Then I turned over the presidency of the senior class to the incoming president and joined my classmates. I am now ready and willing to reverse that procedure. I would gladly move back to the front row center for another year of the best days of my life!

. . . I value my undergraduate life at Reserve not because of my academic marks but because of the friendly, cooperative and altruistic spirit that prevailed on the campus. That spirit stands out in my mind now more than ever because it is the kind of spirit that the whole world needs if we are going to avert another war. I hope sincerely that other institutions like Reserve realize that only by instilling the qualities of good, clean living into our youth can this world be a peaceful one.

I shall certainly be thinking of Reserve on June 3.[1] My graduation day stands out as a big day in my life. I hope that before another year rolls around I'll be able to be with you watching the proceedings.

My duty at my present station keeps me quite busy. I am here primarily to handle communications traffic. That in itself is enough. However, I am looking ahead to the days when I'll be competing with millions of other men for a job. I am taking a course in marketing from the University of Tennessee. I hope I'll be able to step back into my job at Goodyear without too much difficulty.

Sincerely,
John A. Church ['30; Age 32]

1. Commencement day.

Somewhere in the Pacific
May 25, 1945

Dear Dr. Hayden,

Many thanks for your letter which I received several weeks ago. I'm very sorry that I have been unable to answer it until now but as you know the navy has a habit of keeping one busy.

You may have heard the expression about it being a small world. Well little did I know how true it was until I reported aboard my ship and found Bud Hanks ['38] from Hudson acting as a communications officer aboard. Just prior to that I ran into Bob Hutchinson ['40], who was in the class ahead of me. He is now a pilot on one of the converted carriers out here. Both of them are fine and have no complaints.

There isn't a day that goes by that we don't talk about the times we had back at school. Both Bud and myself get our *Records* regularly and enjoy them very much.

At present I am attached to the USS *Maddox*, a destroyer, and find the duty very interesting. All of us aboard feel she is the best "can" out here, but of course our views are a little one sided. However, she has a good record and a grand skipper.

I have seen some action, enough to last me for quite some time. Say hello to everyone for me and give my best to "Scotch" and "Tebby" [Coach Thiebert].

Yours truly,
Dorsey Thomas [Jr., '41x; Age 22]

Harrie B. Stewart ('29). *Archives* Forrest W. Kenner ('34). *Archives*

June 6, 1945

Dear "Yipper" [David S. Owen]:

 . . . We now have thirty-two Gold Stars on our Honor Roll. Major Forrest Kenner 1934, brother of "Ham" Kenner ['37], has just been reported missing over Luzon. Lt. Harrie Stewart, class of 1930, who you didn't know, died a prisoner in a ship that was torpedoed not long ago when the Japs were hurriedly moving prisoners from the Philippines to the mainland. Lt. Ernie Stifel ['39], whom you knew, has recently been reported missing in action, as was Lt. Jon Izant. Jon was made a second lieutenant right on the field of battle due to his unusual gallantry in action in the Battle of the Bulge; then, a few weeks later, was reported missing in action. There has been no final word. We understand that Bill Calder ['41], who was a prisoner, has been heard from—and so it goes.

We are all hoping that this pesky war, which has now dragged on a long time, can somehow be brought to a finish soon. Lt. Dave Hanson ['36], Pete's ['44] older brother was here for commencement, as was Lt. Bruce Silver ['41], and Dave predicts the end of the Japanese War in a year or less. I hope he's right and I hope it will be much less. . . .

      Cordially yours,
      Ralph W. McGill

June 13, 1945

 . . . You may have heard that Ernest Stifel, Jr ['39]. from Wheeling was missing in the Pacific. We all were relieved to hear that he is safe, interned in Russia, slightly wounded.

      Sincerely,
      Mrs. Richard Stifel

Reese W. Lindsay ('39). *Archives*

June 14, 1945

Dear Mr. and Mr. Lindsay:

Rumor has come to us in a round about fashion to the effect that Bill has been reported killed in action.[1] We hope this is not true, but we would appreciate a note from you giving us the latest information about Bill. He has been on our missing list for a long time and we have been constantly hoping to have more cheerful news at any moment.

Sincerely yours,
Raymond A. Mickel

1. Reese "Bill" Lindsay, Jr. ('39), a first lieutenant in the Army Air Corps since 1943, was first pilot of a bomber when he was shot down over Leipzig on August 16, 1944.

June 14, 1945
Garmisch-Partenkirchen
Germany

Dear Dr. Hayden,

It has been a long time since the Academy has heard from me. I am truly sorry, for I meant to keep you informed as to what I have been doing and where I have traveled. I joined the 10th Armored Division at Trier, Germany. That was the first large German town taken by Patton's Third Army. Little did I imagine that after watching the half-tracks go by Hudson I'd soon be fighting in one!

At this time, I am in the Occupation troops here. I don't believe that it will last long, however, for I don't score too high on points. That will no doubt mean that I will soon be heading for the South Pacific. There is faint (oh, how faint) hope for occupational duties. If I remain here for the

Occupation I have a chance to attend one of the colleges here on the continent or in the United States. . . .

      Best wishes to all,
      Brownie [Charles B.] Ketcham ['44; Age 19]

Ernest J. Stifel., Jr's ('39) father updated the headmaster on Ernest.

              June 18, 1945

Dear Dr. Hayden:

 Today we had a letter from Tom Henney ['34] about a recent visit he had with you at Reserve. He was wondering whether he had told you enough or too little about Ernest, so that in order that you might get the story correct I think that I should give you facts as we know them.

 Ernest has been serving with the 77th Bomber Squadron in the Aleutian Islands since March 1943. For the past year he has been the gunnery officer with the rank of 1st Lt. Some time ago we received a report from the War Department that he has been missing in action since May 10, but just a few days ago we received a second report that he is now safe and interned.

 Naturally we have had no word at all from Ernest, but we are perfectly content to wait as long as we must, just so long as we know that he is safe.

 We can add nothing more to that meager information, for that is as much as we know, and even that much has been given to us confidentially. But I am sure that you will want to know at least that much and that you will use discretion in what you may have to say about him. . . .

 As with so many other boys, there are many gaps that need filling, but that shall have to wait until after all this is over and we can again sit down with them.

 We are so glad that you send us the *Reserve Record*, for it is a lot of fun for both Mrs. Stifel and me to go through it regularly and read about Reserve today. I really wish we might visit it again.

 With warm regards from us both to you and Mrs. Hayden,
    Faithfully yours,
    Ernest Stifel, Sr.

              June 22, 1945

Dear Mr. Stifel:

 . . . It was grand to hear about Ernest. We shall treat the letter with the discretion which you expect of us, and I just want you to know how we appreciate your confidence and how happy we are at the receipt of this kind of news.

 These are very difficult days; I don't have to tell you that. The Commencement season was difficult and every day we get a bit of news of one

William E. Wells III ('36) on the Academy golf team. *Archives*

sort or another which simply keeps us holding our breath and hoping and praying most earnestly for the boys. . . .

      Gratefully yours,
      Joel B. Hayden

                June 22, 1945

Dear Mrs. Wells:

 I just got back to Reserve last night and found the following memo on my desk: "Lt. William E. Wells III, Air Corps, missing over Germany since April 8. . . ."

 It is our hope and prayer that the coming weeks will bring you definite information that Bill ['36], or "Tiger", is just missing—no more than that. That will mean that pretty soon you will be hearing from him. As I say, that is our hope and prayer.

 As you remember Reserve, it was a small school; it always will be. That is one reason why we have gotten to know each other so well. There is a sense of kinship and understanding between the boys and the men which is precious beyond words. We can all "see" Tiger and actually "feel" him in terms of his residence here and the fun we had together and the way he had to work and how he learned to work. We think of those two cousins, "Tiger" and Joe, and they clearly left their stamp on the whole generation of school boys who lived together with them.

      Affectionately yours,
      Joel B. Hayden

Philippines
June 24, 1945

Dear Dr. Hayden,

... Gosh, school and Hudson and Ohio for that matter seem so far away.... The Japs left the Philippines in quite a mess as they retreated—and are still doing so whenever possible. What they can't loot and carry with them, they destroy by either burning or shell-fire. Some of the villages were left more or less intact, but they looted the homes, or should I say huts, of anything they desired—burned their rice, and kept or killed their livestock.

Manila is the worst example of the war I have yet to see—there isn't a building left standing—those that are are mere hollow shells. The harbor is full of scuttled and bombed ships. It looks like a hopeless job of restoration, but the people have already started with a zeal that makes one marvel at. I arrived there after the fighting was over—while climbing through the ruins of a section called the Walled City we came across plenty of dead Japs and their equipment, and I suppose they're still there. There are so many important things that come first, that they'll just have to wait I guess. All in all it doesn't take very long to bury them though; they use a bulldozer. If I ever have to see a city that is in the plight that Manila is, I only hope it's Tokyo.

I am with the 32nd Division and at the present time we're in a rest camp not too far from the front. Most of the fighting is now being done in the mountains—consider that along with rain, caves, and jungle, and you can see why it takes a while. Few tanks, artillery or airplanes to help you—because it's usually impossible to use them. Just tooth and nail, inch by inch, blasting them out of their caves and trying to get them in the open. They seem to be getting more fanatical and go in big for trying to scare you at night. They seem to prefer to fight and sneak up on you at night. Talk about "girding up your loins," Wow!

The Philippines as a whole is not too bad. This is the winter here, which means nothing more other than it's the rainy season. The days are very hot and the flies are thick, but the nights are cool, nothing is too bad as long as you can sleep at night. This is a Malaria area, but the mosquitoes are no more numerous than in the States. Plenty of palm trees, coconuts, bananas and pineapples. If you're lucky you can even get a monkey or parrot for a pet.

The people are friendly and act almost humble to the troops; I guess that comes from three years of oppression. They're always calling you sir and bowing and scraping etc., but they always seem to have a big smile. Nearly all of them can speak English. They have a great love for the American dollar, and are always after it. Prices over here are terrific.

Today is Sunday, but unfortunately I had to miss church this morning, because I had to take a patrol out hunting for Japs. Unfortunately our luck was nil. The Japs in this area that were by-passed hide in the hills during the day, and come down at night looking for food. Once in a while the boys capture one or two. If a Flip gets one first it is usually too late to ask him any questions. The natives are great lovers of huge knives which they always carry. They can really use them too.

I don't know when the division is moving up on the line again. Maybe not for quite a while. The other divisions are pushing them out of the mountains and down into the lowlands, where it should be, comparatively speaking, duck soup. There artillery, tanks and planes can be used to help the doughboy. It is not so very glamorous, or bright and shiny, but I'm really proud of our infantry. I think the foot soldier really takes a beating wherever they are in the world—even in the States.

We're all watching Russia, and certainly hope she comes in. I have no great desire to visit China. . . .

Yours very truly,
Bill Glover ['42x; Age 22]

Wasseralfingen Aalen Kreis
Wurttemburg
June 24, 1945

Dear Mr. Hayden:

This battered German steel [typewriter] will probably give me some trouble before I finish this letter because the "z" and "y" have been interchanged and I was unfortunately brought up on the American touch system. Your letter reached me only recently because I have been moving around quite a bit—through seven countries as a matter of fact. Part of my Cook's tour of Europe was due to a clerk's mistake, but I am very grateful to him because I would have missed Luxembourg, Belgium, Aachen, Cologne, Dusseldorf, Essen, Muenster, Kassel, Wurzburg and Nuremberg if he hadn't been confused! As it is I am an authority on victory through air power as well as on the infantry fighting I know only too well.

With all Reservites, wherever they are, I am saddened by the news of Dean Wood's sudden death. We can be sure that few are privileged to lead as exemplary and satisfactory a life as his. I remember the two occasions he was forced to discipline me, because all he did was explain why certain things aren't done by gentlemen. The effect on my subsequent actions was greater, of course, than if he had berated me and meted out punishment.

My wound was so little bother that any good Britisher would have murmured, "Just a scratch, old chap," and when I saw what was left of the original company I felt even more fortunate. Everybody in the infantry

Philip Narten ('41) on right with his army buddy, Bud Wiley, at Tidworth Barracks, England, November 1944. *Courtesy Phil Narten*

gets hit sooner or later anyway. At present we are garrison soldiers again, pulling guard on the German 19th Army, which our division had the grim task of stopping single handed last January north of Strasbourg. Using the theory that the attack is the best defense, we stopped them cold for a couple weeks, but then there was so little left of us that we were pulled back and reorganized. This is the 12th Armored Division, by the way, and we have only three battalions of infantry compared to three regiments or nine battalions in an infantry division. I hope we never have to stop an army with three battalions again. I got through that semi-organized mayhem all right and then found myself on the wrong end of a machine gun on the relatively easy job of cutting off the Colmar pocket. So it goes; thank you for your long letter, perhaps I'll be dropping in at Hudson before long.

                Yours,
                Phil Narten ['41; Age 22]

Earlier in May the Izant family received the confirmation of the death of their son, Jonathan. Dr. Hayden presided over the memorial service in the chapel on June 24 and sent his personal condolence to them the next day.

Jonathan G. Izant ('41). *Archives*

June 25, 1945

Dear Grace and Bob, Mary and Bob, Jr.:

It makes me sick at heart to realize how little I have been able to see you and be with you. Enclosed I am sending you the best copy I can make of the service of yesterday afternoon.

Our hearts and minds are with you and always will be, just as Jon is with us and always will be.

I bring you assurance of the unfailing love and devotion of the Hayden family and all of us here on campus and in village who have known and loved Jon.

Devotedly yours,
Joel B. Hayden

❧ July–August 1945

With every ending is a new beginning. So far thirty-five boys had been lost to the war. Since October 1944 the trustees were considering "a suitable war memorial for our boys in the present conflict." During the summer, plans were well underway to launch a memorial campaign "like the school had never known," with the goal of raising the funds—a projected one million dollars—to provide for an addition to the gymnasium and a new library and science building. The gymnasium was to be known as the Memorial Gym with a bronze tablet to be dedicated to the alumni who had lost their lives in the war and to those who had served. The campaign was to be launched in mid-October 1945 with a projected date of completion in 1951, when the school would celebrate its 125th anniversary.

John A. Church ('30). *Courtesy John A. Church*

Dr. Hayden did not go to Maine immediately following commencement as he had in past years. There were many details to tend to in relation to the fundraising campaign. The birthday greetings he had so diligently sent to the boys in the service were tended to by Dean Mickel. Surely it wouldn't be long until he could wish them all well in person as the boys returned from Europe. But there was still a victory to be won in the Pacific.

The jubilation of V-E Day in May gave way to horror with the liberation of the death camps in Europe. On July 5 General MacArthur reported the liberation of the Philippines. The U.S. fleet began the first heavy bombardment of the home islands of Japan on July 13. On July 26 in Potsdam, "The Big Three"—Harry Truman, Joseph Stalin, and the newly elected British prime minister Clement Atlee—sent an ultimatum to Japan, demanding an immediate and unconditional surrender. Three days later Japan turned down the ultimatum.

On August 6 the first atomic bomb was dropped on Hiroshima; two days later another was dropped on Nagasaki. President Truman warned Japan on August 9, "Quit or be destroyed." On August 14 the Japanese government communicated their acceptance of the Allied peace terms. One of the first of the Academy boys to learn of this was John A. Church ('30). A communications officer stationed at Pearl Harbor, he decoded the message of peace that was soon heard around the globe: the war was over.

Schorndorf, Germany
July 4, 1945

Dear Mr. Mickel,

According to the latest reports, the 100th Division is to remain in Germany until March of next year. Of course, this status is liable to change at any minute, so don't be surprised if I walk into your home someday soon.

Harrie B. Stewart ('30) and John Church ('30) during their school days. *Archives*

The weather has been cold and rainy for the past week. I haven't been able to go swimming because of that. The sun has finally broken through and it is beginning to warm up a bit.

Today is the Fourth of July and we were supposed to have a big celebration, but due to rain in the earlier part of the day, it was called off. We all had the day off anyway so I can't complain too much.

I am getting very homesick for the states, but I think I'd much rather sweat the war out here until March than have my furlough now and join the forces in the Pacific.

Well, all for now, Sir. Write soon, won't you?

                Very sincerely yours,
                David Spear ['44; Age 19]

                                            July 19, 1945

My dear Dean Mickel,

I have been away for a while, and upon returning home yesterday, I found your kind letter. No, I am sure I didn't receive your note. However, I did receive a fine letter from both Dr. Hayden and Mr. McGill. I haven't answered either of them for the reason that [my son] Bill [Wells '36] is still reported missing. And I've been hoping and praying that I might still have some message from the War department. They said Bill's objective was an oil depot at Derben, Germany and that he went down over that place. The second message said his plane was crippled from the heavy flak and was seen by his squadron commander to peel off and go over Central Germany in a spin. Before disappearing from view in a cloud bank, no person was seen to bail out.

William E. Wells III ('36) in the army.
Courtesy Elizabeth M. Young

One boy has arrived home, he apparently the one that parachuted from the plane. While he was still in England, he wrote his mother that he was the only survivor. Since he's been in this country, he has refused to give out any information, saying he has been sworn to secrecy by the government. Three of Bill's crew have been identified and reported killed (Bill was the pilot of a B-17).

My most recent letter from the Army Air Force headquarters assures me that "our commanders in the conquered areas are making intensive searches in the areas in which our airplanes are known to have disappeared. And the civilian population of the areas are carefully interrogated." Six boys are still listed as missing in action. The only hope as I see it lies in the fact that the government hasn't accepted as final "Bucky" Templeton's statement, that he was the only survivor. However, even though some of these boys may be living, they must be very badly injured, as it's now over three months since the accident.

Perhaps you know that Bill was married in 1943 to Gertrude Wright, whom he met while attending Special Service school at Washington and Lee University. . . . He transferred, just before his marriage, to the Air Corps. He has a lovely baby daughter, aged ten months. Everyone says she's the image of Bill.

Your and Dr. Hayden's and Mr. McGill's letters all illustrate to me the fine kinship and close feeling that exists between the boys and the men at the head of Reserve. I have always felt that Bill had a deeper feeling and affection for his masters in "prep" school than in college. You all exercised a wonderful influence in him most formative years.

Thank you for your kind interest and good wishes, and when I receive further word I'll send it to you.

Very sincerely,
Grace G. Wells

Hollandia
July 25, 1945

Dear Dr. Hayden,

Thought I'd drop a few lines of greeting now to let you know that all remains well with the New Guinea branch of the Hopkins clan. After nearly four months under a New Guinea sun (and rain) I fear that the aforementioned "branch" may have taken on some similarity in appearance to the natives of this island—but the heart remains where it was—back in those United States!

Being the wandering type—and also because the War Department has a way of issuing orders—I wound up at Hollandia shortly after my last letter to you—and here I have stayed ever since. I've been doing essentially the same work as when in Australia—but there is a difference in environment —and what a difference! I guess I never really appreciated civilization before—but I certainly do now.

It isn't that we have a lot to complain about here—for this is a well built-up base, and with electric lights, movies, etc. It could be a lot worse, and when I think of what other fellows are going through, I realize how easy we have it here. Also, we feel that we've gotten quite a bit accomplished, and that, of course, is the main and only consideration. I am very thankful, however, that my stay in New Guinea is nearly ended. In the very near future I'll be at a new location—and one which I think will be very interesting. I'll be able to say where it is, etc. when I write from there—but for the present, "we don't talk about that." These censors and their scissors! . . .

I continue to be temporarily thwarted in my attempt to do some graduate work through the Armed Forces Institute while overseas, as my last information from their headquarters at the University of Wisconsin said that my case had been turned over to DePauw, and that I would be hearing from them in the near future. That was two months ago, and since then I've had no word, but there may be news from them when I reach my next destination—for since we've been in New Guinea, most of the mail has been sent directly there, where it is being held. Thus, there is a rather sad mail situation here, but it will be wonderful when I arrive at my new "home!" I do hope that there will be information concerning graduate work awaiting me, for I'm way anxious to do anything and everything I can now that might help later on. I want more than ever to make education my life work—and while I do not expect to be able to do much studying while overseas, I feel that even the little I can do now will be of great value. . . .

The war news is certainly encouraging, isn't it?—with the increased tempo of air attacks on Japan, and Admiral Halsey roaming up and down the Japanese coast at will, and leaving a few "calling cards" along the way. Perhaps it is wishful thinking (and how wishful it is!) on my part, but my opinion is that the end is very definitely in sight. We can hope, anyway.

      Very sincerely yours,
      Walter Hopkins ['37; Age 26]

                August 7, 1945

Dear Paul [Barstow '43]:

It was great to see the little circular of "Mauthausen of the Donau." I am profoundly grateful it is not now Deutschland. I think that Deutschland will have to have a long vacation from adult responsibility until all of us, as Christians, have learned the significance of both repentance and forgiveness. Repentance cannot be separated from forgiveness, nor can forgiveness be separated from repentance. They are organically one and desperate brutality in thought and action has no place in this universe, and that is one thing we have got to learn—all of us.

Let me say that your father did a perfectly splendid piece of work for us in May. It was a real treat to have him here . . . the last word from him said that you have had a grim daily duty helping the Chaplain handle the tragic situation at a concentration camp now in your hands.

Of course, I haven't heard how long you may be in Europe. America will be in Europe one way or another as long as time shall last. That holds for other parts of the world, too, because isolationism of any kind has been shattered by the realities which we confront. We have to live all over the world now and learn as we've never learned before to understand, to be patient, to be tolerant, to be just, and to be basically realistic about man's capacity for decency and man's capacity for brutality. Whether we like it or not we are our brother's keeper and that sets our personal and corporate progress on a plane which we've never before tried to reach.

Blessings on you from all of us. You'll be hearing from the school shortly. We are going to honor all of you—the living and the dead—and also the unborn generations, with a memorial and anniversary program for this school which should put it in a position to serve as it has never served before.

      Ever yours,
      Joel B. Hayden

Paul Barstow was one of the three students who had left the school in January 1943 to begin college early. In January 1997 I received a communication from him that included his memories of the war years:

> On December 7th, 1943, the second anniversary of the Japanese attack on Pearl Harbor, I was inducted into the Army of the United States. . . . [I] had clamored for induction as soon as I was eighteen. So I memorized the eye-chart . . . and even refused the three-week "wind up your affairs" furlough standard after induction ceremonies . . . I insisted that I had no affairs except to save the world from monstrous tyrannies. Under a war-time accelerated program I had completed my freshman year at Williams College, intending a major in Political Science and a career in public service. . . . My outfit, the 65th Infantry Division, landed at Le Havre on January 22, 1945. We became part of General George S. Patton's Third Army and fought across Germany. V-E Day found us at Linz, Austria. After all the battles and casualties, my most searing experience of the war was at Mauthausen, south of Linz—an encounter with evil too inconceivable to be apprehended at the time or even now. . . . Mauthausen *lager* was a factory whose product was death. . . . We estimated that more than 200,000 people had been exterminated there. . . . It is not for me to describe the documented horrors. But never believe this holocaust did not happen. I was there. I saw it. . . . In the final weeks the Nazis simply fed the exhaust fumes into the busses transporting the victims to mass graves. As the American armies approached, bull-dozers dug great pits, and the victims were herded into them, most not even shot because ammunition was low. My first peace-time assignment was to be in charge of burial details. Despite all that the Army Medical corps could do, the skeletal survivors kept dying. . . .

August 9, 1945

Dear Bill [Glover]:

This being the 9th of August, you and I are both thinking about the atomic bomb and the entrance of Russia into the war. We hope and pray that the 32nd Division will be spared much suffering and everything that goes with that. It is just one of those things that makes you realize what a whale of a big effort this war has been and what a toll it has taken, and the dimensions opened by the atomic bomb make it clear that we who call ourselves human have simply got to get together now and stop this kind of cosmic suicide. I use "cosmic" advisedly. . . .

Ever yours,
Joel B. Hayden

John B. Chandler ('41x). *Archives*   Calhoun "Pete" Narten ('38x). *Archives*

News reached the school that John B. Chandler ('41) had been missing in action since March 18. No mention was made of his branch of service or location. His death was later confirmed by the War Department. The death of another boy was confirmed with the notification in the August 12 *Cleveland Plain Dealer* that Calhoun "Pete" ('38x) Narten was lost at sea between New Guinea and Australia in February 1944, while co-piloting a *Liberator* bomber.

August 17, 1945

Dear Mr. and Mrs. Narten:

On behalf of the Academy I want to extend to you our most sincere and heartfelt sympathy in the reported death of your son, "Pete." I have communicated with Dr. Hayden about it and he wishes me to say for him that he and Mrs. Hayden are with you in spirit. They wish they might be nearer at this moment to give you their assurances more personally. . . .

Pete was a grand boy. His wholesome, friendly spirit, winning smile, and clean sportsmanship made many lasting friendships on this campus. Hard as it is for you to make this sacrifice, you are indeed fortunate in the wonderful memories he has left you as an upright and loyal son and a national hero.

This is the thirty-fourth son of Reserve to make the supreme sacrifice, and there are still seven on the "missing" list, five of whom I fear will never come back.

We join you in our thoughts and our prayers.

Sincerely,
Raymond A. Mickel

Newell, West Virginia
August 21, 1945

Dear Mr. Hayden:

... All that you said concerning Bill I deeply appreciate and will cherish it always in my heart. I'm so glad that you and some others at Reserve knew Bill intimately. He had such a wonderful capacity for making friends because he loved people. Not just young friends, but friends his father's age.

I've had no further word from the government. Bill is still, as are five other members of his crew, listed as missing. Perhaps I may never know what happened to Bill. I still hope and pray that he may arrive home on one of the incoming boats possibly carrying wounded. The possibilities of what may have happened to him—even the idea that he may be an amnesia victim—frightens one beyond words.

I'm as thankful the war is over—at least it means that no more families need suffer the agony of permanent separation.

Most sincerely yours,
Grace G. Wells

Eight months after learning of the confirmed death of their son, the parents of David Read ('43) received a reply to a letter they had sent to a friend of David's inquiring about the circumstances of his death on December 18, 1944, during the first days of the Battle of the Bulge.

Bamburg, Germany
August 21, 1945

Dear Mr. and Mrs. Read:

Although I received your letter quite awhile ago, I haven't answered until now because I've been involved in a series of transfers from one division to another, and also because I wished to get for you as much as possible information about your son and my friend.

You see, I was not with David at the time of the shelling, and to correct a misunderstanding that I believe you have, David was not in his hut at Elsenborn at the time of the shelling either. I'll explain the whole thing as easily as I can, hoping that you'll take it more as history, or as an explanation, rather than a very bad and sorrowful remembrance....

David was a radio operator in our company—one of the toughest and most hazardous assignments in combat—and being such he was automatically involved in any or all patrol and reconnaissance work. Our division was ordered into an attack in December and David took his place on the front lines with his radio to relay all fire artillery orders back to our company. After the attack had been in effect for about three days, the Germans threw a counter-attack which was heavier and more forceful than ours. The Jerries threw everything at us and our casualty list grew larger each day....

The class of 1941 as sub-freshmen. Five members, standing in the back row, died in the war. *From left:* Jonathan Izant, John Chandler, and Robert Prior. *From right:* John Knight, Jr., and Harold "Tug" Hoffman. *Archives*

When about five days of the worst type of fighting was finished, it became necessary for someone to pick up the supper rations for the men who were on the front lines. There were three men in Cannon Co.'s outpost party—David, Lt. Smith, and a Corporal Billman. Of those three men it was the duty of the corporal to secure the evening meal. David, however, saw that the corporal's nerves were just about at an end and so he volunteered to bring the food to the corporal's place. . . .

It was while he was receiving the rations that he was killed. It was quick—all over in a second—and any soldier that you will ever meet will tell you that if your time is up, that is the most desirable way to meet the Creator. . . . David had just picked up the rations when he was hit directly in the chest with a German 80mm mortar shell. The shell killed David instantly, and in exploding from his body, also killed eight other men. . . . He was buried right on the field of battle because of the terrific opposition that the Germans were putting up against us. As I said, casualties were tremendously high, and it was all that we could do to protect the wounded and spot-bury the dead without many more lives being sacrificed . . . .

I'm sorry I had to write this letter because it hurts me to recall it and I can realize how it must torture you to learn it, even though it happened such a [long] time ago. A dearly loved one is not easily, and sometimes never, forgotten.

My buddies and I will always remember David for being just himself, the height of a fine man.

Thank you for your invitation to spend some time with you, and if I ever can, I will be sure to stop and speak with the parents of one of my dearest and closest friends.

Yours very sincerely,
[Name unknown]

Bill Conrad ('32x) died in the first days of the Normandy invasion on June 12, 1944. His mother confirmed his loss in a letter to Mr. Mickel. He had been inducted into the army on March 14, 1941, and released after six months of training due to illness in the family. He was called back into the service in December 1942. In January 1944 he went overseas and eventually to France on D day, where he was killed six days later while attacking a "crack German unit." His commanding officer, who was wounded by the same shell that killed Bill, said in a letter to Bill's mother that he was a wonderful man, and he didn't know any man that did the job better than her son, of whom one could be very proud. According to his mother, Bill never spoke of the army in his letters home. "His letters to us were always to get it over so he could come home to his wife and little girl who is now three years old."

THE SCHOOL YEAR 1945–46
The War Is Over

🍂 Fall Term: September–December 1945

With the unconditional surrender of Japan and the signing of the terms of surrender on the USS *Missouri* in Tokyo Bay on September 2 (V-J, or Victory-over-Japan, Day), the war ended. The day was cloudy as the brief ceremony began. Twenty minutes later, as the last document was signed by Gen. Douglas MacArthur and Japanese officials, the clouds gave way to a burst of sunshine. Peace at last. On September 18 Secretary of War Henry L. Stimson resigned. His recommendation to designate the war as "World War II" was approved by President Truman three days later.

Nineteen forty-five marked the twentieth anniversary of the school being all male. It was also the fifteenth year under Dr. Hayden's leadership. Dean Mickel began his nineteenth year, Mr. McGill his seventeenth.

The first editorial of the year in the *Record* reported that this was the "120th opening day of school to occur on the campus." The editorial continued:

> In all the opening days there probably has never been a more fitting occasion for thanksgiving than at the present time. The years previous to V-J Day were years of anguish and sacrifice—times when the day of commencement was followed by immediate military service. How thankful we are that that day has passed, and that soon our graduates can once again plan for a happy and normal college life. With wartime restrictions relaxed we may hope that this year will be one of the best ever at Reserve.

It remained unclear what changes were to be made in the draft laws. Of the fifty-eight boys who graduated in the class of 1945, only seventeen entered the armed forces.

The September 27 *Record* carried the first formal announcement of the plans for the Memorial Campaign "to honor the heroes, living and dead, of

School calendar 1945–46. *Student Handbook*

Western Reserve Academy." One month later, on October 27, the campaign opened with a Parents' Day gathering. The festivities included a football game with Chagrin Falls High School and a turkey dinner. After dinner the opening meeting of the campaign was held in the chapel "to acquaint the Academy family with the background of the effort." After a speech by Board of Trustees president Robert S. Wilson, Capt. George Manlove ('32) spoke of how much his prep-school days meant to him and all alumni, especially to those in the war.

One man noticeably not in attendance was the one responsible for staying in touch with George Manlove and the hundreds of alumni who served; the one who worked tirelessly to see that a proper memorial to the boys became a reality; the one who anxiously awaited the return of all of the boys from the war. On the evening of October 13, just two weeks before the campaign's kick-off meeting, Dr. Hayden was stricken by sudden illness. One of the last letters he wrote to the boys as a group appeared in the *Record* on October 18, giving advice with regard to admission to college upon their return, inviting them to write their concerns or to come to Hudson to discuss their future plans. "All of the Reserve masters and I want to remind you," he wrote, "that our interest in you and in your educational growth is undiminished by the cessation of hostilities."

One of several local surrender ceremonies, September 2, 1945. R. C. Allen ('32), top right, was present at the one aboard the USS *Rhind* off the coast of Pagan Island. *Archives*

USS *Lesuth*
September 3, 1945

Dear Mr. Mickel,

This is written, of all places, in Tokyo Bay, where we are anchored about five miles off the Yokosuka Naval Base. Why we are here, none of us know[s]. It is very hard for us to understand after a couple years of trailing around the Pacific far behind everything, to find ourselves right in the midst. But here we undoubtedly are.

Had anyone suggested after we left the States a couple of months ago that we would have ended up here, I would have surveyed him as crazy, without even looking at him. We all thought that there would be an invasion of Japan, but we never figured that we would get any closer to it than provisioning some of the ships that would be in on the operation. All this would happen back somewhere in the weeds. And things started out just that way.

We hit Ulithi first and hung around there for a couple weeks. We were supposed to go up to Okinawa, an idea that made none of us very happy; that place has a bad name with the navy. We had seen several ships that had gotten clipped up there, and they didn't look good. Then all of a sudden we were chased off to Leyte. We got in there just about when that peace rumor business began to become concrete. But we still couldn't see anything unusual ahead. But it was there, and we are here—and have been for four or five days now. At last something to tell the grandchildren!

As a matter of fact, there has been nothing very much out of the ordinary in coming in here. The coastline, except for the fact that the mountains arise rather more suddenly, might very well be the California coast that we left behind two months ago. To be sure, there is Fujiyama, but there is no snow on it now, so it isn't really official, and furthermore we have been able to see it only one day since we've been here. The rest of the time it has been raining, which has also a certain similarity to California.

The noble emotions that are supposed to have infused the breast of stout Cortez on the shores at Darien have also been notably lacking. We are, I fear, an essentially prosaic bunch. The only two things that really interest us are getting back to the States, and getting out of the service. There is very little sense of triumph or accomplishment, partly, I guess, because we have never actually been fighting the war, and most of the time haven't even been doing much to help those who were. We expect no one to be foolish enough to break out the "Hail the Conquering Hero" when we steam around and would probably tell them to knock off the nonsense if they did. A hell of an attitude.

Since a sizable portion of the U.S. Navy is in here now, there are no doubt all sorts of people around whom I know. But it will be some time until I find out about it. Have seen or heard of no one from Reserve since I saw Bob [Gulick, Jr., '34] in February. I heard from the family that he was back in Hawaii, which doesn't make me very jealous. But then, I've not been up to Iwo; after that I'm sure that Hawaii would be an annex to paradise.

The situation we are in now is the most comfortable we have hit out here—the first place where it is cool enough to be comfortable. After sweltering for two years in diverse harbors out here, we are quite happy about that. As long as I have to be out at sea, I would just as soon be here as anywhere.

Lest I'm thought to be totally lacking in curiosity, I will confess to a desire to get ashore and into Yokohama and Tokyo. But I'm afraid that is due to be frustrated; they are not encouraging the tourist trade just yet. I have been over to the naval base, which is nothing much to see. There is one badly battered up battleship—The Nagato—an ugly hooker to start with, and not markedly improved by the bombing she has taken recently. There are also several escort vessels and a mess of subs of various sizes. Aside from that, very little.

The Japanese scarcity of mechanical resources is evident here, as it has been everywhere. Considering what they had to fight it with, the Japs fought a pretty rugged war. They have missed some bets here and there, but they have certainly been working on a shoestring—and one that was badly frayed to start with.

. . . You were very likely listening to the broadcast of the signing of the peace treaty. That broadcast originated on the *Missouri*, about four miles astern of us. Ironically, we had to get it from the States, just as you did.

Frankly, I would much rather have been listening to it at a radio back there with my wife. Being in the Medical Corps, I have no immediate prospect of becoming a civilian again, so all my interest is centered on getting back. I am hoping still that I will be pulled off here soon. There never has been much reason for my being aboard, and the end of the war has removed whatever there was. You may be sure that a trip to Hudson will be on the agenda while I am in Cleveland. Can't say that I expect the visit to be within the next couple days, unfortunately. But until things do break that way, I do my best to keep occupied and patient.

      Sincerely,
      Malcolm Finlayson ['34; Age 28]

                                                  Manila
                                        September 3, 1945

Dear Dr. Hayden:

It was wonderful to receive your letter of June 26 when I arrived here a few days ago, and I wish that there were some way to tell you how much it means to me, and to thank you for the help and advice which I need so much. Your letter has been read and re-read many times, and I've gotten so much from it—more than I can say or thank you for.

Now that the war is over and the time when I'll be coming home is definitely in sight (my calculations tell me that I will be returning to the "old country" sometime within the next six months, and certainly not much after that) I am more concerned than ever about the immediate future—and more anxious than ever, too, to make education and coaching my life work—and to begin that work just as soon as I possibly can after my return home. My increasing desire to educate and to coach, is another of the many things for which I have to thank you, for your advice and your interest and encouragement have helped so much. . . .

I would like very much to be able to tell you some things of interest about Manila—but having arrived here just a week ago, I'm still a stranger. We are located about fifteen miles from the center of town, and except to go to the stadium yesterday to see a football game, I've seen very little of Manila so far. I have seen enough, though, to have some idea of the terrific beating this city has taken, for I've seen hardly a building that isn't scarred and tattered and burned in a thorough and brutal destruction that's impossible to describe or to even imagine. Manila has been so completely destroyed that there is talk of changing the site of the city, and that

John Ashton ('38) before his discharge from the army. *Courtesy Mrs. J. Ashton*

is easy to understand after even a brief look at what has happened. The Filipinos will never forget the Japanese.

Seeing Manila as it is makes me more thankful than ever that the war never physically reached the cities at home—and more thankful too that the war ended as suddenly as it did. The atomic bomb is a terrifying weapon—but, in my opinion, it has been a gift of God, because of the continued loss of life, and the destruction that it has saved. I've realized even more in the last few days, too, that there must never be another war or even the threat of one, and that we must all work as hard to preserve the peace as we did to win the war.

I hope that this will find you and Mrs. Hayden enjoying the best of health—the very best of everything—and that you're beginning the happiest, most wonderful year ever at Reserve. I'm looking forward so much to our seeing each other again in the near future—and perhaps then I'll be able to find a way to thank you for your advice and interest and encouragement—and to tell you how much they mean.

Very sincerely yours,
Walter Hopkins ['37; Age 26]

Somewhere in the U.S.A.
September 3, 1945

Dear Mr. Mickel,

Was swell of you to send me a birthday greeting with the news of Reserve—one of these days I hope to get back there to look the place over again. As you can see, I am now back from Europe—and am sweating out a discharge. When it will come, nobody knows.

John Ashton ('38), left, and Bill Heyman ('38) in a 1938 track meet. *Archives*

Trip to Europe was not exactly a pleasure jaunt—but it did make me realize what a blessing it is to live in the States—where your neighbors are peaceable—where we haven't been very greatly affected by the war, and where hates and prejudices at least do not become a national political program. . . . Am intending to do graduate work at Chicago under the [G.I.] Bill of Rights as soon as I get out—in fact am all set along that line. Give my best to your family and to all the Reserve family.

              Sincerely,
              John Ashton ['38; Age 25]

                                  Somewhere in China
                                    September 8, 1945

Dear Mr. Mickel,

By the time that you get this note, the new school year will have begun. Now that peace has come again, the war problems have vanished and given way to post-war ones, which themselves are not irrelevant.

At present I am at a training center where we were and still are training Chinese officers and enlisted men. However, because of the termination of hostilities, we are about to turn the whole thing over to the Chinese. I imagine I'll be here for a month or so more until the thing actually winds up. As I have been over here a comparatively short time, I don't look for my immediate return to the States. However, I do hope to be back as soon as possible. . . .

              Sincerely,
              [W.] Don Richards ['39; Age 25]

Bill Horner ('39x). *Courtesy Bill Horner*

Hawaii
September 14, 1945

Dear Dr. Hayden:

... Since I last wrote you, my experiences have been varied and many. After we left the States a year ago, we spent quite some time shuttling from island to island, and covered almost all of them. They are all alike, and please don't believe those "enchanting" posters. Then we went to Leyte, getting in on the last part of that action. We were there about a month and then joined a small task force and sailed north, our objective being to invade and secure the Kerama Retto group of islands six days before the main invasion force arrived at Okinawa, thirty miles away.

In the early morning of March 29, in bright moonlight, a Jap dive bomber got his sights on us and we were hit forward and a near miss aft. We were towed to the nearest island where temporary repairs were made, and from there went over to Okinawa to discharge our cargo, remaining there thirty-four days. Then the long haul back to the states for dry dock and repairs, and a two day's leave for all hands. Right now we are in Hawaii and will soon be on our merry way again.

My leave couldn't have come at a more opportune time. We got in on June 6 and on June 7 I was eating supper at the farm. My brother, Bob, who was graduated from the Naval Academy on June 6, was married on the 9th, and I was best man. He is now aboard the USS *Lexington*, which is at Tokyo. [My brother] Rick is also there, on the USS *Wenatchee*, and a great reunion that will be! I may be there myself soon.

Now that things are getting back to normal, all reserves are looking forward to civilian life and the future we've dreamed of for over three years. As you know, I left college to enlist on January 7, 1942, and still have about a year to go to get my degree. But I will be twenty-six before I am discharged, and although I want to go back to finish, I have been wondering if perhaps I would be better off to start to work right away and get that much of a start on life. I haven't any definite plans, but I do eventually want to get into some small business and live in a small town or in the country. . . .

Yesterday I went over to the officer's club at Pearl Harbor for a swim and who should I meet there but Lt. "Huey" Long ['38]. He looked fine and we had a wonderful time chatting about our Reserve days. He has just been transferred off the carrier USS *Randolph* and will soon leave for the States to be discharged. He wanted to be remembered to you and all of his friends in Hudson.

      Sincerely,
      Bill Horner ['39x; Age 25]

In September 1997 I received a letter from Mr. Horner that included his remembrance of a chance reunion with his brother James ("Rick," '41):

It was customary (necessary) for ships at sea to share any fuel surplus with others running low. So it was on a day on the Pacific Ocean when a ship came in close and asked for fuel. It was routine and I didn't pay much attention, but did notice that one of the men sitting on top of the pilot house during the refueling looked familiar. [I] put the glasses on him, then looked at the bow letters on the ship, and guess what? The ship was the U.S.S. Wenatchee and the fellow taking it easy on the pilot house roof was my brother Jim, who after his college at [Western Reserve University] served as business manager of [Western Reserve Academy] for 10 years from 1957–1967.

      September 17, 1945

Dear Blaine [Rawdon]:

It certainly was a sad twist of fate that the Haydens should be gone from Hudson when you got here with Gene Lindsay ['42] and Lew Ball. Our whole summer, as a family, has been filled with "fits and starts." I think you can understand that because you've gone through *real* combat and at its highest and lowest levels. But Wallie[1] has given me a graphic description of your reunion here in Hudson. He just roars and then weeps over the whole thing, but you know Wallie.

Dick Theibert is back home for a while; I think he will be mustered out early in October. Bob Cone ['43] is here for thirty days resting up, then

Blaine Rawdon, Lewis Ball, Bill Hancock, and Gene Lindsay (all '42) had a short reunion in the spring of 1945. *Courtesy Lewis Ball*

he'll probably return to Texas and just how soon he will be mustered out nobody knows. I can give you more news later and the *Alumni Record* will be in your hands soon, and that will give you news from approximately 350 boys.

We have a real campaign on—an Anniversary and Memorial Campaign which I hope will be the biggest thing to date in the history and work of WRA. Your dad has taken the chairmanship of the New York area, for which "God Bless him!" I don't know any family that understands any better what Reserve has in mind and what it is trying to do than the Rawdon family.

Ever yours,
Joel B. Hayden

1. Robin S. Wallace, science and math master and bookstore manager (1932–59).

Headmaster Hayden wrote the following letter to Lewis Ball's father.

September 27, 1945

Dear Mr. Ball:

. . . It was certainly nice to see you and be brought up to date. I hope that the news from Blaine, Jr. will be good news pointing shortly to his release from the armed forces.

A 1934 boy at WRA who was a German prisoner for two-and-a-half years[1] showed up yesterday. He came originally from Honesdale, Pennsylvania and that is still his home. He graduated from the University of Pennsylvania. He looks all right now, but he told us that only the Red

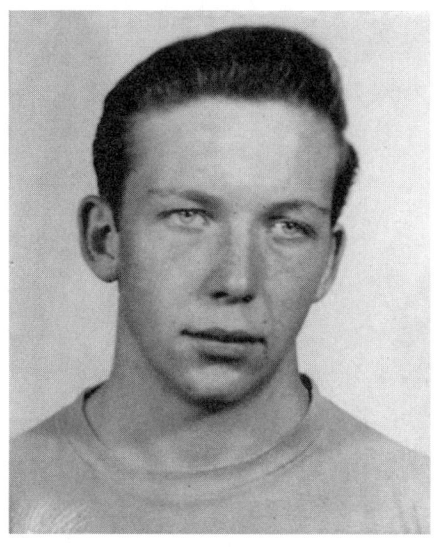
John A. Palmer ('45x). *Archives*

Cross seeds in particular and Red Cross service in general kept him and his buddies alive until the day that he was released by allied armies. . . .

We get bits of news nearly every day—news which now is heartening—and I understand just how all parents must feel because Mrs. Hayden and I feel that way ourselves. . . .

                Sincerely,
                Joel B. Hayden

1. Robert Katz ('34).

News reached the school on October 10 that John A. Palmer ('45x) died in the Pacific. A memorandum from Dean Mickel to Director of Admissions Harlan Parker quoted from a conversation the dean had had with Ledyard "Bud" Baxter ('44), a family friend: "After having graduated from training as a pharmacist, where he finished at or near the top of his class, [John] was sent to Japan on a destroyer as mate. In the Okinawa campaign, a Kamikaze struck his ship, sinking it, and killed several of the crew including John. Before his death, he managed to save three or four of his fellows." Dr. Hayden's letter to John's parents turned out to be his last letter of condolence, for three days after writing it he was stricken with illness.

                October 10, 1945

My dear Mr. and Mrs. Palmer:

All of us at Western Reserve Academy join you with understanding and sympathy in your loss of John.

The faculty of this school, staying on year after year, has known all of these boys—the thirty-six of them who are now represented by Gold Stars. It wants each family who has suffered to realize that they are not alone.

The close and intimate relationship between boy and boy, and boy and man, on this campus is something which is of eternal significance for all of us who live, and it must be much the same for those who go on and live more richly and more gloriously both in the mind and in the plan of God. . . .

   Very sincerely yours,
   Joel B. Hayden

              Somewhere in the Pacific
              October 11, 1945

Dear Dr. Hayden,

. . . You sure bowled me over when you said that you quoted my last letter in Chapel. I almost didn't mail it because it was such a lousy job of writing. However, I have always heard that inspiration comes at the oddest times.

This time I will try to give you a little news of what has been happening over here. My outfit is a sort of roving battalion in that it may be hooked on to any Division headquarters the Marine Corps may designate. So far we have been working with the 4th Division. But that does not mean that the next operation will be with them also.

It is funny how Reserve seems to jump up and meet me at the strangest times. The most recent is in connection with our recreation program. You may or may not remember my endeavors at the Academy motion picture emporium. When I graduated, I fancied myself a rather experienced movie operator. Lo and behold if the other day a set of 35mm movie projectors arrived for use by the camp. Since we are the only ones in camp, and since I am the only person who has ever seen a motion picture projector, you can easily surmise that I have been calling on my information gained at Reserve. And every time I go into that booth, I remember the Saturday night shows and the new Simplex portables I talked the school into buying—I think. I seem to remember reading in the *Record* about a local commercial theatre taking over.

To get back here. We have weathered the Marshalls, Saipan, and Tinian with the fewest number of casualties of any other battalion in the landing forces. I can't give you the numbers, but we are almost intact, keeping the same outfit we had when we left the states. It is a darned good bunch of men now, and all of them know "what the score is." That is the reason why I am not afraid to pat ourselves on the back—the more battle experience a group of men get, the more chance they have of pulling through unscathed.

I received a letter from [my brother] Newt ['34] in which he tells of his landings on Guam, so you can see that the Vradenburgs are out here doing their darnedest to get this fracas over with so that we can get back there and live what we're out here fighting for. In fact, I am sure that if Newt and I were to be given a tractor each, we could just about take the old Homeland all by ourselves. Of course, a little help from Nimitz and a few of his many fleets would help.

        Sincerely,
        George [Vradenburg, '37; Age 26]

        Sasebo, Kyushu, Japan
        October 11, 1945

Dear Dr. Hayden,

Greetings from Japan. We arrived here in Sasebo two and a-half weeks ago. We are attached to the Fifth Marine Corps, which has the job of occupying Kyushu. Our CIC [Counter-Intelligence Corps] detachment, a metropolitan team composed of fourteen men, is waiting for orders to move to Yawata, about 130 miles northwest of here. We expect to move into Yawata with elements of the 32nd Army Division. In the meantime, we are biding our time here helping out the CIC detachments assigned to this metropolitan area.

About eight CIC detachments, including the 95th, were attached to the VAC when it left Hawaii on 1 September. We were on the water twenty-four days. At Saipan about twenty more ships joined our convoy and we picked up more ships between Saipan and Japan. By the time we reached Sasebo our convoy totaled about fifty ships.

Sasebo was an important naval base during the war. There were several Jap ships in the harbor when we arrived. They were partially sunk as a result of our naval dive bombers several months ago. There were three aircraft carriers which were partly submerged and gutted. Sasebo was hit by B-29's in June and most of the city was burned out then. It is hard to describe the wreckage left by our bombers. The whole center of town was wiped out, and only a few buildings are standing which are even partially intact.

Yesterday I talked with some CIC boys who just returned from Nagasaki, which is 100 miles south of Sasebo. They say the place was virtually leveled by the atom bomb and some of the residents have red faces—result of the intense heat generated by the atom bomb.

A typhoon hit Sasebo yesterday afternoon and raged all night. The wind blew in thousands of windows throughout the city and it was risky driving about in a jeep. It was my first typhoon and was an experience I will never forget. The wind has gone down a lot today, though it is still raining hard. I understand the ships in the harbor took an awful beating last night. We were fortunate in not encountering a typhoon after leaving Saipan.

When we arrived here two weeks ago it was warm and sunny. Now it is cold, the first real cold I've experienced in over three years. The people here in Sasebo face a hard winter. They have inadequate clothing and food, and many have been bombed out. It is a pitiful sight to see so many people wandering aimlessly about. All the people I have seen so far look emaciated, cold and hungry. The marines have given them some food and candy, and it is a sight to see how eagerly they snatch food and candy from your hands. The children look underfed and are constantly shivering from the cold. I understand AMG [American Military Government] will try to provide food and clothing for them this winter.

So far I have seen no signs of hatred toward the occupation forces. The Japanese seem to have resigned themselves to whatever is in store for them. Our work—investigation of subversive activity, secret organizations, war criminals, etc.—keeps us in contact with what is going on here. In general, the people seem to be dead set against the militarists and industrialists who they are now convinced led them into a war which they never wanted. It is an unforgettable experience to talk to "Jap" naval officers who only a few months ago commanded submarines ranging as far east as Hawaii and even farther.

A Liaison Committee of civilian officials, government men, and army and navy officers has been established in all major cities. The committee is supposed to serve as a buffer between the people and the occupation forces and the problems caused thereby. But there is a gap between the civilian population and the Japanese government. I have talked with civilians who claim the government has not acquainted them with the actual situation. The people just don't seem to know what is going on. The result is that they have hesitated to voice an opinion about anything.

The emperor is everything. Everything he says is obeyed and treated with the highest respect. MacArthur is relying on the emperor and the government to advise the people about what is going on and how they should conduct themselves under the present trying circumstances. The people were apprehensive about the conduct of the American troops. They have now seen and admitted that their fears were unfounded on that score.

I have often thought what Japan would be like, and I have read a lot of material on what we might expect to find here. But I never dreamed I would come here so soon after the end of the war. Japan is like another planet. I know of no "yardstick" by which to measure my first impressions. Everything is so different. The standards of living are unbelievably low. There is an odor of filth and garbage that is stifling at times. The bulldozers have cleared away most of the wreckage in the center of town. The bodies buried under the debris accounted in part for the stench that permeated the atmosphere here in Sasebo when we arrived. The people are so poor and under-nourished that it is impossible to see how they thought they could ever wage a war, especially against the United States.

I realize that my first impressions of Japan have so far been limited to Sasebo, but from reports I have read from other cities and from conversations with other CIC boys, I guess conditions here are similar to those in other large cities throughout Japan. The people gape at the massive equip-

Devastation in Sasebo, Japan. *Courtesy E. S. Babcox, Jr.*

ment the marines and seabees brought ashore after our convoy arrived. They are literally flabbergasted at the size of our bulldozers, excavators, huge tractors, trucks, derricks, et. al. which are busy clearing away the debris from the center of town.

We have two Nisei[1] boys attached to our detachment as interpreters. They are doing a magnificent job helping us get information from the people, officers, and government officials. They are fine boys, both young and both born and educated in Hawaii. Their parents were born in Japan and one of the boys visited Fukuoka about ten years ago.

Our detachment will be leaving any day for Yawata, which is on northern Kyushu and is the center of industrial Japan. It too was hit by B-29's and was devastated and practically burned out. We have a real job awaiting us there. As in Europe, CIC throughout Japan has been cooperating with AMG. I have met some competent men in AMG. AMG has a tough and long assignment here.

. . . I am hoping to be home by Christmas. I have been overseas three years plus. I was in the states in August and September 1944, to attend an intelligence school in Chicago, after which I returned to Hawaii. Until I do leave for home, I am storing up experiences I will never forget nor tire of relating. . . .

                      Sincerely,
                      Edward S. Babcox, Jr. ['35; Age 28]

1. Over twenty-five thousand Nisei, second-generation Japanese from Hawaii and the United States, fought in Europe; several hundred served with the CIC as spies, interpreters, and interrogators in the Pacific.

Vincent W. Allin ('36).
Courtesy Vincent Allin

> Aboard USS *LST* 1105
> At Sea: Destination Japan
> October 16, 1945

Dear Mr. Mickel,

Was sorry to miss you at Hudson when I passed through last June. Still, it was nice to see your wife, Mr. and Mrs. Jones, the McGills, and some of the other masters. Was on my way home then from the Philippines, where I'd had command of a sub chaser.

Had a grand leave. All leaves are "grand." While I was home I went down to Rochester, Minnesota and saw Dave Jennings ['35]. He is working and studying as a young doctor at the Mayo Clinic. Eye work—his father's field. Dave asked to be remembered to you and his other Reserve faculty friends. On the transport ship that took me back to the States I met a younger former Reservite named Fred Havens ['40]. We often played bridge together.

After my leave was up, I started out to the Pacific again. Then the war ended. Those of us leaving the States about this time used to kid that first, it was the atomic bomb; second, it was the Russian entry into the war with Japan; and third and finally, the "crushing" news that we were coming back again, that made the Japs give up.

For nearly two months now I've been chasing the *PC* 807. Was at Samar, Leyte, Manila, and Subic Bay in the Philippines. No ship. Then they decided that it must have gone to Okinawa area. Am now on my way there—by way of Japan, as they thought I should be able to get to Okinawa easier that way than by waiting for a direct trip at Subic.

During the trip north we got word of a terrific typhoon ahead on our course. We turned back and steamed in the "wrong" direction for several days. It is well that we did keep that storm at a safe distance!!! That was the typhoon that wrecked Okinawa! Now those of us going to ships that were supposed to be in that area are wondering whether or not our vessels were among the many damaged.

We expect to arrive in Tokyo Bay tomorrow. It will be interesting to see the location where the Jap surrender was signed—and this war ended. We are glad of this chance to see the land of the "setting sun." Then we'll have to begin chasing our elusive ships again. It's a tiring business—and the bases are over-crowded with men going home. Aboard ship it is nicer—especially being an officer.

. . . One of the officers just came into the wardroom and said that they've just picked up the first Japanese island on the radar. Am sure glad this is not several months ago! We are changing course now, so the ship is beginning to roll more. That will put an end to this letter . . . . Hope all is going well for you, your soccer teams, and all of Reserve.

Yours sincerely,
Vincent W. Allin ['36; Age 28]

By the time the letters from George Vradenburg, Edward Babcox, and Vincent Allin reached the school, Dr. Hayden was ill. According to the brief announcement in the October 18 issue of the *Reserve Record,* he had just returned from the train station in Hudson "where he said farewell to friends on Saturday evening." He stepped out of his car, collapsed, and was assisted into Pierce House. "Dr. Weidenthal [school physician, 1931–71] was immediately summoned and diagnosed the headmaster's illness as a cerebral hemorrhage. While Dr. Hayden's condition is serious, there has been some improvement and the outlook is considered hopeful."

October 25, 1945

Dear Eddie [Babcox]:

. . . I wonder if you have heard by this time that Dr. Hayden suffered a serious cerebral hemorrhage on the evening of October 13. For a few days we almost despaired of his life. Since that time he has made some improvement which seems to be continuing. At the very best, his recovery will take a long hard pull, and he will need all of the prayers and spiritual support that his multitude of friends can give him.

The Trustees have decided to go ahead with the campaign for expanding the plant and deepening the usefulness of the Academy. No doubt by this time you have heard about those plans. We are all sure that Dr. Hayden would wish to have it no other way than to proceed, because that was

The Athenaeum. *Archives*

very close to his heart and up to the time of his illness he had expended himself unstintedly on behalf of the campaign.
    Sincerely,
    Raymond A. Mickel

The Athenaeum, or the "A," was one of the original buildings on the campus. Built in 1843, it served as the natural science building and later as a recitation hall. In 1917 it was converted to the dormitory, which is still in use today. While planning for an addition to the gymnasium, rumors abounded that the building might be moved some two hundred feet. Kenneth Zonsius, Jr. ('43), rose to the building's defense from Rapid City, South Dakota, where he was a lieutenant in a reconnaissance squadron with the Army Air Force.

                                        Rapid City, South Dakota
                                             November 13, 1945
Dear Mr. McGill:
    I understand through indirect sources that Dr. Hayden is very ill. This naturally is a cause for consternation for all of us who were his students. I would appreciate very much some enlightenment on his condition so that I might write him a letter.
    I sincerely hope that the plans for the construction of the new buildings are materializing rapidly. There is one little matter in relation to that which has been troubling me, however.

Last month, while I was visiting Reserve, I understood Mr. Parker to say that the construction of these buildings might result in the moving or removing of the Athenaeum. I would like to defend the Athenaeum's right to remain part of new Reserve by pointing out that it is a vestige of old Reserve—and therefore a symbol of a heritage which every sincere Reserve student should be proud of.

I admit that the Athenaeum is not too attractive (largely due to a rather repugnant paint job); there also may be some doubt as to its stability. However, it seems to me that every effort should be made to correct these foibles. In my humble opinion it is the Athenaeum—and not its foible—that is inexorable.

Your friend and student,
Kenneth Zonsius [Age 20]

Dean Mickel offered the Thanksgiving message in the November 15 *Record*. "How far away Thanksgiving a year ago now seems when we think of what has happened since!" he reflected. Mr. McGill's reply to Kenneth Zonsius explained the tentative plans for the Athenaeum.

November 17, 1945

Dear "Kenzius":

Yes, Dr. Hayden is a very ill man. He had a stroke five weeks ago tonight and a very hard one; was unconscious for forty-eight hours and then gradually began to "come out of it." He has made some improvement but there has been no change in his paralysis. He is paralyzed on the left side.

Your comment about the possible fate of the Athenaeum in our new building program is very interesting. I might say that I don't believe the bulk of the people who have lived in the Athenaeum feel quite as you do about it. You may or may not know that it was reconditioned internally some twenty-five years ago, the job being done hastily and at minimum expense. The result is that the cross-timbers and other materials are rather lighter than they should have been, which makes the place a noisy, vibrating old shack.

However, the present thought is not to destroy it. Our Board of Trustees are more or less of the opinion that they will try to have it moved about 200 feet to the south in order to create room where it now stands for the proposed new addition to the gymnasium. My private opinion is that it will neither be moved nor torn down[1]—but please don't quote me on this.

Your observation about its "repugnant paint job" is interesting. You will recall how dingy its external appearance was some years ago. Well, Mr. Wilson, Chairman of our Board, thought it ought to be possible to brighten it up a bit by painting its exterior and this was done—and you are the first guy to ever observe to me that you consider the building more "repulsive" now than before it was painted. However, everyone for his own opinion—in a democracy! . . .

       Cordially yours,
       Ralph W. McGill

 1. The building still stands in its original location.

Winter Term: January–March 1946

When Dr. Hayden fell ill, Scotch McGill was named acting headmaster. At that time it was hopeful that the headmaster's recovery would, at best, take a number of months. Although news of his slow and steady improvement was encouraging, it became apparent in early January that he would not recover sufficiently to continue his administrative duties. Mr. McGill acknowledged this fact in a letter of January 16, 1946, to one of the boys: "Dr. Hayden's condition is such that a new headmaster is going to be employed and Dr. Hayden given Emeritus status . . . ."

The same letter expressed McGill's concern over the matter of "reabsorbing some seven men back into our faculty next fall who have been away in the armed service," and cited the main problem as housing.

Mr. McGill's "Postwar Reflections" in the January issue of the *Alumni Record* included a description of the devastation suffered at L'Ecole du Montcel in France. For many years a number of Academy boys had the opportunity to study there during the summer. For nearly four years the school had been the headquarters of the German chief of aviation for the Versailles area; when the Germans left it was reopened on a small scale. A quote from the school's headmaster stated, "Fundamentally, except for the horrible destruction of the beautiful and historic chateau, we are among the fortunate and privileged of the French people. Life is beautiful!"

The first *Reserve Record* of the new term brought the news of Charles Tice, Jr. ('39x), an infantryman in the Ninth division of the First Army, who was killed in Germany on February 28, 1945, and the final assumption of the deaths of Devin Gilchrist ('40), who had been listed as missing since December 1943, and Charles "Boots" Killian ('40), reported as missing in January 1945.

On January 26 the father of Boots Killian informed the school that, after a year of hopeful waiting, the War Department now listed him as presumed dead. "Nevertheless," Mr. Killian stated, "we still feel that some day 'Boots' and the entire crew will be found. . . . May God grant our continued hope and prayers for the safe return of the entire crew in the near future."

Mr. Killian enclosed a copy of the official notice of his son's death:

Charles A. Tice, Jr. ('39x). *Archives*

January 11, 1946

Dear Mr. and Mrs. Killian:

Since your son, Second Lieutenant Charles J. Killian, 0558573, Air Corps, was reported missing in action 10 January 1945, the War Department has entertained the hope that he survived and that information would be revealed dispelling the uncertainty surrounding his absence. However, as in many cases, the conditions of warfare deny us such information.

The record concerning your son shows that he was a crew member of a B-24 airplane based on Morotai Island off the northwest coast of New Guinea, which participated in a mission over Grace Park Airdrome, Luzon, in the Philippine Islands, on 10 January 1945. Following the completion of the mission, his plane refueled on Leyte Island, and departed thence for Morotai Island. Contact was maintained with the plane for nearly five hours after leaving Leyte. Thereafter, no trace of either the plane or any member of the crew has been discovered.

Full consideration has recently been given to all available information bearing on the absence of your son, including all records, reports, and circumstances. These have been carefully reviewed and considered. In view of the fact that twelve months have now expired without the receipt of evidence to support a continued presumption of survival, the War Department must terminate such absence by a presumptive finding of death. Accordingly, an official finding of death has been recorded under the provisions of Public Law 490, 77th. Congress, approved March 7, 1942, as amended.

The finding does not establish an actual or probable date of death; however, as required by law, it includes a presumptive date of death for the termination of pay and allowances, settlement of accounts and payment of

Edgar S. Ingraham, Jr. ('27). *Archives*

death gratuities. In the case of your son this date has been set as 11 January 1946, the day following the expiration of twelve months of absence.

I regret the necessity for this message but trust that the ending of a long period of uncertainty may give at least some small measure of consolation. I hope you may find sustaining comfort in the thought that the uncertainty with which war has surrounded the absence of your son has enhanced the honor of his service to his country and of his sacrifice.

> Sincerely yours,
> Edward F. Witsell
> Major General
> Acting the Adjutant General of the Army

In February, the school learned of the death of Edgar S. Ingraham, Jr. ('27), who was killed in a plane crash on a mission in India. And with notification of his death, forty-one Gold Stars appeared on the Service Honor Roll.

> Clearwater Beach, Fla.
> February 7, 1946

My dear Mr. Mickel:

Your letter asking for information about Edgar was forwarded to me down here and should have been answered much sooner.

Edgar's death was such a terrific shock to me, as we had thought he was in a comparatively safe place, that I have not regained my poise yet and hence fail to do many things I should do.

He had entered the army on October 1, 1941 and was stationed in Washington first, as a pathologist in an army medical museum. From there he went to Fort Bragg and later to Battery General Hospital in Rome, Georgia where he was chief of laboratory service. He had been made a major before being ordered overseas in February 1945.

He was, at the time of his death, chief of the laboratory at the 142nd General Hospital in Calcutta and was making a routine flight from his own hospital to a nearby one to do some work for them on the death of five soldiers—the cause of which had not been determined. His plane crashed in landing and none of the thirty-two persons on board were saved.

We yearn and hope that Edgar died instantly as the plane seemed to explode, so say eyewitnesses, and they think no one except the crew even knew anything was amiss.

Edgar had had such fine preparation for his life work—four years undergraduate work at Colgate, four years of medical work at WRU in Cleveland, two years of internship at Presbyterian Hospital in Philadelphia followed by three years in the Institute of Pathology in Cleveland preparing for his specialty. When he entered the army he was Resident Pathologist in Montreal. Jr. had married a lovely Canadian girl in November, 1942 and has left two sweet baby girls. They are with me here in Clearwater Beach where we are both trying to regain strength and courage to go on.

I think very fondly of WRA—as our boys both did—and am grateful that you were interested and cared about Edgar. [His brother] Bill ['34] is home after three years in the Pacific. His wife and little girl have been living with us. Please give my very kindest regards to Dr. Hayden and all the others who remember us in Hudson.

    Most sincerely,
    Edith R. Ingraham

               Lima, Ohio
               February 14, 1946

Dear Dr. Hayden,

I think I am perhaps two months behind in my correspondence with WRA, and especially you. A lot has happened in the last couple of months—from the end of hostilities until the middle of January I was stationed in Japan—then I was sent home, and effective 1 February '46 I was made a civilian again—and so I guess it was all to the good.

I was in Lima only four days, but in that time I read the war news of our alumni from cover to cover. I had no idea what a high price Reserve had to pay in the way of boys. Is there any way I could get information on what happened to the Barnes boys—Doug and Paul? Possibly you could give me a little.

I personally came out luckier than many—outside of a little shrapnel in the leg which has never bothered me. I feel a very strong tendency to call myself lucky. Whoever said "there are no atheists in foxholes" certainly

John P. Seaman ('43). *Courtesy John Seaman*

knew what he was talking about; I have never seen nor heard of one—and the platoon I took into combat had men from every walk of life imaginable. I often wonder how long it will stay with those that are left. I wonder if they are as God-fearing today or as religious as they were while crouched in the bottom of their holes "sweating out" the artillery, waiting for the beginning of another push and so on. But there I go again rattling on. Enough of that. . . .

                Sincerely,
                Bill Glover ['42x; Age 23]

                              Philadelphia, Pa.
                              February 24, 1946

Dear Mr. Mickel,

I would like to apologize for not having expressed my thanks for the thoughtful birthday greetings from WRA the past two years. Perhaps I was too close to graduation to appreciate fully the interest WRA has taken in its service personnel. Each day finds me valuing those days spent at Hudson more and more. My only regret as I reminisce is that I did not take full advantage of all the opportunities, but I don't doubt that is a regret common to many.

At the time of our last short conversation my knowledge of what the navy had in store was very vague. It so happened I had the good fortune to spend all the intervening time at an experimental laboratory in the Philadelphia navy yard, where I expect to remain until discharge in June. Work involved everything from slide rule to molding plastics; consequently, I never suffered from monotony, rather the tantalizing effect of never knowing what was next in store.

> Sincerely,
> John Seaman ['43x; Age 21]

February 27, 1946

Dear Zimmie [Oseland, '43]:

It was nice to know that you appreciate the birthday notes which we have been sending. When our fellows started into the service, Dr. Hayden began writing individual notes to the men, but when the number mounted to several hundred, the responsibility broadened to such an extent that he had to alter the technique in writing the birthday notes. As you know, there are more than 875 [Academy] men in the service and, to date, we have done our best in trying to remember the birthdays of all of them. It is no little task but we are very glad to do it if we know that the fellows appreciate it, and we have heard from so many of them to the effect that they do that there is no doubt that we shall continue the practice until all of you have returned.

... The year has gone along exceedingly well in spite of the cloud cast over the campus by Dr. Hayden's tragic illness. Just now we are in the process of trying to recover from a big house party weekend for the upper classmen and their girl friends. It seems to have been very successful and all the boys say they are very glad they had it, but many of them were very glad that it ended on Sunday. As one boy's date drove away Sunday afternoon, he turned around towards Cutler, threw up his hands and yelled, "Whoopee, I'm free!" Maybe that little touch will bring back some recollections to your own mid.

All your friends on the campus join in sending greetings and very best wishes.

> Sincerely,
> Raymond A. Mickel

March 1, 1946

Dear John [Seaman, '43]:

... I am glad you feel increasingly as time goes on that the Academy has been an important factor in your life. ... You can be assured that our thoughts and our interest follows you wherever you go and as long as you live. ...

I shall not go into any report on the campaign because the *Record* carries that story from time to time. ... Suffice it to say that the Trustees are planning to start on the building program this coming summer.

> Sincerely,
> Raymond A. Mickel

The groundbreaking ceremony for the Memorial Gym did not take place until May 14, 1949, and the addition was completed in 1951, as planned. Wood House, the dormitory named in honor of Harlan Wood, was completed in 1953. The library and science building was dedicated in 1963 and named in honor of Robert S. Wilson, president of the board of trustees from 1941 to 1966.

Spring Term: March–June 1946

Williamsport, Pa.
April 7, 1946

Dear Dr. and Mrs. Hayden,

In the last week or so I've had so many reminders of Reserve and Hudson that I really can't put off writing any longer. I think that it has been almost exactly three years since you last heard from me. I was just finishing Reserve Officer's School in Quantico, Virginia, then, and, if I remember, was thinking that the next assignment would be radar school at Harvard or M.I.T. And, in as much as what has happened subsequently is absolutely as different as can be, I'll try to square the records with you and Reserve.

Within two months of the time you received that last letter they put me ashore on Tinian, between Saipan and Guam, in time for the fireworks. I was assigned as a replacement rifle platoon leader in "A" Co., First Battalion Eighth Marines, Second Marine Division—and got through okay. Then our battalion was left on Tinian as the Garrison Force until shortly before the Okinawa operation when we went to Saipan to rejoin the Division. The work there was hard, continuous patrolling. I never want to see another cave so long as I live! But the work afforded excellent training for all of us. Lord knows I needed it and of my platoon—forty-six men—only nineteen were experienced men and none of those were non-commissioned officers at the beginning of the training phase. The combination of both Saipan and Tinian was very expensive so far as men and energy are concerned . . . [ellipses in original] I was the fifth officer to take over the platoon. But after eight or ten weeks training we had a pretty efficient team again. It was a lot of fun to watch 'em develop and learn to work together.

And then I was assigned as Battalion Intelligence Officer of the same battalion. This was just before leaving Saipan for Okinawa. The Second Division was the unit that made two first landings against the southeastern beaches of Okinawa on D Minus One and again on D-Day. These were the landings that the Japs claimed to have repulsed. We had planned to go ashore after these landings, but, when the landing went practically unopposed, we were left afloat. After fourteen days of floating around we were ordered back to Saipan.

Late in May, last year, my Regiment was called up to Okinawa to seize two small islands needed for the air warning system. These were planned in a rush but came off in fine shape—no opposition. We were engaged in these operations at about the same time as the breakthrough at Shuri Castle, over on the main island.

Then the Regiment was assigned to the First Marine Division. We landed just south of the town of Maha and went into the line on the Kunishi Ridge. We got there just in time to see the results of some real rough fighting, but Lady Luck led us through, without too much trouble, to the southern end of the island. We were the first outfit to break through. You may remember, General Buckner was watching this breakthrough from the Regimental Observation Post when he was hit. And from there we went back to Saipan. That has been practically my watch word, "Back to Saipan!" And how I loathe that place!

There the bunch of us sat betting that the war would be over within seventeen years, when it happened—and we chop-chopped up to Kyushu for the occupation. We landed at Nagasaki—rather where Nagasaki used to be. Since I moved right out of the city I can't speak with any authority about atomic bomb effects. We were told that we were landing at the main docks of a big port—they weren't impressive; where the warehouses ought to be there was ashes and rubble, and when you looked for the town you could smell it all right, but you surely couldn't see a great deal. Within a few weeks time we'd worked our way down to Kagashima, the southernmost large city in Kyushu. There I have been up until the third of February, when a surprise rotation draft caught up with me.

I really have enjoyed the occupation. My intelligence job kept me busy—plenty busy—but after the first year overseas, if you don't find something to keep you busy you're sunk! There is much, much work to be done in Japan, too, believe me. After my return to the States I have read enough articles in the magazines and Sunday papers to convince me that many people are publishing opinions after a weekend in Tokyo. On the other hand I didn't see much of Japan, either, and I hope that some of the optimists are right. Had a very pleasant voyage back aboard the USS *Monrovia*—sixteen days from Sasebo to San Diego. . . .

Sincerely,
Chuck Cooper ['40; Age 23]

One by one the boys were coming home. Although he did not live to see the day, Dean Wood's wish for their return to a "normal life" was coming true. Bob Gulick's ('34) letter might just has well have been written by any number of the hundreds of alumni who had been away.

Arlington, Virginia
May 22, 1946

Dear Doc,

I've thought of writing to you often, but the difference between thought and action is often marked. Too, I'm rather ashamed for waiting so long. Especially in the light of so many remembrances from the Academy during the long days at sea.

The latest *Record* brings heartening news that you are steadily improving. Just such an item as that carried by the *Record* has cheered me as I know it cheered hundreds of the boys, now men, who have known you and been your friends. Young Bobby and I tonight remembered you in our prayers and hope for such news of improvement.

Sally and I now have two youngsters, Bobby, three (a future husky at 45 lbs.) and Susan, six months, redheaded and strictly a pleasure. I missed Bobby's babyhood during '43 and '44, so Susan is new and delightful. Of course I expect the fact that she is a girl has some effect too, but she finds all the world she lives in a joyous place and communicates that joy through her smiles and crowing.

Fortunately we bought a nice little home eleven minutes up the Potomac on the Virginia side of the river. The neighborhood is pleasant, almost countryside development, so we have our own roof overhead.

My work in the Bureau of Aeronautics is in Engineering—aircraft power plants and specifically the accessories and gadgets that go on the engines. Demobilization has hit as it has everyone, and it will be an uphill grind getting replacements trained. But it can be done. Too, I like to be busy, and I'm that.

Sally joins me in sending wishes for return of your health, and regards to Mrs. Hayden.

Sincerely,
Bob Gulick [Age 29]

In his 1972 book, *The Growing Years*, J. Fred Waring described the first commencement held in peace in five years (and the last to be held during Dr. Hayden's fifteen-year term): "Dr. Hayden did not come to the Commencement exercises. The Acting Headmaster, Mr. McGill, presided with characteristic dignity and simplicity. A beautiful 'Citation for Dr. Hayden,' by Lucien Price of the class of 1901, was read.... Prizes and diplomas were awarded. New graduates and old filed out to the front of the Chapel and sang the Alma Mater. It was all over" (161).

The July 1946 edition of the *Alumni Record* carried a tribute to Dr. Hayden, also written by Waring. In it he described the scene at Pierce House,[1] the headmaster's Academy home since 1931, at the end of the school year.

Dr. Hayden with the boys in his study in Pierce House shortly before his illness. *Archives*

All during the last term of school the seniors have been going up to Pierce House in groups to visit with Dr. Hayden and say goodbye, and Old Boys have been coming back to delight him with accounts of their experiences in the war and their new ventures in college or business. It has been something we hardly dared hope for since that night last October when he was stricken, but always we have believed he would pull through. 'I'll beat this thing yet,' he said once in the early days after the accident when he could hardly move at all. With most extraordinary patience and good humor he has won back objective after objective and consolidated his position. It has been a struggle that our 875 veterans will understand. He has wanted to talk with each one of this graduating class personally, and he is doing it. . . .

When we think of the Headmaster, unconsciously we include his home. . . . the book-lined library, the green leather chair, a bright fire, apples, good talk—and always Mrs. Hayden, as devoted a partner as a man could hope for. . . . To her may be attributed much of that kindly and stimulating atmosphere that old boys will remember at Sunday morning breakfasts and Mugwump parties and informal dinners.

Pierce House in 1931. *Archives*

LaRue Piercy, former English master, alumni secretary, and faculty adviser for the *Reserve Record*, returned to Hudson in 1943 after two years of personnel work at the Martin Bomber Plant in Maryland. He became editor of the *Hudson Times,* the local newspaper known today as the *Hudson Hub.* In the June 14, 1946, issue, Piercy paid a tribute to Dr. Hayden that also included memories of the Haydens' home:

> To Pierce House, the Haydens' home, came a stream of guests—old friends of the school, old friends of the Haydens, and many friends of both. . . . Pierce House was also open to students and faculty. Groups gathered there for meals and informal meetings. Masters and boys went individually to the study in the north wing, sat in red-upholstered chairs or [the] davenport by the fireplace, viewed the great library stretching from floor to ceiling, and chatted personally and profitably with their headmaster and friend. And parents came there too to talk over their sons' problems. Inspiration and wisdom flowed freely in Pierce House. . . . Every summer the Haydens spent at their summer home, Faraway Farm, East Stoneham, Maine. . . . There the Haydens will go again this summer before settling at Middlebury, Vermont.

1. Pierce House, named in honor of the school's second president (George Edmund

Pierce, president 1834–55) was purchased by the Board of Trustees and remodeled in 1931 to provide a campus residence for the headmaster. It has since served as the home of four headmasters who succeeded Dr. Hayden.

As Mrs. Hayden tended to the final details of leaving the home she so dearly loved for the past fifteen years, she jotted down a note to Director of Admissions Harlan Parker:

July 22, 1946

Dear Harlan:
 . . . The house is a thing to leave right now—but the leaving is not without heartache. I do believe, however, that Joel will have a good recovery. He improves all the time. We leave tomorrow . . .
 Just Middlebury, Vermont after October 15 . . .
> Affectionately,
> Hazel

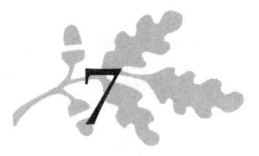

AFTERMATH

If Your Boy Has Not Come Home

On August 29, 1946, Dean Mickel wrote to parents of those boys who were still listed as missing in action and asked for the latest news. "If your boy has not come home," he wrote, "we want you to know that you have our deepest and most sincere sympathy. I wish we were able to see you and let you know more directly where our hearts lie. We hope, however, the news from you will be good." The replies brought an end to the uncertainties surrounding the whereabouts of four Academy boys who had been missing.

A letter from the aunt of Eugene C. Pomeroy ('30) contained details of his life and the circumstances of his death. After graduation from the Academy he returned to the French concession of Shanghai, China, where he had lived for three years as a young boy. He eventually worked at the *China Press*, an American newspaper in Shanghai. When Japan declared war on China in July 1941, the newspaper folded and Eugene joined the British army. He was sent to India for military training, and when Britain declared war against Japan on December 8, he was sent to Malaya, where he was imprisoned by the Japanese. He and two British soldiers were shot and killed while attempting to escape.

Canadian citizen D. Ronald Hardy ('38), a member of the Royal Canadian Air Force, was stationed in India. On the night of November 11, 1944, he was lost over Burma while distributing mines with a squadron. At five hundred feet above ground, his plane swerved, then plunged into a hill and was assumed to have been shot down. No one on the plane was ever heard from again.

September 3, 1946

Dear Mr. Mickel:

The War Department notified us last April 9 that our son Jim [James A. Saalfield, '33x], who was reported missing November 14, 1944, was now considered lost for good.

W. Harold Kennedy ('42), Dr. Hayden, and D. Ronald Hardy ('38). *Archives*

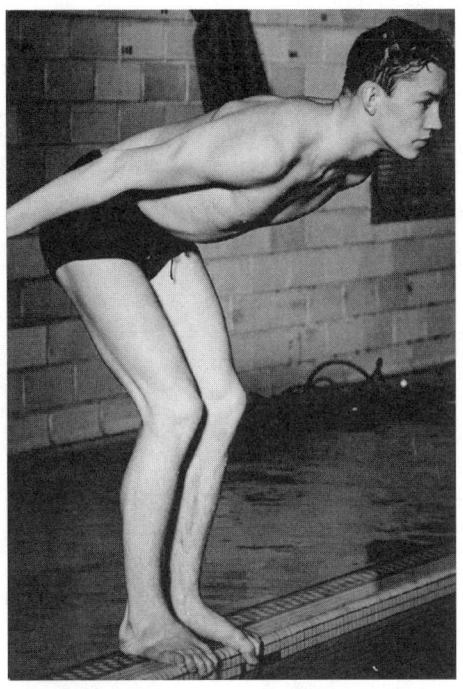

D. Ronald Hardy ('38) on the Academy swim team. *Archives*

Jim, who was a major and squadron leader in the AAF, led a raid of twenty-six *Liberators* from Morotai to Brunei Bay in Borneo. Three machines including Jim's, which was leading the squadron, were shot out of the air. Some men were rescued out of the other two machines, but there was never any word from any of the men on Jim's machine. One report we received indirectly from the navy stated they had received a radio from the operator on Jim's machine to the effect that he, the operator, was badly wounded as was the pilot (we don't know whether that pilot was Jim or not) and all the other members of the crew were dead.

Another report we received from the army stated that the plane had landed on some river and all the members of the crew were killed by the Japanese. We probably never will know his and his crew's fate.

We deeply appreciate your interest.
                Sincerely,
                A. G. Saalfield

                                      November 29, 1946

Dear Mr. Mickel:
    . . . The War Department has given us little information concerning Bill's [William E. Wells III, '36] death. Bill was reported missing April 13, 1945,

and on December 15, 1945, his family was officially notified that he was killed in action.

Perhaps you know Bill was a *Fortress* pilot and completed several missions before he was shot down. The War Department has not been able to tell us exactly where Bill's accident occurred but it was someplace in the southern part of Germany. . . . If we receive any more information concerning this tragedy, we will be glad to forward it on to you.

Kindly give my regards to all my old friends at Reserve.

Sincerely,
J. M. Wells, Jr.[1]

1. Joseph M. Wells, Jr. ('35), was Bill's cousin. The boys grew up together, and everyone mistook them for brothers.

December 7, 1946

Dear Dean Mickel:

The letter which confirmed Bill's death came just about a year ago. And, I believe, I wrote Dr. Hayden about it [August 21, 1945, p. 24]. They never identified Bill's body. They based their assumption on a report by the Germans that there were four identified and three unidentified bodies recovered following the crash on April 8, 1945 near Krusemark, Germany. Also on the testimony of one boy who returned. He claimed he was the only survivor.

As he was able to leave the plane and as his testimony seemed variable, we all hoped some others may have gotten out too. After the final report came I went to Washington to get more definite information. There were ten boys on the plane—one bailed out, seven bodies were found which left two unaccounted for. I hoped for so long that Bill might be one of the two and would still come back. However, the major in the Air Corps to whom I talked said the others could have been entirely cremated. The plane's engines were severely damaged by flak. And I understand an 88mm shell tore loose a wing. They went into a tail spin which, I suppose, hindered them from bailing out.

I'm so sorry that you didn't hear of this long ago, as I know you were interested in hearing about Bill. . . .

Very sincerely yours,
Grace G. Wells

December 23, 1946

Dear Mrs. Wells,

I am sorry to get the news of finality which your letter contained.

All of Bill's old friends here on the campus continued to hope with you that encouraging news might eventually come. We just could not

Reserve's War Dead Honored In Memorial Gym Dedication; Mr. Izant And Mr. Stevenson Speak In Honor of Soldiers

Sharply at 2:00 P.M., last Sunday, after a very pleasant dinner in Cutler Hall, the students, alumni, parents, and friends of Western Reserve Academy congregated in the Memorial Court, opposite the tablet which bears the names of the forty-six Reserve graduates who gave the last full measure of devotion to their country. Immediately in front of this tablet, between the United Nations and the United States flags, was the speakers' platform, from which Mr. Robert H. Wilson, president of the Board of Trustees officially presented Reserve with its new Memorial Gymnasium.

After Mr. Hallowell had accepted the Gym on behalf of the school, Mr. Robert J. Izant of Hudson spoke briefly, representing the parents and relatives of those whose names are inscribed on the great bronze tablet. He was followed by Mr. James D. Stevenson, of Cleveland. As a classmate of many of those who gave their lives, Mr. Stevenson spoke for the many friends made by these honored dead during their stays at Reserve. Next, as president of the senior class, Tem Taylor spoke briefly on the student body's response to the challenge of their predecessors. The Reverend Mr. John Walbridge of the Hudson Congregational Church then concluded the brief but very impressive ceremony with prayer.

Memorial Court Crowd Listens to Mr. Izant

Memorial Courtyard Dedication. Reserve Record, *May 1951*

believe that it would not be so. Nevertheless, as time went on, sober realization forced us to come to the conclusion that such good fortune was not likely. We are, indeed, sorry that it has so occurred and all of your friends at Reserve join in sending you our most heartfelt sympathy. Bill was one of forty-six reserve men lost in this war, all fine young leaders whom this country could ill afford to give up. We hope and pray that this will be the last time when our young men will be called upon to make this sacrifice.

      Sincerely yours,
      Raymond A. Mickel

In September 1997 I received the following letter from Stephen B. Lamb ('40). His closing sentence intrigued me.

      Friday Harbor, Washington
      September 4, 1997

Dear Ms. Piekutowski:

A few days after graduation in 1940 I came back through Hudson on my way east for the summer and on to Princeton in the fall. I stopped on the edge of the campus, near the infirmary, and looked across behind Cutler, past the soccer field, past the Chapel to the far end of the campus. The late afternoon sun was glinting through the trees. There was not a soul in sight, not a sound, not even a car. I stood there for a long time, transfixed by the peace, the beauty, and the memories. France had fallen, England was besieged, Lend Lease was in the air, and war was inevitable. My war. I knew this. But for that moment, all I could think of to ask myself, when, if ever, will I have this moment again?

This magic moment I have relived many times in my mind, and remember every detail. The good men who shaped me, [faculty members] Parker, McGill, Roundy, Cleminshaw, Jones, Eaton, are all long gone, but I remember each and every one of them. And, oh yes. I did relive that moment when I went back to the class of 1940 50th reunion in 1990. I waited until the campus was empty, stood in the same spot, and it was June 4th, 1940 again. Not a thing had changed.

Stephen B. Lamb [Age 75]

APPENDIX A
Gold Stars

1938
    Frank K. Thompson '29
1940
    John H. Eakin '31
1941–42
    William M. Bishop '36
    Carl A. Weiant, Jr. '33
    James D. Tew, Jr. '30x

1942–43
    John B. Gillespie III '36
    Torrey W. Eaton '37
    Edward D. J. Morris '36
    Harold K. Hoffman '41
    Robert F. Heinrichs '38

1943–44
    Harry Allchin, Jr. '39
    John W. Richey '36
    William M. Ashley '40

1944–45
    Daniel R. Hanna III '41x
    William H. Heyman '38
    Neil S. McPhail '33
    Roderick A. Gillis, Jr. '42x
    Paul H. Barnes '42
    Edward W. Kelsey III '40x
    Valentine A. Fries '43

    David A. Read '43
    Ramon L. Spooner '42
    H. Douglas Barnes '43
    Charles F. Kennedy, Jr. '40
    Robert S. Prior '41x
    Abner O. McDaniel '39
    Dan W. Climer '43
    John S. Knight, Jr. '41x
    David L. Bennell '40x
    James H. Cooper, Jr. '41
    Jonathan G. Izant '41
    Harrie B. Stewart '30
    Reese W. Lindsay, Jr. '39
    William P. Conrad '32x
    Calhoun Narten '38x
    John B. Chandler '41x
    Forrest W. Kenner '34

1945–46
    John A. Palmer '45x
    Devin H. Gilchrist '40
    Charles J. Killian, Jr. '40
    Charles A. Tice, Jr. '39x
    Edgar S. Ingraham, Jr. '27
    Eugene C. Pomeroy '30x
    James A. Saalfield '33x
    D. Ronald Hardy '38
    William E. Wells III '36

APPENDIX B

Faculty Masters, 1940–46

IN ORDER OF APPOINTMENT:

Ralph B. Simon 1919–51   Biology; Superintendent of Evamere Farm
  B.S., Ohio State University
Mary E. Eilbeck 1925–45   Librarian
  Drexel Institute Library School
Harrison M. Kitzmiller 1925–54   German, French
  B.A., Ohio State; M.A., Columbia University
Howard R. Williams 1925–55   Chemistry; Science Department Head
  A.B., Hiram College; A.M., Western Reserve University
Angus M. Frew 1926–41   Director of Physical Education
  M.D., University of Louisville
Harley Holmes 1926–41   Orchestra
  LL.B., New York Law School
Chandler T. Jones 1926–61   English
  A.B., Amherst College; M.A., Columbia University
Raymond A. Mickel 1926–60   History, Physical Education; Dean
  A.A., Juniata College; A.M., Columbia University
Ralph W. McGill 1928–59   Math; Assistant Headmaster
  A.B., Ohio Wesleyan; A.M., Columbia University
Harlan R. Parker 1929–59   Latin; Director of Admissions
  A.B., Oberlin College
LaRue W. Piercy 1929–41   English; Alumni Secretary; Publications
  A.B.; A.M., Western Reserve University
Ralph E. Clewell 1930–57   Piano; Glee Club; Music Department
  Mus.B., Baldwin-Wallace College
Brooks Shepard 1931–45   English, Natural Philosophy
  Ph.B., Yale University
Louis C. Tepper 1931–48   Director of Machine Shop
  former Production Engineer for the Studebaker Corporation

Roscoe J. Theibert 1931–59   Math, Physical Education
    A.B., DePauw University
Kurt Weidenthal 1931–71   School Physician
    A.B., Adelbert College; M.D., Western Reserve University
Paul C. Roundy 1932–70   History, Math
    A.A., Amherst College; Ed.M., Harvard University
Robin S. Wallace 1932–59   Science, Math; Bookstore Manager
    B.S., Western Reserve University
Glenn W. King 1933–73   Music Theory
    Mus.B.; Mus.M., Oberlin College
Russell H. Cleminshaw 1934–60   Physics, Science
    M.E., Cornell University; M.A., Western Reserve University
Stacey E. Eaton 1934–42, 1943–44   French, Spanish
    A.B., Clark University; A.M., Bates College; Ed.M., Harvard University
McClean C. Russell 1934–41   Vocal Music; Music Appreciation
    A.A., Amherst College
Raymond C. Burns 1935–43   Religion and Ethics
    A.B., Colgate University; B.D., Union Theological Seminary
Shirley E. Culver 1935–57   French
    A.B., A.M., Brown University
Charles T. Mears 1935–47   Arts and Crafts, Activities
    A.A., Ohio Wesleyan; M.S., Western Reserve University
J. Frederick Waring 1935–67   English, History
    A.A., Yale University; M.A., University of Wisconsin
William W. Kirk 1936–44   French, Spanish
    A.B., University of Delaware, University of Paris; M.A., Middlebury College
Robert T. Morse 1937–42   History
    A.B., Yale University
E. Mark Worthen 1938–71   History, English
    A.A., Harvard University
George S. Dickey 1939–41   English
    A.B., Oberlin College
Charles P. Fehl 1939–48   Orchestra
    A.Mus., Oberlin College
Max W. LaBorde 1941–69   English
    A.B., Allegheny College
Edwin G. Caldwell 1941–43   History
    A.A., Notre Dame; A.M., Ohio State University
Marvin E. Walker 1941–42   Publications; Alumni Secretary
    A.B., Denison University
Glenn H. Fredenburg 1942–43   Latin, English
    A.B., Colgate University; M.A., Western Reserve University

Francis C. Lindaman 1942–43   English
   A.B., A.M., Gettysburg State University
Donald E. Wilson 1942–44   History; Publications
   A.B., A.M., University of Missouri
Robert B. Auld 1942–46   English
   A.A., Oberlin College; Ed.M., University of Pittsburgh
Willis E. Dodge 1943–54   Latin, English
   A.B., Bowdoin College; A.M., Bates College
Edwin L. Ellis 1943–49   Math, Science
   A.S., Davidson College
Charles F. McKinley, Jr. 1943–46   English
   B.A., Kenyon College
John C. Pflaum 1943–46   History, English
   B.A., M.A., University of Pennsylvania
Homer I. Cleary 1944–47   Spanish
   A.B., Dartmouth College
Elmer A. Habel 1944–48   Mathematics
   A.B., Wofford College; A.M., George Washington University
Franklyn S. Reardon 1944–62   English
   A.B., A.M., Colgate University
Richard Scibby 1944–45   Mathematics
   A.B., Western Kentucky State Teachers College; A.M., University of Kentucky
Otis O. Wheeler 1944–45   Manual Arts
   Stout Institute
William J. Barr 1945–46   Mathematics
   A.B., Ohio State University; M.A., University of Akron
Samuel F. Husat 1945–64   Spanish, Latin
   A.B., Mt. Union College; M.A., University of Michigan
William Moos, Jr. 1945–80   Art, Manual Arts, Photography
   A.Arch., St. John's University
Mounir Sa'adeh 1945–46   History
   A.A., M.A., American University of Beirut

APPENDIX C

Board of Trustees, 1940–46

IN ORDER OF APPOINTMENT:

Rev. William M. Fincke 1916–55
Frank A. Seiberling 1916–55
Warren Bicknell 1916–55
Harold T. Clark 1923–65 (Secretary)
R. H. M. Robinson '92 1923–51
William R. Hopkins '92 1925–59
Lincoln Ellsworth 1925–51
William D. Shilts 1928–71
Lewis B. Williams '98 1928–66
Alfred M. Corcoran 1936–54 (Treasurer)
Robert S. Wilson 1936–70 (President, 1941–66)
Joel B. Hayden 1937–50 (Headmaster, 1931–46)
Harry L. Findlay '98 1939–43
William H. Gerhauser 1939–52
Warren Bicknell, Jr. 1941–75
Dr. Robert H. Bishop 1941–55
Robert C. Brouse '31 1941–79
Roland C. Allen 1945–48

APPENDIX D

Academy Boys Who Died during Military Service after World War II

JOSEPH S. ALLEN, '38

He was one of four brothers to attend the Academy. A commander in the navy, he was killed in 1956 during helicopter training off the coast of San Diego, California.

JOSEPH T. ERK, '41

A soccer player and star of the senior play, he was a navy lieutenant fighter pilot with the U.S. Seventh Fleet stationed on the USS *Kearsarge*. He was killed during a training mission on March 6, 1958.

ROBERT C. CROMWELL, '42

He was the stepson of Assistant Headmaster Scotch McGill. The father of two children and a second lieutenant in the Army Air Force, he was killed on June 11, 1953, when his jet crashed during a secret mission.

IRVEN A. HISSOM, '43

A marine pilot known as "Whitey," he was killed on January 25, 1956, while on a navy training mission in Texas.

ARTHUR G. CALLAHAN, JR., '49

Known at the Academy for his sense of humor, Callahan, a lieutenant (junior grade) navy pilot, died during a landing aboard the aircraft carrier USS *Bon Homme Richard* in August 1956.

NORMAN E. MALONE, JR., '51

He was a study hall prefect and athletic manager while at the Academy. His jet plane crashed on takeoff on October 10, 1960; Malone had been a first lieutenant in the Army Air Force.

JOHN D. PEACE III, '53

Captain of league basketball while at Reserve, he enrolled in the U.S. Naval Academy after graduation. A lieutenant (junior grade) Skyhawk pilot, he was listed as missing in action in Vietnam in February 1968.

RICHARD C. THUM, '61

He was a prefect, varsity athlete, and president of the senior class. His father and four of his brothers graduated from the Academy. A lieutenant in the U.S. Navy, he was based on the USS *Constellation* when he was shot down over North Vietnam on November 25, 1968.

Index of Names

Abbey, Robert L. '35, 179–80
Alexander, Marvin G. '39, 138–39
Allchin, Harry, Jr. '39, 16, 20, 74–75, 79–80, 113, 133, *134*; mentioned, *114*, 132, 174; in narrative, 73, 111, 116; recommendation for, 17
Allchin, Tom '46, 73, 74–75, 133
Allen, J. Scribner '39, 131, 186–87
Allen, James H. '41, 190, 195, 197, 216
Allen, Joseph S. '38, 10–11, 292
Allen, R. Craten '32, *253*
Allin, Vincent W. '36, 266–67
Anderson, John U., Jr. '39, 64–65, *66*, 115
Ashley, Frederick W., 39, 40, *41*
Ashley, William M. '40, 143–44
Ashmun, Russell F. '42, 131–32
Ashton, John '38, 41–42, 57–58, 151–52, *256–57*

Babcox, Edward S., Jr. '35, 59–60, 62, 100, 109–10, 263–65, 267–68
Babcox, Reid B. '29, 24, 28, 59–60, 62, 100, 109
Babcox, Tom B. '37, 16, 45–46, 59, 62, 75–76, 100–101, 110
Ball, Lewis C. '42, 20, 166, 171–72, 195, 196, 197, 259, *260*
Barlow, Franklin S. '30, 191, 213–14, 224–25
Barnes, Doug '43 and Paul '42, 86, 96–97, 193–94, 204, 273
Barnes, H. Douglas '43, 99, 122, 135, 141, *193*, 220–22; and Paul '42,

Barnes, Homer F., 14
Barnes, Paul H. '42, 134–35, *139*, 179, *192*, 202–3, 205
Barrett, Richard H. '35, 182–83
Barry, "Chubb" '43, 122
Barstow, Paul R. '43, 55, 104, 119, 150, 245–46
Bauer, Richard J. '43, 129
Baxter, Ledyard M. '44, 261
Bell, Hugh F. '37, 88, 110, 151
Bell, Hugh F., Jr. '62, 110
Bell, Lawrence G., Jr. '36x, 150–51
Bennell, David L. '40x, 184, 223, 224
Bennett, Geoffrey '44, 133
Berman, William H. '42, 189
Bishop, William M. '36, 8, *9*
Black, Reid C. '42, 194–95, 197
Blackstone, George V. '41, 112–13
Bliss, Richard H. '38, 99–100, 141
Blossom, Mrs. Dudley S., 5
Bluem, Robert A. '39x, 50, 80, 92–93, 98, 135–36, 144–45
Borden, Bob '38, 125
Bowerfind, Edgar S. '42, 223
Boyer, Robert J. '42, 199
Brough, Brian I. '39, 17, 203
Brouse, Ned '38, 216
Burns, Raymond, 75, 163, 172–73

Calder, William I. '41, 184
Caldwell, Edward G., 20, 110, 172, 233
Callahan, Arthur G., Jr. '51, 292
Carter, Keith '43, 125

Chandler, John B. '41, 247, *249*
Cheyney, Charles '35, 32
Christy, Earl B. '41, 68, 69–70
Church, John A. '30, 231–32, *241, 242*
Clapp, Roger, E. '37, 12
Cleminshaw, Russell, 286
Clewell, Ralph E. 39, 40, 108
Climer, Dan W. '43, 183, 184, *217*
Cobbledick, William G. '43, *215*
Cone, Bob '43, 259
Congdon, Rowland C. '42x, 55, 191
Conrad, William P. '32x, 183
Cooper, Charles F. '40, 276–77
Cooper, James H. '41, 184, 227–28
Cromwell, (McGill), Bernice, 31, 32–33, 161, 177
Culver, Shirley, xviii, 39

Danforth, John H. '33, 189–90
Danforth, William H., '34, 23–24, 154–55
Dennison, David S., Jr. '36, 49, 50–55, 93
Dickerson, J. Spencer '38, 56–57
Dickerson, John '42, 28
Dickerson, Willard D. '36, 207
Dinsmore, Raymond P., Jr. '43, 150, 191
Doyle, Dorothy, 68

Eakin, John H. '31, 8, *9, 10*
Eaton, Stacey E., '35, 75, 152, 163, 286
Eaton, Torrey W. '37, *31*, 32, 34, 47, 48, 63–64; mentioned, 33, 46, 57, 62, 67, 101
Edwards, Richard P. '38, 87
Ellis, Ed, 122, 127
Ellsworth, James W., xvii, 22, 146
Erk, Joseph T. '41, 292

Fairchild, George '88, 28
Fehl, Charles P., 172
Ferris, Henry '37, 216
Findlay, Harry L., 36
Findlay, Malcolm W. '38, 36
Finlayson, A. Neil '40, 57, 136, 137–38
Finlayson, Malcolm W. '34, 253–55
Forbes, Jerry '32, 82
Fornshell, Bob '43, 223
Frew, "Doc", 199

Fries, Valentine A. '43, 178–79, 181–82, *192*, 205
Fuzy, Paul '40, 126, 216

Galbreath, William W. '38, 180
Garman, Mayor Guy F., 24
Gerhauser, Merton F. '35, 107–8
Gilchrist, Devin H. '40, 111, 113–14, 116–17, 153, 166–69, 270
Gillespie, John B. III "Jack" '36, 42, 45, 46, 47, 48–49, 98; mentioned, 57, 62, 80, 145
Gillis, Roderick A. '42x, 153, 174–75
Glover, William H. '42x, 30–31, 36–37, *38*, 123–24, 237–38, 246, 273–74
Goldsmith, Ken '43, 99, 122
Grant, G. G., Jr. '39, 203
Gregory, Bill '41, 195
Gressle, A. Keith '48, 189
Gressle, Mrs. Jerrie, 188–89
Griffin, Johnny '38, 100
Guarnaccia, Gina, 33, 115, *162*
Guarnaccia, Jean Hayden, xv, 33, 115, 127, 131, 146, *162*; wedding, 5; mentioned, 130, 160
Guarnaccia, Sam, 5, 33, 115, 127, 131, 145
Guarnaccia, Sam, Jr., 127
Gulick, Robert A., Jr. '34, 109, 254, 277–78

Hamilton, Bob '42, 55
Hancock, Bill, '42, *260*
Handyside, Douglas P. '38, 62–63, 72–73
Hanks, "Bud" '38, 232
Hanna, Daniel R. '41x, 163, *164*, 165, 174
Hanson, Dave '36, 233
Hanson, Peter S. '44, 118, 189
Hardy, D. Ronald '38, 282, *283*
Havens, Fred '40, 266
Hayden, Hazel, xxii, in Hawaii, 5, *6*, 59; her note, 281; mentioned, 66, 79, 118, 146, 179, 197; and Mrs. Tepper, 22; remembered, 279–80; in Vermont, 131
Hayden, Joel B., Jr. '39, xv, *162*; whereabouts, 42, 66, 100, 111, 115, 113, 118, 145

Hayden, Dr. Joel B., profile, xxi–xxii; 6, 41, *162*
Hayden, Ralston '42, 20
Heinrichs, Robert F. '38, 80–81
Henney, Tom '34, 235
Hess, Carl M. '33, 108–9
Heyman, William H. '38, 153, *164*, 174, 257
Hirshberg, [A.] Walter '44, 88
Hirshberg, Herbert '41, 88
Hirshberg, Richard L. '36, 58, 88, 130
Hirshberg, Robert L. '36, 88, *89*, 180
Hissom, Irven A. '43, 177, 292
Hoffman, Harold "Tug" '41, 68, 69–70, 249
Holstine, Philip M. '42, 184
Holtkamp, Walter H. '47, 79
Hopkins, Walter A., Jr. '37, 244–45, 255–56
Horner, James "Rick" '41, 258
Horner, Walter "Bob" '40, 258
Horner, William A. '39x, 61, 258–59
Hutchinson, Bob '40, 232

Ingraham, Edgar S. '27, 272–73
Ingraham, William R. '34, 124–25, 273
Iredell, Robert, Jr. '34, 190
Izant, Jonathan G. '41, 122–23, 199, 214, 215, 219–20, 233, *240*, 249

Jahant, John W. '43, 49, 98–99, 220
Jennings, Dave '35, 266
Johnson, John T. III '35, 89–91
Jones, Chandler, T. 33, 100, 108, 266, 286

Katz, Robert W. '34, 184, 260–61
Kelsey, Edward W. '40x, 176, *181*
Kendel, William F. '27, 77
Kennedy, Charles F., Jr. '40, 76, 156, 183, 199, 200–202, 205–6, 230–31
Kennedy, W. Harold '42, 127–28, 129–30, 133–34, 148–49, *283*
Kenner, Forrest L. '34, *78*, 184, *233*
Kenner, Hamilton W. '42, *78*, 233
Ketcham, Charles B. '44, 234–35
Kidgell, Burt, *146*

Killian, Charles J., Jr. '40, 73, 125–26, 183, 206–7, 212, 270–72
King, Glenn W., 35, 75, 173
Kirk, W. W., 83, 172
Kitzmiller, Harrison, 32, 94, 100, 108
Kitzmiller, Helen, xiv, 32
Klump, William H., Jr. '39, 117, 118
Knight, John S., Jr. '41x, 184, 218, *219*, 249
Kuhn, Harley, 146, *147*

Lamb, B. Stephen '40, 66–67, 73, 126, 285–86
Lightner, Donald G. '35, 214
Lindaman, Francis, 173
Lindsay, Eugene '42, 259, *260*
Lindsay, Reese W., Jr. '39, *234*
Lingle, Nan, 20
Long, "Huey" '38, 259
Lothrop, Richard P. '44, 189
Loughry, Bob '35, 108

McConky, Fred '43, *99*, 122
McCuskey, Charles L. '28, 190
McDaniel, Abner O. '39, 183, 212–13
McGill, Ralph W. "Scotch", profile, xxiii
McIntosh, John C. '39, 140–41, 195–96
McKay, James M. III '39, 203–4
McKay, "Kay" '43, 204
McPhail, Neil S. '33, 121–22, 153, 173–74, 175, 177–78, 210–11
Malcolm, John A. '42, 183–84, 210
Malone, Norman E., Jr. '51, 292
Manlove, George K. '32, *xvii*, 43–44, 81–82, 118, 185–86, 207–9, 252; to brothers, 94–96; to father, 230; to mother, 156–60, 197–98, 228–29
Manlove, William F. '44, 82, 94, 96, 118
Marshall, Richard S. '41, 39
Mears, Charles T., 36, 71, 152, 173, 187
Meese, Bob '40, 125, 126
Mell, Marvin '43, 99, 122, 129
Metcalf, Edward I. '42, 83, *84*, 85
Mickel, Raymond A. profile, xxiii–xxiv
Millar, Joseph H. III '34, 87, 94
Miller, "Dek" '39, 66
Miller, J. Ledlie, Jr. '42x, 174

Montgomery, George '41, 125
Mooney, Jack '43x, 177
Moore, Alan A. '39x, 175, 184
Morris, Edward D. J. '36, 8, 47, 48, 58–59
Morse, Robert T. 35, 172, 216

Narten, Calhoun "Pete" '38x, 119, 120, 121, 247
Narten, Philip C. '41, 238–39
Newberry, William B. '37, 104, 110
Newstetter, Wilber I., Jr. '41, 126–27
Noyes, John H. '40, 216–17
Nussdorfer, Ade '41, 195

Oseland, Zimri C., Jr. '44, 275
Owen, David S. '42, 55, 102, 122, 233

Palmer, John A. '45x, 261–62
Parker, Harlan, 4, 69, 82, 148–49, 269, 281, 286
Peabody, Dwight V. '43, 204–5
Peace, John D. III '53, 293
Peace, William D. '41, 212
Pendleton, James L. '34, 191
Piercy, Larue, 26, 32, 280
Pomeroy, Eugene C. '30x, 282
Pope, Edward J. '37, 138–39, 197, *211*
Powers, James H., 44–45
Price, Lucien '01, *3, 41*; from Hayden, 70; mentioned, 4, 8, 223; from Wood, 1, 13–14, 18–19, 22, 34–35, 44–45, 69, 97
Priestley, James F. '34, 8, 11
Prior, Robert S. '41x, 211, *249*

Rakowsky, Rudolph '44, 118, 177
Rawdon, Blaine N., Jr. '42, *19*; in letters, 166, 171–72, 197, 217–18, 219, 225–27, 259–60; mentioned, 20, 184, *193*, 196, 223; from Shepard, 13
Read, David A. '43, *192–93*, 248–49
Reardon, Franklin S., 163
Rich, Norman '38, 151
Richards, W. Donald '39, 152, 257
Richey, John W. '36, *120*, 121

Rideout, Alfred L. '38, 145–46, 163
Roundy, Paul, 68, 100, 177, 286

Saalfield, Arthur J. '38, 169–70
Saalfield, James A. '33x, 282–83
Sadler, "Sad" '38, 100
Sawyer, Tom '36, 142
Schmahl, Frank D. '43, *99*
Seaman, John P. '43, 119, 150, 274–75
Seely, Worcester W. '41, 111, 151, 165
Shaw, John B. '40, xviii, xx, xxi
Shepard, Brooks, 13, 152
Shepard, Brooks, Jr. '39, 66
Shultis, Agnes D., 224
Shultis, Lester D. '43, 119, 224
Silver, Rabbi, xx
Silver, R. Bruce '41, 119–20, 155, *156*, 161–62, 233
Silver, Richard L. '38, 88–89, 162
Silver, Stu '45, 162
Simon, Ralph, 108
Sisson, Richard N. '44, 118
Smith, Tony '44, 175
Spear, David A. '44, 241–42
Spooner, Byron G. '45, 105–7
Spooner, Ramon L. '42, 19–20, 105–7, 192–93, 196
Spring, Herb '38, 125
Sprow, August W. '33, 103, 104
Sprow, William J. '40x, 101–2, 103–4, 105, 115–16, 121, 128–29, 184
Stevenson, Jim '43, 122, 184
Stewart, Harrie B. '30, 27, 28, *233, 242*
Stewart, Joe H. '30, 76, 78–79
Stifel, Ernest A., Jr. '39, 233, 235–36
Swan, George '37, 100
Sykes, Carl '43, 125
Sykes, Nelson '41, 125

Tanner, Charles H. '44, 24, 114–15
Tanner, Harvey '38x, 24–25, 30, 34, 114–15, 161, 198
Tepper, Herbert J. '39, 66, *162*, 190
Tepper, Louis, xvii, 5, 10, 24, 60, 126, *142*, 153; mentioned, 102; tribute,

136, *137*, 138; from War Production Board, 77
Tew, James D. '30x, *26*, 27, 49, 61–62
Theibert, Dick '42, 55, 66, *125*, 259
Theibert, Jack, '40, 55, 66, 125
Theibert, "Tebbie", 33, 55, 122, 127
Thomas, Dorsey O., Jr. '41x, 232
Thompson, Frank K. '29, 8, *10*, 27
Thum, Richard C. '61, 293
Tice, Charles A. '39x, 270, *271*
Tillinghast, Charles M. '35, 93
Tilt, Russell, 108
Tolan, Bernard E. '40, 118, 164–65
Tucker, Benson '42, 184

Upson, George '43, 122

Varley, Dave '40, 66
Vilas, Malcolm B., Jr. '35, 67–68, 71, 141–42
Vogel, Ted '39, 108
Vradenburg, George A., Jr. '37, 160–61, 163, 176–77, 262–63, 267
Vradenburg, Newt '34, 262

Walker, Marvin E. '35, 11, 35, 71, 109, 110, 173
Wallace, Bob '39, 216
Wallace, Robin S. "Wallie", 68, 122, 123, 161, 163, 177, 203, 259
Ward, W. Alan '36, 63–64, 67
Waring, J. Fred, AFS, 40–41, 49, 50, 75, 82–83; *Alumni Record*, 279; *The Growing Years*, 5, 278; mentioned, xviii, 35, 88, 100, 104, 163; return, 110, 122, 126–27, 152, 153, 161–62
Weiant, Carl A., Jr. '33, *26*, 27–28
Weidenthal, Kurt, 267
Weitz, Joe '40, xx, 216
Welles, Carder '25, 77
Wells, Bradford '44, 38, 133, 148, 175
Wells, Howard M., Jr. '41, 38, 148
Wells, Joseph M., Jr. '35, 283–84
Wells, William E. III '36, 184, *236*, 242, 243–44, 248, 283–85
Whitaker, Louis S. '43, 91, 149
Williams, H. R., 97, 108
Williams, John R. '42, 209–10
Wilson, Donald E. 152
Wilson, Robert S., 118, 252, 269, 276
Winkler, Charles H. '34, 190
Winterling, John B. '43, 40
Wood, A. Walter '42, 99
Wood, Harlan N., profile, xxii–xxiii; 3, 147, *188*
Woodruff, Lincoln H. '39, 190
Worthen, E. Mark, xviii, 111, 152, 173, 209

Yang, Tien Wei '41, xviii, xxi, 76, 175, 230–31
Yardley, Jack '44, 60, *61*, 102, 126

Zonsius, Kenneth C., Jr. '43, 99, 268–70

Remembering the Boys
was designed by Christine Brooks;
composed in 9.5/13.5 Palatino
on a Macintosh G4 using PageMaker 6.5;
printed by sheet-fed offset lithography
on 50# Supple Opaque stock,
Smyth sewn and bound over binder's boards in Arrestox cloth,
and wrapped with dust jackets printed in three colors
by Thomson-Shore, Inc., of Dexter, Michigan;
and published by
The Kent State University Press
Kent, Ohio 44242